Wesley Cole

December 5, 1989

GRUMBLES
FROM THE GRAVE

By Robert A. Heinlein
Published by Ballantine Books:

Between Planets
Citizen of the Galaxy
The Door into Summer
Double Star
Farmer in the Sky
Friday
Have Spacesuit—Will Travel
Job: A Comedy of Justice
The Puppet Masters
Red Planet
Rocket Ship Galileo
The Rolling Stones
Space Cadet
The Star Beast
Starman Jones
Time for the Stars
Tunnel in the Sky
Waldo & Magic, Inc.
Grumbles from the Grave

GRUMBLES FROM THE GRAVE

Robert A. Heinlein

Edited by Virginia Heinlein

A Del Rey Book

BALLANTINE BOOKS • NEW YORK

A Del Rey Book
Published by Ballantine Books

Library of Congress Cataloging-in-Publication Data

Heinlein, Robert A. (Robert Anson), 1907–1988
    Grumbles from the grave / Robert A. Heinlein.—1st ed.
      p.   cm.
    "A Del Rey book."
    ISBN 0-345-36246-2
    I. Title
    PS3515.E288G7   1990
    813'.54—dc20   89-6859
                                   CIP

Design by Michaelis/Carpelis Design Assoc. Inc.

Manufactured in the United States of America

First Edition: January 1990

10 9 8 7 6 5 4 3 2 1

For Heinlein's Children

❖

CONTENTS

❖

❖

FOREWORD

❖

This book does not contain the polished prose one normally associates with the Heinlein stories and articles of later years. It has been taken from the day-to-day correspondence between the author and his agent, and from letters from several others, many of which have been excerpted.

Such cutting eliminates a great deal of tedious back-and-forth correspondence concerning details of contracts, discussions about royalty rates, and other items which would hold up the flow of information about the writing business (and other things). This book has been abstracted from enormous files, which run millions of words long, much of it boring to those not concerned with the daily business of writing and selling.

Many people have asked me to consider writing Robert's biography, or a joint one—his and mine—but I am not ready to do that yet. Perhaps, one day.

Meanwhile, this correspondence covers mostly the years from the time when Robert first began writing until the period 1969–1970, at which time he found that his writing time was effectively cut down to zero by the continuing details of his business and subsequently, grave illness . . . Over the years, I had taken over record keeping, information on sales, taxes, and some of the correspondence. In 1970, Robert was very sick for the entire year, and it was then essential that I keep the business running. It was fortunate that I had begun doing so the previous year.

In order to follow the various subjects, I have excerpted these letters to put together as many as possible of the remarks and ideas on those subjects. Each letter did have a number of topics in it, these have been separated where possible. Some of the topics are: juveniles, adult novels, publishers, travel, fan mail, time wasters, Robert's writing methods, and so forth.

Some names have been left out for legal reasons.

There are places where there are only notes on telephone conversations. It would be impossible to reconstruct those. They have been omitted.

There are a few sparse excerpts from letters which were written after I took over running the business end of Robert's writing . . . most of those letters written by Robert. He talked to Lurton Blassingame, his agent, now and then, but mostly he spent his time reading for his work, or writing. During the last eighteen years of his life, he had many illnesses. But, in between, he continued working.

I was his "first reader"—the person who read each work first and made suggestions for cutting, revisions, and so on. It was a great responsibility. When Robert came down with peritonitis in 1970, *I Will Fear No Evil* needed more cutting, but it was obvious that he was (and would be for a long time) in no condition to do that. And his publisher was calling for the manuscript, so I had it Xeroxed and sent it in. I take full responsibility for that. With further cutting, it might perhaps have been a better story. In spite of this, it has sold more than a million copies in U.S. paperback alone, and has been translated into more than half-a-dozen languages, and is still in print in all of those, including English.

At one time, Robert wrote to his agent about the possibility of writing a memoir-autobiography: *Grumbles From The Grave* by Robert A. Heinlein (deceased).

This is that book. It covers many years, many subjects, and some personal comments—taken mostly from letters between Robert and his agent, Lurton Blassingame.

Virginia Heinlein
Carmel, California 1988

❖

A SHORT BIOGRAPHY

OF

ROBERT A. HEINLEIN

BY VIRGINIA HEINLEIN

❖

Robert Anson Heinlein was born July 7, 1907, the third of seven children of Bam Lyle Heinlein and Rex Ivar Heinlein, in Butler, Missouri. The growing family moved to Kansas City during his childhood.

When Robert learned to read, he read everything he could lay his hands on. He did, in fact, read on his way to school, going along the street, up and down curbs, up to the schoolhouse. He attended junior high school, Central High School in Kansas City, and spent one year at a local junior college. His next older brother had gone before him to the United States Naval Academy, and Robert set his sights on going there. He collected many letters of recommendation from people and gained the appointment from Senator James Reed to enter the Naval Academy in 1925.

Following his graduation and commissioning in 1929, he served aboard the *Lexington* under Captain E. J. King, who later became Commander in chief of the U. S. Navy during World War II. When his tour of duty on the *Lexington* was about to end, Captain King asked that he be retained as a gunnery specialist. However, Robert was given duty as

Heinlein's birthplace in Butler, Missouri.

Robert A. Heinlein (lower right) with his sister Louise (lower left) and his brothers Lawrence Lyle (upper left) and Rex Ivar (upper right).

Robert A. Heinlein, 1929.

Heinlein at the time of his high
school graduation.

gunnery officer on the *Roper*, a destroyer. Destroyer duty was difficult because of the rolling of the ship, and seasickness was a way of life for him. He lost weight and came down with tuberculosis. After he was cured, the Navy retired him from active duty.

At twenty-seven years of age, he found himself permanently ashore, with a small pension. It was necessary for him to find some way to augment that money. He tried silver mining, politics, selling real estate, and further study in engineering. One day, he found an ad in a science fiction magazine for a contest. So he sat down and wrote a story ("Life-Line"). He felt it was too good for the magazine he had written it for, so he sent it to the top magazine in the field—*Astounding Science Fiction.* John W. Campbell, Jr. bought the story.

The next several stories he wrote were less salable, and it was only

Heinlein gets the ball rolling, 1934.

on his fifth or sixth try that Campbell again purchased one. The second and following stories eventually sold, but Robert was hooked for life on writing. Originally, his purpose in writing was to pay off a mortgage on a house which he and his wife of a few years had purchased. After that mortgage was paid off, he found that when he tried to give up writing, he felt vaguely uncomfortable, and it was only when he returned to his typewriter that he felt fulfilled.

❖ ❖ ❖

During World War II, Robert left his writing to do engineering work for the U.S. Navy. For three years he did such work in Philadelphia. The war over, he returned to his writing. By this time, he was looking for wider horizons. He was persuaded to begin the juvenile line, and he sold stories to the *Saturday Evening Post*. His second juvenile was picked up by television, in a series that ran for five years. He also wrote the classic film, *Destination Moon*, and he began to think about writing serious adult novels to open up that market to science fiction.

Robert thought that the possibilities of mankind going into space were sufficiently important and feasible that before he left Philadelphia, he wrote two letters urging that the Navy begin space exploration. One letter went through channels as far as the head of the Philadelphia Naval Air Experimental Station, who killed the proposal. The second went (also through channels), via a friend, through Naval Operations, and got as far as a Cabinet meeting. It was reported that then-President Truman took it seriously enough to ask whether such a rocket could be launched from the deck of a ship. No, the President was told. And that killed the project.

In 1947 Robert was divorced from his wife, and when he received his decree nisi, he married me. During World War II, I had gone into the Navy, as a WAVE, and my second tour of duty was in Philadelphia, where I met Robert; we worked in the same section.

One day Robert spent hours searching for some tear sheets for an anthology. In an effort to help, I decided that his files needed to be organized. So I set about that, setting up a system which I still use today. This began my involvement in the literary business.

By the time Robert found himself too busy to do more than overhead work (keeping up correspondence with his agents, keeping records,

The Soviet Union's May Day Rocket, 1960. The slogan reads "Earth-Mars-Earth—we will get there first."

answering fan mail, and all the other chores attendant on being a literary figure), I was well enough acquainted with his business that I could take over those chores for him. We worked together as a team, discussing what to do about offers, and I would answer the letters for him.

❖   ❖   ❖

With the juvenile series well launched, and selling many copies primarily to libraries, Robert became the darling of librarians. He was asked to give endless speeches, and when his annual books for boys came out, he did a special program for general radio distribution on each new book.

But he still yearned to do serious writing for adults, rather than for the specialized science fiction market. So, in 1960, he finished writing *Stranger in a Strange Land*. That book became his best known work. When the boys who originally read his juveniles grew up, they kept looking for more of the science fiction which Robert had made so popular. So he set out to write adult novels for them. For some years, he regularly wrote two books a year, one adult and one juvenile. In addition, there were always requests for other things in the way of nonfiction. Many of those requests had to be turned down for lack of time.

Between books, we did a good deal of foreign travel. We went around the world four times, spent time in Europe. One of the most interesting, but not to be repeated trips, was to the Soviet Union. In 1960, we saw the May Day parade, then took off for Kazakhstan. Soon after our arrival in Alma-Ata, we were told of the U-2 incident. Things turned frosty for us, but there was no way out, so we continued the trip, going on to Samarkand, which was the real reason we went all that way into the USSR. While we were in Vilno, just before a summit conference between Khrushchev and President Eisenhower, the Soviet Union sent up a rocket which to this day we cannot be certain was unmanned. On the way down from seeing some castle in Vilno, we encountered a group of Red Army cadets, who were extremely excited about it and had to tell us. We were heartsick about the development and returned to our hotel.

❖ ❖ ❖

In 1970, there was a serious illness, from which it took him two years to recover his health. Then, he sat down at his typewriter and turned out *Time Enough for Love.*

Always a man of fragile health, illnesses became more frequent, and there was less time for writing. We both had a taste for travel, and we saw a good deal of the world; anywhere there was transportation, we went. We visited Antarctica and went through the Northwest Passage to Japan. When China opened up to travel, we went there, among other parts of the East. *To Sail Beyond the Sunset* was eventually published on Robert's 80th birthday. Questions began to come in—Was this to be the final book from his typewriter? (But by this time it was a computer.) He had intended to write more, but again illness intervened, and *To Sail did* become his final story.

❖ ❖ ❖

I will leave it to others to evaluate the influence of Robert's work, but I have been told many times that he was the "Father of Modern Science Fiction." Those books have been published in many languages, in many lands, and some of them seem to have been landmark stories.

During his lifetime, Robert received many honors, including four Hugo awards for the best novel of the year. The books so honored were: *Double Star* (1956), *Starship Troopers* (1959), *Stranger in a Strange Land* (1962), and *The Moon Is a Harsh Mistress* (1966). He was also the recipient of the first Grand Master Nebula Award from the Science Fiction Writers of America. There were also many other awards: The Sequoyah Award, given by the Children of Oklahoma for the best children's novel of the year (*Have Space Suit—Will Travel*); many awards for the blood drives we did; *Tomorrow Starts Here*, given by Delta Vee, Inc.; Robert perennially won first rank among popular writers in the *Locus* inquiries. But the thing which pleased him most, it seemed, was being invited to be a Forrestal Lecturer at his alma mater in 1972.

In October 1988, I was asked to come to Washington, D.C., to receive, on Robert's behalf, the Distinguished Public Service Medal. My greatest regret is that he could not have known of that.

Heinlein's Distinguished Public Service Medal (awarded posthumously).

GRUMBLES
FROM THE GRAVE

CHAPTER I

❖

IN THE BEGINNING

❖

April 10, 1939: Robert A. Heinlein to John W. Campbell, Jr.

I am submitting the enclosed short story "Life-Line" for either *Astounding* or *Unknown*, because I am not sure which policy it fits the better.

EDITOR'S NOTE: *Robert always told the following story when asked how he began writing. He had seen an ad in one of the pulp science fiction magazines, offering $50.00 for the best story by a beginning writer. He wrote "Life-Line," then decided that it was too good for that particular magazine. So he sent it to John W. Campbell, Jr., who had been editing* Astounding *for approximately two years at that time. Campbell was always looking for new talent and apparently recognized it in Robert's first work. Robert claimed that he took a look at the check for "Life-Line" and said, "How long has this racket been going on?" His second story was also accepted, after some revisions. Thereafter it was some months before Campbell accepted another story.*

Robert was one of a group of writers whose work is now called "The Golden Age of Science Fiction." John Campbell helped his writers along with suggestions and brought them along to make Astounding *the foremost science fiction pulp magazine of the time.*

April 19, 1939: John W. Campbell, Jr. to Robert A. Heinlein

. . . I like your story, "Life-Line," and plan to take it at our regular rate of 1 cent a word, or $70.00 for your manuscript.

Heinlein's first story, "Life-Line," John W. Campbell, Jr.'s *Astounding,* August 1939. Art by Isip.

August 25, 1939: John W. Campbell, Jr. to Robert A. Heinlein

At about this time you should receive our check for $310.00 for "—Vine and Fig Tree—" ("If This Goes On—")—which title will have to be changed to give it more umph. The story, by practically all that's good and holy, deserves our usual unusually-good-story 25% bonus. It's a corking good yarn; may you send us many more as capably handled.

But—for the love of Heaven—*don't* send us any more on the theme of this one. The bonus misfires because this yarn is going to be a headache and a shaker-in-the-boots; it's going to take a lot of careful rewording and shifting of emphasis.

❖ ❖ ❖

I genuinely got a great kick out of the consistency and logic of the piece. You can, and will, I'm sure, earn that 25% bonus for unusually good stuff frequently. I'm very much in the market for short stories and novelettes. This piece can't appear until after E. E. Smith's "Gray Lensman" finishes, so I'd like more stuff in between whiles.

December 15, 1939: John W. Campbell, Jr. to Robert A. Heinlein

I was wrong, evidently, in believing you had difficulty working out "Lost Legacy" [published in *Super Science Stories* as "Lost Legion" by Lyle Monroe], but you are definitely wrong in suggesting that "If

The second NOVA story Astounding has offered—a story so exceptional in its presentation, so powerful and logical, that it wins the rare NOVA designation!

A tale of Dictatorship in America—but dictatorship carried to its logical, deadly end! The ultimate of the "leader principle" is—The Prophet! Dictatorship hiding behind the mask of a false cult!

Heinlein's story, "If This Goes On," *Astounding*, February 1940. Art by Hubert Rogers.

Heinlein at his desk with plate from "If This Goes On."

This Goes On—" is, or has any tendency to be, hack. It has flavor, a roundness of background that makes it lovely.

EDITOR'S NOTE: John W. Campbell, Jr. started writing pulp science fiction stories while still in college. He was a large, tall man who threw off ideas like a sparkler and was addicted to various hobbies and hospitality to authors. Some of his hobbies were photography, ham radio, and dianetics.

Robert did not admire his writing style and objected strenuously to the various changes JWC made in Robert's stories. Despite their differences in personality and style, the two men became good friends after Robert began writing for Astounding. *John turned down a number of Robert's stories after the first one had been published. Those were changed slightly and later sold to other pulp magazines. Whenever John considered a story particularly good, he was allowed by the higher-ups at Street and Smith to give the writer a bonus. Rates, in those days, were very low, and the bonus added nicely to the writer's income.*

Each month Astounding *carried a reader poll, which rated the stories which had appeared in an earlier issue. Those stories vied against each other for placement in the "Analytical Laboratory." Robert's first story, "Life-Line," was second in the reader poll three months following publication.*

During the three years Robert wrote mainly for Astounding, *he often placed first and second (using his own name and a pseudonym) with his stories. He quickly became John's leading writer.*

The stories which appeared in Astounding *had blurbs written by the editor, both on the contents page and at the beginning of the story. Robert complained that John often gave away the point of the story in these blurbs. However, Robert learned much about the art of writing from John.*

January 23, 1940: John W. Campbell, Jr. to Robert A. Heinlein

Now, the idea I'd like to have you mull over a while before giving me a definite answer. I think you're one of the writers who can work up someone else's ideas into a logical story with enthusiasm. Some can, you know, and some definitely can't. You are in a position to know, and that's why I'd like to have your own reaction to this.

February 23, 1940: Robert A. Heinlein to John W. Campbell, Jr.

Here is the story about the atomic engineers and the uranium power plant ["Blowups Happen"]. I had intended to send it to my friend in Lawrence's radiation laboratory at Berkeley for a final technical check-over, but decided to send it to you promptly instead. As you pointed out, things are happening fast in this field. The quicker a story laid in it sees print, the better the chance that some assumption in the story will not already have been invalidated.

❖ ❖ ❖

I presume that this story herewith will give you some idea as to whether or not I can work out another man's ideas. If you decide that I can, then I would be interested in taking a crack at your idea of scientists going insane over the uncertainty of truth in the "sub-etheric" field. But not just at present, not before fall. It does not seem to me to be a good idea for me to do another story about scientists going crazy too soon—neither for me as a writer trying to build a commercial reputation, nor for the magazine.

Furthermore, it is a big idea; I would want to use not less than fifty thousand words. I have a serial on the stands now; I don't suppose that

"Blowups Happen," *Astounding,* September 1940. Art by Charles Schneeman.

you want to publish another serial by me for a year, at least—or have I incorrectly estimated the commercial restrictions.

EDITOR'S NOTE: During the summer of 1940, Robert visited John Campbell in the east, the two became fast friends. Letters went back and forth, at great length.

November 2, 1940: Robert A. Heinlein to John W. Campbell, Jr.

. . . I turned it down, stating that the rate for my own name was higher than that. (I may let them publish "Lost Legacy" under a pseudonym, as it is one that I really want to see published. I am going to give a slight amount of rewriting to make it science fiction rather than fantasy, but still let it say the things I want it to say.)

Having touched on my personal policy to that extent, I feel obliged to be more specific, since it concerns you, too. I am going up, or out, in this business—never down. I don't want to write pulp bad enough to slip back into a lower word rate, and a hack attitude. As long as you are editing, at Street and Smith or elsewhere, you can have my stuff, if you want it, at a cent and a quarter a word, or more if you see fit and the business office permits. I won't use an agent in dealing with you, although I now have one. Neither my name nor the name of Anson MacDonald will be made available to any other book at the rate at which you buy from me, and, if I get an offer of a better rate, I will let you know and give you refusal, as it were, before switching. I write for money and will sell elsewhere for a materially higher word rate, but I feel a strong obligation to you. No other editor will get the two names you have advertised and built up at the rates you pay.

❖ ❖ ❖

I seem to have drifted a long way from stating my own policy and intentions. I will probably go on writing, at least part time, indefinitely. If you someday find it necessary to start rejecting my stuff, I expect to take a crack at some other forms, slick perhaps, and book-form novels, and in particular a nonfiction book on finance and money theory which I have wanted to do for a long time, also some articles on various economic and social problems. I have an outlet for such things, but it would be largely a labor of love—maybe ten dollars for an article into which has gone a week of research, and slim royalties on books in that field. Howsomever, I might crack the high word rates on general fiction at the same time. One never knows—I never expected to be writing pulp, or fiction of any sort, but it has paid me well . . . to my surprise!

❖ ❖ ❖

Addendum to remarks about my own policy: You may possibly feel that my wish to get out of the field of science fiction and into something else smacks of ungratefulness, in view of the way you have treated me. That is the very reason why I am looking forward to another field. I dislike very much to have business relations with a close personal friend. The present condition in which you like and buy everything I write may go on for years. If so—fine! Everybody is happy. But it would be no pleasure to you to have to reject my stuff, and certainly no pleasure to me. And it can happen at any time—your editorial policy may change, or my style or approach may change, or I may simply go stale. When it does occur, I want to cut it off short without giving it a chance to place a strain on our friendship. I don't want it to reach a point where you would view the reception of one of my manuscripts with a feeling of, "For Christ's sake, why doesn't he peddle his tripe somewhere else. He *knows* I hate to turn him down." And I don't want to greet a series of returned manuscripts in my mailbox with a feeling of, "Good God, what does he *expect* for a cent and a quarter a word? The New Testament?" Nor do I want you taking borderline stories from me simply because you hate to bounce them. I suspected that might be the case with the tesseract story ["—And He Built a Crooked House"].

Right now I know I am a profit-making commercial property, because the cash customers keep saying so in the Analytical Laboratory, but I don't intend to hang on while slipping down into fourth or fifth place. No, when I quit, I'll quit at the top, in order to insure that our business relations will never become unpleasant or disappointing to either of us. Which is a long and verbose way of saying that I value your friendship very highly indeed and intend to keep it if I can.

February 13, 1941: John W. Campbell, Jr. to Robert A. Heinlein

. . . We'll pay you $1\frac{1}{2}$ cents a word for your stories. Your guarantee that your *name* will not appear in other science fiction or fantasy magazines. And, naturally, your keeping the said arrangement strictly under the lid. Since "Anson MacDonald" is as much your name now as "Robert Heinlein," built up in and by *Astounding*, that goes, too. If you get an offer at $1\frac{3}{4}$ or 2 cents a word—grab it. It will promptly dispose of competition, or it will fade out very quickly. That's steeper than any modern scf. book can economically pay for anybody.

February 17, 1941: Robert A. Heinlein to John W. Campbell, Jr.

. . . One exception to the above that might amuse you—I have a phony name [Lyle Monroe] and a phony address, fully divorced from the RAH persona, under which and from which I am trying to peddle the three remaining stinkeroos which are left over from my earliest writing. For such purpose I *prefer* editors whom I do not like. It would tickle me to sell off the shoddy in that fashion. I don't think it is dishonest—they examine what they buy and get what they pay for—but I'm damned if I'll let my own name even appear on one of their checks.

❖   ❖   ❖

. . . I think my meaning is clear, and I will, as I believe you know, live up to it. Let me add this: If the going gets tough and the business office tells you to cut rates, I will go back to a cent and a quarter a word without murmur, *provided it is the highest rate you pay anyone.* As long as you pay anyone a cent and a half, I want it. If my stuff starts slipping and is no longer worth top rates, I prefer to quit rather than start the downgrade. Same thing I had to say once before with respect to rejections—I don't like 'em and will quit the racket when they start coming in. I know this can't go on forever but, so help me, having reached top, in one sense, I'll retire gracefully rather than slide downhill.

September 6, 1941: Robert A. Heinlein to John W. Campbell, Jr.

From your last two letters I am forced to conclude that you and I are talking somewhat at cross-purposes—you are apparently under the impression that I am still writing. To be sure, I did not drop you a card saying, "I retired today." I could not—under the circumstances it would have seemed like a childish piece of petulance. Nevertheless, I knew that I would retire and exactly when and why, and I sent a letter to you a number of months back in which I set forth my intention and my reasons. Surely you recall it? I know you received it, for you commented on it. The gist of the matter was that I intended to continue to make the writing of science fiction my principal occupation until I received a rejection slip, whereupon I would retire. I told you about it ahead of time so that you would know it was not pique, but a thought-out plan, which motivated me.

You will remember that in 1940 I was already looking forward to retiring in a few months. Well, the time came when I should have retired, but I couldn't—I couldn't afford to; you were buying everything I wrote at nice fat rates. A day's work paid me at least thirty dollars and usually more. I couldn't enjoy loafing; if I stayed away from the mill it had to be for some reason I could justify to my residual puritan bias. So I took myself to one side and said, "Look here, Robert, this has got to stop. You haven't any need for more money; the possession of more money simply leads you into expensive tastes which in no way increase your happiness. In the meantime you are getting fat, short-winded, and soft, and ruining your digestion to boot." To which Robert replied, "Yeah, boss, I know. But look—it's the money machine. Just punch it, and the dollars fall out. Money, money, money, money!" So I had to speak to him sternly, "Money! Sure, money is nice stuff, but you don't need much of it. We settled that when we entered the navy, and we proved it the time you got stung buying that silver mine." To which he answered, "Yeah, but look—you could buy the GE Home Workshop. You could put it right over there—and it costs only $110." "Another gadget! You know what I think of gadgets. When would you use it, anyhow?" "Don't give me that stuff! You know you like gadgets." "Well, within moderation, but the lust for them is a vice." "It is, eh? You've got it pretty bad then." "I have not," I answered with dignity. "I can take them or leave them alone. Besides, I would rather make them than buy them." The argument went on and on. He pointed out to me that money did not have to be spent; it could be loaned or given away. (We were both agreed that it should never be saved, except for specific short-term purposes.) I said, "When did you ever give or loan money that the deal didn't turn sour?" He mentioned a couple of times, and I was forced to admit he was right; "—besides, we could be more careful about it," he added hopefully.

The upshot of the matter was a compromise. I agreed to let him continue to punch the alphabetical slot machine just as long as he hit the jackpot every time; the first time he failed to get his nickel back we would quit.

So—at long last came the envelope I had been looking for, a rejection instead of a check [for "Creation Took Eight Days," later published as "Goldfish Bowl"]. I had a quick pang of regret over the money I didn't get, which was washed away by the pleasant knowledge that school was out at last. I spent the whole day taking pictures. I spent the next day starting the excavation for a swimming pool, a project which I have had in mind for five years, which I have been ready to commence for some months, but which takes time, lots of it. I could hire it done by staying at the typewriter, but that was not the idea—I wanted the heavy physical exercise [that] a pick, shovel, and wheelbarrow provide.

Besides that, I have had a number of typewriter projects in mind which have been indefinitely postponed because I was busy with S-F. In particular a short book on monetary theory which should have been written eighteen months ago. That is a "must" and will probably be finished this winter. I expect it to be published but I probably won't make any money out of it. Besides that, I have been urged to tackle a primer of semantics and general semantics. I am moderately well prepared for the task, having had five seminars in the subject; nevertheless there is a lot of research to be done and a monumental task of devising lucid pedagogical methods in a most difficult field, involving as it does a very nearly complete reorientation in methods of thinking even for the "educated" reader. I estimate that it may take from two to five years to complete. Incidentally, if you are interested, I would be willing to do a popular article or two on the subject for *Astounding*. I offered to do so once before, you may recall, but you made no answer.

Besides the above, I am going to try to do at least one novel for book publication and will probably try a flyer in slicks, most likely through Virginia Perdue's agent. I haven't had much luck with agents up to now, and it seems to be agreed that a good agent is almost a *sine qua non* for such endeavor.

The above plans, although numerous and involved, are leisurely in their nature—which is what I have been wanting. I want to be able to stop, sit down, and "invite my soul" for an hour, a day, or a week, if I feel the need for it. I don't know yet what my principal task in this world is, if I have one, but I do know that I won't find it through too much hurrying and striving . . .

. . . I have gone on, wordily, because it is important to me that you should understand my motives—I want your approval. Let me pose a rhetorical question: What incentive is there for me to remain a full-time writer of science fiction? At the present time I am the most popular writer for the most popular magazine in the field and command (I believe) the highest word rate. Where is there for me to go but down? I can't go up in this field; there is no place to go . . . Frankly, the strain is wearing on me. I can still write, but it is a terrific grind to try each week to be more clever than I was the week before. And if I do, to what purpose. First is the highest I can stand; a cent and a half a word is the most I can hope to be paid.

I will not attempt to pep up my stories by introducing a greater degree of action-adventure. It is not my style. It seems to me that the popularity of my stuff has been based largely on the fact that I have continually enlarged the field of S-F and changed it from gadget motivation to stories more subtle in their themes and more realistically motivated in terms of human psychology. In particular I introduced the regular use of high tragedy and completely abandoned the hero-and-villain formula. My last story, the one you bounced ["Goldfish Bowl"], does not represent a change in the sort of thing I have been doing, but

SIXTH COLUMN

"Sixth Column" also ran as a serial in *Astounding* in 1941.

When Ardmore reached the secret, buried Citadel, only six men were alive there. PanAsia has just completed the total conquest of the United States, and the men are despondent. The scientists have just discovered and begun exploring three new spectra beyond the electromagnetic—the electrogravitic, the magnetogravitic and the electromagnetogravitic. These could create seeming miracles—levitation, simple transmutation, instant cure of any germ- or virus-caused disease, etc. No one knows what to do with them. But Ardmore, with an advertising man's imagination, suggests the start of a new "religion," since the PanAsians do not interfere with the religions of the "slaves."

And with the new science and enough mumbo-jumbo, they go forth to bedazzle, frustrate, and drive the PanAsians back to their homelands. (This was Heinlein's first full novel.)

a logical and (for my taste) artistic extension of the theme. I don't blame you for bouncing it; if you did not see the point of the story, you have no reason to think that your customers would. Nevertheless, the story had a point, a most important point, a most powerful and tragic one. Apparently I expressed the point too subtly, but you and I have rather widely divergent views about the degree of subtlety a story can stand. For my money you have damaged a great many excellent stories you have printed by telegraphing the point of the story on the contents page, in the blurb under the title, and in the subtitles under the illustrations. And you damn near ruined "Requiem" by adding four lines to the end which led the reader up a blind alley, clear away from the real point of the story.

Anyhow—I'm not trying to sell you that last story; I'm just trying to say that it was not a pointless story, but one of the most daring themes

I have ever tackled, and, so far as I know, never before attempted in science fiction.

Returning to our muttons: I am extremely grateful to you for the help you have been to me in every way during this two-year try at commercial writing. And I don't want you to feel that I have taken what I wanted and walked out. One of my reasons for the continual scouting I have done for *Astounding* and *Unknown* has been that I anticipated my own retirement and wanted to be able to say, "Okay, John, I'm quitting, but here are half a dozen other writers, my protégés, who take my place several times over." I expect to continue that scouting indefinitely.

Besides that, I have laid down no hard and fast ultimatum to myself that I won't write science fiction at all. If I get an idea that really intrigues me, I'll write a story about it and submit it. Naturally, I don't expect you to maintain the former financial arrangement. I won't take a rate cut, but you are welcome to buy at a cent a word under the Lyle Monroe name, a cent and a quarter for Caleb Saunders, or, if you think a story merits it, a cent and a half for Heinlein or MacDonald. If one of the latter two makes the grade in slicks, it will be withdrawn from pulp entirely, but that is still a remote possibility.

SIXTH COLUMN

September 16, 1941: Robert A. Heinlein to John W. Campbell, Jr.

My own work—I am taking you at your word that "Creation Took Eight Days" ["Goldfish Bowl"] can be fixed up to sell to you in either one of two ways, by changing the ending or by changing the earlier part to make the ending less of a surprise. Of the two I prefer to change the earlier part; otherwise it is a completely different story and not my kind of a story. I have never written a World-Saver story of the usual formula, because I don't believe in them. Even in "Sixth Column" I was careful to point out that the job was just started and never would be finished. This particular story was intended to give an entirely fresh angle on the invasion-by-alien-intelligence theme. So far as I know, every such story has alien intelligences which treat humans as approximate equals, either as friends or as foes. It is assumed that A-I will either be friends, anxious to communicate and trade, or ene-

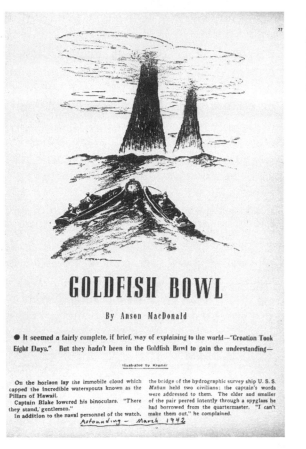

''Goldfish Bowl,'' published in *Astounding* March 1942, under pseudonmyn Anson MacDonald. Art by Kramer. ''Goldfish Bowl'' had originally been rejected by Campbell, but eventually Heinlein and Campbell agreed on revisions.

GOLDFISH BOWL

By Anson MacDonald

● It seemed a fairly complete, if brief, way of explaining to the world—"Creation Took Eight Days." But they hadn't been in the Goldfish Bowl to gain the understanding—

Illustrated by Kramer

On the horizon lay the immobile cloud which capped the incredible waterspouts known as the Pillars of Hawaii.

Captain Blake lowered his binoculars. "There they stand, gentlemen."

In addition to the naval personnel of the watch,

the bridge of the hydrographic survey ship U. S. S. *Mahan* held two civilians: the captain's words were addressed to them. The elder and smaller of the pair peered intently through a spyglass he had borrowed from the quartermaster. "I can't make them out," he complained.

Astounding — March 1942

mies who will fight and kill, or possibly enslave, the human race. There is another and much more humiliating possibility—alien intelligences so superior to us and so indifferent to us as to be almost unaware of us. They do not even covet the surface of the planet where we live—they live in the stratosphere. We do not know whether they evolved here or elsewhere—will never know. Our mightiest engineering structures they regard as we regard coral formations, i.e., seldom noticed and considered of no importance. We aren't even nuisances to them. And they are no threat to us, except that their "engineering" might occasionally disturb our habitat, as the grading done for a highway disturbs gopher holes.

Some few of them might study us casually—or might not. Some odd duck among them might keep a few of us as pets. That was what happened to my hero. He got too nosy around one of their activities, was captured, and by pure luck was kept as a pet instead of being stepped on. In time he understood his predicament, except in one respect—he never did realize to its full bitterness that the human race could not even *fight* these creatures. He was simply a goldfish in a bowl—who cares about the opinions of a helpless goldfish? I have a fish pond in my patio. Perhaps those fish hate me bitterly and have sworn to destroy me. I won't even suspect it—I'll lose no sleep over it. And it seems to me that the most esoteric knowledge of science would not enable those fish to harm me. I am indifferent to them and invulnerable.

I used a working title of "Goldfish Bowl" but changed it because, in my opinion, it tipped the story. Now it appears that you want the story tipped more quickly. Perhaps the working title is almost the only change it needs. In any case, John, you habitually give the key idea of a story in the blurbs—sometimes, I think, to the detriment of the dramatic punch of a story. That was my reaction to the blurbing on "By His Bootstraps." (But you're the editor! I ain't complaining; I'm expressing an opinion.) I'll look the story over in a day or two and try to see where I can do some planting in the early part. If you have any specific ideas, please mention them right away; I am not quite sure what you want— the degree, at least. Maybe we'll have to ship this story back and forth a couple of times yet.

It will please me to sell this story for a reason that has developed since I last wrote to you. As you know, I have been gradually selling off the half-dozen stories you have rejected since I started writing. Last week I sold two in one day—the last two ["Pied Piper" and "My Object All Sublime," both under Lyle Monroe. Heinlein never permitted reprinting these]. Utter dogs they were, written in the spring of 1939. That leaves me with an absolutely clean sweep of having sold every word I have ever written from the first day I sat down to attempt commercial writing . . . So—a clean sweep right up to this last story. The opportunity to fix it up to sell is very pleasant.

September 17, 1941: John W. Campbell, Jr. to Robert A. Heinlein

I had forgotten that little point of yours. And now, of course, the thing sticks me at a wonderfully tender spot. Item: We went to large size, with about a 70% increase in consumption. Item: We have novelettes, but are atrociously short of short stories. Item: We've had one good author who could really produce wordage. And now—now of all times!—that one wants to retire! Just when, it so happens, we haven't a single thing of yours on hand. Your protégés, helpful as they are, can, together, produce about as much, but not the quality, that you can. So—we launch the large-size, large-consumption book with the loss of the top one-third of our authors—the one man with three names.

Look—how about at least making it a new year's resolution, or something? By that time, maybe we can get shaken down into a better order.

On that story-that-bounced: Science fiction is normally read as light, escape literature. The reader does not expect or seek heavy philosophy; particularly, he does not expect or prepare himself for heavy philosophy when he reads a story that shows every sign of being action-adventure. Bathyspheres—alien something-or-others—men vanishing and men killed—heavy menace, with Navy personnel called in to look into it—something powerful and active under way here, with violent action ending in a solution—

Or at least that seemed the setup. The answer you gave was utterly unexpected, the right answer to the wrong question, so to speak. Therein it was a seemingly pointless question-and-answer, and disappointing to the reader. At Heinlein-MacDonald $1^1/_2$ cent rates, I can't disappoint; alteration of either the answer—so it fitted the question the reader was asked—or of the question into a form that more evidently called for the type of answer provided, would make it click. The answer provided did make a highly interesting point, but a point overwhelmed in the rush of unfulfilled expectation of action-adventure.

In general, if you retire abruptly at this particular moment, *Astounding* is going to feel it in much the way one's tongue feels a missing tooth just after it's been yanked.

So far as going up goes, I'll agree you can't very well. I can agree with your desire to retire, under your circumstances. But look—when you don't have to, writing's a lot of fun. When you have to fill magazines, as I do, good manuscripts are godsends. Be god for a little while more, and send more, willya?

I know one thing: I'm going to get some loud and angry howls from readers.

September 19, 1941: John W. Campbell, Jr. to Robert A. Heinlein

In re your own stories. Novelettes are your meat—those and short serials, which will be, under the new setup, short novels complete in an issue. You need elbow room to develop the civilization background against which your characters act. I know that, and have suggested shorts to you mainly when I was kinda desperate for short stories that couldn't be smelled before opening the book.

September 25, 1941: Robert A. Heinlein to John W. Campbell, Jr.

I think I've got it. Darned if I don't think so. The serial, I mean—the one I've been looking for ["Beyond This Horizon"].

Like this—for some time I've been wandering around in a blue fog, trying to get a theme, a major conflict suitable for a novel-length S-F story. I wanted it to be fully mature, adult, dramatic in its possibility—and not used before. Naturally, the last requirement was the sticker. Perhaps the possibilities in S-F have not been exhausted, but they have certainly been well picked over; for me, at least, it is hard to find a really fresh theme. But I started searching by elimination. First, I elim-

"Methuselah's Children," Heinlein's tale of a super-race, *Astounding*, July through September 1941. Art by Hubert Rogers.

inated space travel. Old hat, and it tends to steal the scene from any-thing else. Then I assumed that the basic problems of economics and politics had been solved. Thus, in one sweep, I got rid of almost every type of story I have done up to this time.

Okay—in a world that is all peace-and-prosperity, what will men and women have left to struggle for? Problems of sex and marriage obvi-ously, but I am not writing for *Ladies' Home Journal*. The basic problem of esthetics? Wide open for S-F treatment, and new, but the issues are subtle and it would be difficult to convince the readers that the prob-lems of esthetics are susceptible to scientific analysis and manipulation. Same for metaphysical problems.

I seemed to be up against a dead end, when a possibility occurred to me which, while not new, has been futzed with rather than dealt with—the possibilities of genetics, and in particular, What Are We Go-ing to Make of the Human Race? Mr. Tooker discussed it ably in the March '39 book, Stapledon has dealt with it on the grand scale in "Last and First Men," Taine-Bell suggested some possibilities in "The Time Stream," numerous superman stories have been written, and lots of stories of the mad-scientist-in-the-laboratory-creates-new-species type have been done. [Aldous] Huxley did a beautiful satire in *Brave New World*, and even Heinlein has brushed the edges of the subject in "Me-thuselah's Children." But it seems to me that there remains a different and in some ways better story yet to be written.

September 30, 1941: Robert A. Heinlein to John W. Campbell, Jr.

Herewith is a piece of utter hoke which you saw in its original form in 1939. I shortened it to fit an immediate market ready to buy it, but I am not obligated to sell it there. In its shortened form it seems somewhat improved and it occurred to me that, if you are still having trouble getting short stories "which can't be smelled before the book is opened," as you put it, this item might stand a chance. It isn't good, I know, but it may be no worse than the competition.

It is offered to you at one cent a word, under the Monroe name which appears on it, or under the name of Leslie Keith. God knows it is not worth a cent a word, but I believe that is your lowest rate. If you can't use it, place it carefully in the enclosed receptacle and bounce it back to me at once, so I can shoot it off to the low-pay, slow-pay market for which it is intended.

I suppose it is silly of me to waste time revising and selling these

A scene from "By His Bootstraps," *Astounding*, October 1941. Art by Hubert Rogers, an artist closely associated with *Astounding* and with Heinlein's works.

He took a wild swing, hisself ducked, and himself collected the haymaker—

tant to you and to me is the effect they had on the human psyche. One twentieth-century style go-getter can accomplish just about anything he wants to accomplish around here— Aren't you listening?" "Huh? Oh, yes, sure. Say, that's one mighty pretty girl." His eyes

dogs, but this is the last of them, and it is a source of satisfaction to have disposed of all of them. And none of them took more than one rewriting, which isn't bad, since most writers do two drafts in any case.

Tomorrow I start revising "Creation Took Eight Days" ["Goldfish Bowl"], which *won't* take me eight days and will leave two whole months for the serial. I've continued research every day and have a stack of notes *that* high. I'm going to like this serial, I think.

October 1, 1941: John W. Campbell, Jr. to Robert A. Heinlein

Re "By His Bootstraps." It's taking first place away from "Common Sense" . . . "Bootstraps" is not hack; it's the first all-out, frank attack on the circle-of-time story. It's a magnificent idea, and it's been worked out beautifully. You've taken a minute, but highly intriguing point in the whole theory of time-travel, and built it up to the proportions it deserved. Reasons it's good, among others: you follow the thoughts of each of the several returns of Wilson, showing why he did, each time, say what he said, though he might well have tried to change from his remembered speech. You have a story in which, each time, the man from the future who knows more, says, "It's too long a story to explain," and brushing off the explanation, both intrigues and annoys the reader—and makes him like it.

October 4, 1941: Robert A. Heinlein to John W. Campbell, Jr.

I have been beset by insomnia while trying to get the serial started, and was forced last night to the expedient of twin beds and barbiturate. Under the influence of drugs I was awake only three times in the night, but got over eight hours sleep, by damn, and feel fine today. But serial still looks hopeless. The idea is grand, wonderful, and I see more interesting angles to it every day. But each day it looks a little more impossible to work out than the day before—for pulp. The events would take place with such geologic leisureliness. And there are other difficulties, which will be obvious to you. I don't know—I don't know.

. . . "By His Bootstraps" is still hack—a neat trick, sure, but no more than a neat trick. Cotton candy.

CHAPTER II

❖

BEGINNINGS

❖

October 16, 1941: Robert A. Heinlein to John W. Campbell, Jr.

I can write my own story with great speed when I start, but I am not yet satisfied as to the central conflict. I have several different central problems in my mind, any of which would make a story, but as yet do not have one which fully satisfies me. I want this story to be high tragedy rather than horse opera—full of gore and action as a Greek tragedy, but tragedy in the Greek sense. (Necessarily a tragedy, because wisdom required to control genetics wisely is superhuman, and I'm no superman.)

EDITOR'S NOTE: As the use of working titles was frequent, titles of stories are not always given. Now and then a final title to a story was affixed by the author, but, more often, the editor changed the title before the story saw print. It would only cause confusion here to show all the title changes some stories went through.

November 9, 1941: Robert A. Heinlein to John W. Campbell, Jr.

Here are the first ten thousand words of the current struggle ["Beyond This Horizon"]. Confidentially, it stinks. But I am and have been doing my goddamndest to turn out printable copy for you. My worst trouble is to get enough illustrative action into the story and to keep it from bogging down into endless talky-talk. I have stacks of notes on this story, more than twice as much as on any story I've ever

"Beyond This Horizon," by
"Anson MacDonald,"
Astounding, April and May 1942.
Art by Hubert Rogers.

done; the ideas it suggests really interest me—but I am finding it hard as hell to beat a *story* out of it.

But I am turning out copy and will continue to do so, at about two thousand words a day or more. Those spots on the right margin are my blood, a drop per line.

November 15, 1941: Robert A. Heinlein to John W. Campbell, Jr.

Here is another hunk of hack ["Beyond This Horizon"]. I think it well to let you see it in weekly chunks, as I am by no means confident of its quality and would like for you to look it over and comment on it as I turn it out. Then, if you get any brainstorms, I can incorporate them without delay. You appear to think better of this yarn than I do. I think it is going to require a *deus ex machina* to give the ending any real oomph—in my present sterile state of mind you may be elected *deus.*

December 2, 1941: Robert A. Heinlein to John W. Campbell, Jr.

I believe I am correct in assuming that required revisions and corrections can wait until I get to New York. Most of the changes, if any, would need to be made in the second installment. I think I have ducked around the taboos sufficiently; compare this story ["Beyond This Horizon"] with any issue of *Ladies' Home Journal*—this story is much more discreet than the stuff now printed in domestic magazines. I remember a story in Street and Smith's *National Magazine*, in which the hero scrubs the heroine's back—both raw. Me, I did not even suggest that sexual intercourse was an old human custom, and you can search the yarn from end to end without finding any reference to anatomical details.

I *did* include a scene involving telepathy with an unborn child—you suggested it. But I kept the mother off stage. I don't think there is a leer in the story. Lots of boy-meets-girl and some will object to that, but, dammit, there *had* to be—if the story was to be at all true to life.

December 8, 1941: John W. Campbell, Jr. to Robert A. Heinlein

I never meant to give you a feeling of extreme urgency. Perhaps your interpretation—your personal emotional index—of "desire" comes closer to my intent than "need." Partly, that can be due to the situation best expressed this way: I need—in the sense of "must have without fail"—some tall stories. I need manuscripts. I desire some tall stories from you; I ardently desire manuscripts of the quality you produce.

(Curious—you and I each possess a vocabulary of perhaps 300,000 words, with a pretty fair ability to distinguish between the shades of meaning involved. And I can't quite adequately express the exact tone and intensity of value of the basic thought "I want you to write stories for *Astounding*.")

But for the future. I don't know what you'll be doing. I have no idea what pressure of work will be on you. I don't know whether you can ever write a story as a method of relaxation. (I can; it's as much fun as reading someone else's work.)

December 9, 1941: Robert A. Heinlein to John W. Campbell, Jr.

This is the first time in forty-eight hours that I have been able to tear myself away from the radio long enough to think about writing a letter. Naturally, our attention has been all in one direction up to now. We are still getting used to the radical change in conditions, but our morale is extremely good, as is, I am happy to report, that of everyone. For myself, the situation, tragic as it is, comes to me as an actual relief and a solution of my own emotional problems. For the past year and a half I have been torn between two opposing points of view—and the desire to retain as long as possible my own little creature comforts and my own snug little home with the constant company of my wife and the companionship of my friends and, opposed to that, the desire to volunteer. Now all that is over, I have volunteered and have thereby surrendered my conscience (like a good Catholic) to the keeping of others.

The matter has been quite acute to me. For the last eighteen months I have often been gay and frequently much interested in what I was doing, but I have not been happy. There has been with me, night and day, a gnawing doubt as to the course I was following. I felt that there was something that I ought to be doing. I rationalized it, not too successfully, by reminding myself that the navy knew where I was, knew my abilities, and had the legal power to call on me if they wanted me. But I felt like a heel. This country has been very good to me, and the taxpayers have supported me for many years. I knew when I was sworn in, sixteen years ago, that my services and if necessary my life were at the disposal of the country; no amount of rationalization, no amount of reassurance from my friends, could still my private belief that I ought to be up and doing at this time.

I logged in at the Commandant's office as soon as I heard that Pearl Harbor was attacked. Thereafter I telephoned you. The next day (yesterday) I presented myself at San Pedro and requested a physical examination. I am an old crock in many little respects—half a dozen little chronic ailments, all of which show up at once in physical examination but which I was able to argue them out of. Nevertheless, I was rejected on two counts, as a matter of routine—the fact that I am an old lunger and that I am nearsighted beyond the limits allowed even for the staff corps. They had no choice but to reject me—at the time. But my eyes are corrected to 20/20 and I am completely cured of T.B., probably more sound in that respect than a goodly percentage now on duty who never knew they had it. Sure, I've got scars in my lungs, but what are scars?

❖ ❖ ❖

My feelings toward the Japs could be described as a cold fury. I not only want them to be defeated, I want them to be smashed. I want them to be punished at least a hundredfold, their cities burned, their industries smashed, their fleet destroyed, and finally, their sovereignty taken away from them. We have been forced into a course of imperialism. So let it be. Germany and Japan are not safe to have around; we are bigger and tougher than they are, I sincerely believe. Let's rule them. We did not want it that way—but if somebody has to be boss, I want it to be *us*. Disarm them and *don't turn them loose*. We can treat the individual persons decently in an economic sense, but take away their sovereignty.

December 16, 1941: Robert A. Heinlein to John W. Campbell, Jr.

So far, I have not been able to peddle my valuable services. The letter in which I volunteered, accompanied by a certified copy of my physical exam report, is wending its way through the circuitous official

Heinlein in his naval uniform, shortly after his graduation in June 1929. Contrary to his wishes, Heinlein did not see active military duty during World War II.

channels. I stuck airmail postage with it with a memo to the Commandant's aide asking him to use same, and the letter asks for dispatch orders; nevertheless, it would not surprise me to be sitting here until January or so. In the meantime, I have been circulating around the offices of local naval activities, trying to find someone who wants me bad enough to send a dispatch asking for me. No luck so far. Damn it—I should have volunteered six months ago.

December 21, 1941: Robert A. Heinlein to John W. Campbell, Jr.

I was interested in your father's comment in re the navy, and in your further comments. Some of the comments he found fault with are real faults, some as you pointed out derive from a lack of knowledge of the true problems. Some of the real faults seem to me to be inherent in the nature of military organization and inescapable. The navy is an involved profession; it takes twenty-five years or so to make an admiral—and older men are not quite as mentally flexible as younger men. I see no easy way to avoid that. Is your father as receptive to new ideas as you are? Will he step down and let you tell him how to run AT&T? Is there any way of avoiding the dilemma? Nevertheless, the brasshats are not quite as opposed to new ideas as the news commentators would have us think. The present method of antiaircraft fire was invented by an ensign. Admiral King encouraged a warrant officer and myself to try to invent a new type of bomb (Note: We weren't successful.) You may remember that one of my story gags was picked up by a junior officer and made standard practice in the fleet before the next issue hit the stands. Nevertheless, there is something about military life which makes men conservative. I don't know how to beat it. Roosevelt has beaten it from the top to a certain extent by insisting on young men and/or men whose abilities he knew, but it is sheer luck that we have a president who has known the navy's problem and personnel since he was a young man. I know of no general solution.

❖ ❖ ❖

I may get sea orders any day—along with a lot of other old crocks who would not have to go to sea if it had not been for that partisan opposition I spoke of . . .

. . . Some of Hamilton Felix's point of veiw is autobiographical. [Hamilton Felix was the protagonist of "Beyond This Horizon."] I would like to have been a synthesist, but I am acutely aware that many of my characteristics are second-rate. I haven't quite got the memory, nor the integrating ability, nor the physical strength, nor the strength of character to do the job. I am not depressed about it, but I know my own shortcomings. I am sufficiently brilliant and sufficiently imaginative to realize acutely just how superficial my acquaintance with the world is and to know that I have not the health, ambition, nor years remaining to me to accomplish what I would like to accomplish. Don't discount this as false modesty . . .

I have just sufficient touch of genius to know that I am not a proper genius—and I am not much interested in second prize. In the meantime, I expect to have quite a lot of fun and do somewhat less constructive work than I might, if I tried as hard as I could. That last is not quite correct. I simply don't have the ambition to try as hard as I might, nor quite the health. But I do have fun!

❖ ❖ ❖

In re mental-ostrichism and boycotting the war news: A long time ago I learned that it was necessary to my own mental health to insulate myself emotionally from everything I could not help and to restrict my worrying to things I could help. But wars have a tremendous emotional impact and I have a one-track mind. In 1939 and 1940 I deliberately took the war news about a month late, via *Time* magazine, in order to dilute the emotional impact. Otherwise I would not have been able to concentrate on fiction writing at all. Emotional detachment is rather hard for me to achieve, so I cultivate it by various dodges whenever the situation is one over which I have no control.

January 4, 1942: Robert A. Heinlein to John W. Campbell, Jr.

You suggest that my thinking about the navy I keep compartmented away from my thinking on other subjects. It is true that I have been oriented and indoctrinated by a naval education and naval experience. It is true that a man cannot escape his background—the best he can do is to try to evaluate it and discount it. But as to your "proof" (by, God save us, Aristotelian logic!) that I keep my mind compartmented—well, much more about that later; much, much more.

In the meantime, I shall "sound general quarters and return your fire." For a long time I have from time to time felt exasperated with you that you should be so able so completely to insulate your thinking in nonscientific fields from your excellent command of the scientific method in science fields. So far as I have observed you, you would no more think of going off half-cocked, with insufficient and unverified data, with respect to a matter of science than you would stroll down Broadway in your underwear. But when it comes to matters outside your specialties you are consistently and brilliantly stupid. You come out with some of the goddamndest flat-footed opinions with respect to matters which you haven't studied and have had no experience, basing your opinions on casual gossip, newspaper stories, unrelated individual data out of matrix, armchair extrapolation, and plain misinformation—unsuspected because you haven't attempted to verify it.

Of course, most people hold uncritical opinions in much the same fashion—my milkman, for example. (In his opinion, the navy can do no wrong!) But I don't expect such sloppy mental processes from you. Damn it! You've had the advantage of a rigorous training in scientific methodology. Why don't you apply it to everyday life? The scientific method will not enable you to hold exact opinions on matters in which you lack sufficient data, but it can keep you from being certain of your opinions and make you aware of the value of your data, and to reserve your judgment until you have amplified your data.

All I said with reference to the Pearl Harbor debacle was that the necessary data for an opinion was not yet in and that we should reserve judgment until the data was available. I added, in effect, that this was no time for the intelligent minority to be adding to the flood of rumors and armchair opinions flying through the country. I still say so. As an intelligent and educated man, you have a responsibility to your less gifted fellow citizens to be a steady and morale-building influence at this time. Your letters do not indicate that you are being such.

I am going to try to take up a number of points one at a time, some from your letters, some from related matters.

"Aid and comfort to the enemy, phui. Morale damage, hell." (From your letter) I am going to have to be rather directly personal about this. It may not have occurred to you that I am a member of the armed forces of the United States at the present moment awaiting orders, for sea duty I hope. Such comments as you have made to me might very well damage the morale of a member of the armed forces by shaking his confidence in his superior officers. There happens to be a federal law forbidding any talk in wartime to a member of the armed forces which *might tend* to destroy morale in just that fashion—a law passed by Congress, and not just a departmental regulation. It so happens that I am sufficiently hardheaded, tough-minded, and conceited not to be much influenced by your opinions of the high command. I think I know more about the high command than you do. Nevertheless, you were not entitled to take the chance of shaking my confidence, my willingness to fight. And you should guard your talk in the future. It might, firsthand, secondhand, or thirdhand, influence some enlisted man who had not the armoring to his morale that years of indoctrination gives me.

Bear in mind that my advice to you is based on a law, specifically intended by the Congress under the Constitution to restrict the freedom of speech of civilians in wartime in their relations with the military. If you don't like the law, write to your congressman about it. If you feel you must express yourself, write it down and save it until the war is over—but *don't* tell a member of the armed forces that his superiors are stupid and incompetent. Don't write to Ron [L. Ron Hubbard] in such a vein. He has not my indoctrination and he *is* in the battlefield. If you feel that the high command is incompetent, take it up with your congressman and your senators. Those of us in the service must work under the officers that are placed over us—it doesn't help to try to shake our confidence in them.

❖ ❖ ❖

. . . I've dug down into my personal funds many times to entertain visiting congressmen, visiting notables, etc. There are no funds appropriated for such things; the commissioned officers pay for them themselves. Naval officers act as scout masters for sea scouts. They are always available to speak before any body of persons willing to listen—travel to and from at his own expense, or charged to ship's service (a *private* fund) by his C.O. We always have had public relations officers and we always have done everything we knew how to do to foster goodwill for the navy. In addition to that, the naval affairs committees of both houses are kept constantly informed in detail of the needs of the navy and the strategic reasons therefor.

Our efforts were pitifully inadequate. How could they be adequate? In the first place, we aren't advertising men and we don't know how. In the second place, even if we knew how, we had no appropriations

Heinlein in his white naval uniform. (early 1930s)

Heinlein's Fencing Champion medal.

to work with. All we could do was to talk, and that got us damned little newspaper space and no billboards. Of course, we could get an occasional scholarly article published—much good that did!

. . . You may consider my reaction as a type form professional reaction; it derives from my orientation and indoctrination. It is quite evident from the suggestion you made and your answer to my reaction that you have not the slightest understanding of the psychology of a professional military man. I don't know quite how to explain this. It is a heavily emotional matter and goes back to some basic evaluations. Let me put it this way: Take a young boy, before he has been out in the business world. Put him into the naval academy. Tell him year after year that his most valuable possession and practically his only one is his personal honor. Let him see classmates cashiered for telling a small and casual lie. Let him see another classmate cashiered for stealing a pair of white silk socks. Tell him that he will never be rich but that he stands a chance of having his name inscribed in Memorial Hall. Entrust him with secrets. Indoctrinate him so that he will consider himself locked up and unable to move simply because his sword has been taken away from him. Feed him on tales of heroism. Line the corridors of his recitation halls with captured flags. Shucks, why go on with it— I think you must see what I am driving at. That will produce a naval officer, a man you can depend on to be utterly courageous in the face of personal danger regardless of the sick feeling in his stomach, but it won't produce an advertising man.

Naval officers, as a group, are no more temperamentally capable of producing the kind of sensational publicity you suggest they produce than they are of sprouting wings and flying.

Furthermore, if they were, they would be no damn good as naval officers. A naval officer is much more than a man with a certain body of technical information. He is a man trained to respond in a certain behavior pattern in which "honor" and "service" have been substituted for economic motivation. I don't know whether I have convinced you or not, but I can assure you that it would be almost impossible to find an officer who has spent his entire adult life in the fleet who could put over the sensationalism you suggest. It is about like asking a priest to desecrate the sacrament.

❖ ❖ ❖

Certainly the navy has specific secrets. In peacetime they are limited to such things as the details of weapons (and occasionally the existence of a weapon), codes and ciphers, the numerical details of gunnery scores, the insides of certain instruments, and similar details in which we are *trying* to keep a little ahead of the next. You spoke of "official spies" being shown things which are kept from the public. Who handed you that piece of guff? I know what you mean—foreign officers. Unless they are allies, they don't see anything that newsreel men don't see. I remember once being ordered to chaperone a British naval officer. I was admonished never to let him out of my sight and was given a list of things he must *not* see. I even went into the head with him. . . .

Of course, in wartime practically everything is secret—and a damned good thing! But the essential matters on which a civilian could make up his mind whether or not we need a big navy aren't secret, never have been secret, and by their nature can't be secret. Geographical strategy, for example, and the relative strengths of the fleets of various nations. *Jane's Fighting Ships* is not a particularly reticent book, and I know you have seen it. Navy yards aren't hard to get into. In normal times, naval vessels run boats for any visitor who wants to come aboard—and the ship's police has a weekly headache to make sure none get into the fire-control stations and similar places.

I am completely bewildered as to what you mean by the "hush hush" attitude of the navy. I would certainly appreciate some facts.

Lots of civilians are necessarily entrusted with certain naval secrets. I've sailed with many a G.E., Westinghouse, and AT&T engineer. The gadget of mine that was taken over by the fleet was developed by one of your father's engineers. I doubt if he personally had any occasion to know about it, but don't ask him about it and don't try to conjecture what it might be. Don't mention it to anyone, lest they do a little guessing. By mentioning the *class* of engineer that developed it I have shown greater confidence in you than I have in any other civilian. Let it stand that it is a proper military secret and that we hope that we are the only navy using it.

It is quite possible that a request for a piece of information is turned down when the questioner can see no reason why it should not be told. To that I can say only that the officers refusing to part with the information are the only possible judges as to whether or not public welfare is involved. Being human, they can make errors of judgment, *but no one can judge for them*. Obviously—if you hold a secret, I have no way of judging whether or not you should share it with me. Consequently, the responsibility for the decision rests entirely with you. A perfectly innocent request for information can be met with what appears to be an arbitrary refusal. How can the questioner know?

But, having been in the navy, and having held both confidential and secret information, I can assure you that it is not the policy of the navy to go out of its way to be mysterious. Decidedly not! On the contrary, it usually seemed to me that we were too frank, aboveboard, and open. It was too easy to get too close to really hush-hush stuff, to such an extent that it used to worry me.

❖　❖　❖

Item: You excuse the somewhat wild remarks of yourself, [Fletcher] Pratt, and company, on the basis that you are sore as hell, especially so as you are navy fans and love ships. (Incidentally, you don't seem to want to be classed as part of the general public, yet seem to resent being advised to act like professionals in the matter.) If you think you're sore and upset, how do you think I feel? Pearl Harbor isn't a point on a floor game to me—I've been there. The old *Okie* isn't a little wooden model six inches long; she's a person to me. I've sketched her fuel lines down in her bilges. I was turret captain of her number two turret. I have been in her main battery fire control party when her big guns were talking. Damn it, man, I've *lived* in her. And the casualty lists at Oahu are not names in a newspaper to me; they are my friends, my classmates. The thing hit me with such utter sickening grief as I have not experienced before in my life and has left me with a feeling of loss of personal honor such as I never expected to experience. For one reason and one only—because I found myself sitting on a hilltop, in civilian clothes, with no battle station and unable to fight, when it happened.

EDITOR'S NOTE: *Robert wrote stories for John W. Campbell, Jr. for* Astounding *and* Unknown *for close to three years. When Pearl Harbor was attacked in 1941, Robert tried to persuade the Navy to take him back on active duty. Failing in that, he went to work in Philadelphia doing engineering at the Naval Air Experimental Station.*

The war over, Robert looked around at the wider horizons for his writing career. Four short stories were sold to the Saturday Evening Post, *then the* most important and highest paying market, and he sold his first juvenile novel to Charles Scribner's Sons. The next market he tackled was motion pictures, and the successful Destination Moon resulted.

"Gulf" was the only story Robert wrote after World War II which was intended solely for the Astounding market. Occasionally his agent, Lurton Blassingame, would send a novel to John W. Campbell, Jr. Some of those were rejected for various reasons with lengthy letters of explanation from John Campbell to Robert. Those stories were never intended for that market, but Campbell would explain why the writing and stories were terrible—from his viewpoint. When Podkayne [Podkayne of Mars] was offered to him, he wrote Robert, asking what he knew about raising young girls in a few thousand carefully chosen words.

The friendship dwindled, and was eventually completely gone. It was just another casualty, probably, of World War II.

CHAPTER III

❖

THE SLICKS AND THE SCRIBNER'S JUVENILES

❖

TRY AT SLICKS

October 25, 1946: Robert A. Heinlein to Lurton Blassingame

The news that you sold "The Green Hills of Earth" to the *Saturday Evening Post* is very gratifying for more reasons than the size of the check. I am happy that we have cracked the top slick market; I am particularly happy that it was done with this story, as it is a favorite of mine which has been growing in my mind for five years.

EDITOR'S NOTE: In the 1930s and 1940s and farther back, the Saturday Evening Post *was the elite market of the short story writer. It paid the highest rates and carried the most prestige.*

The Post *was on every newsstand, and was widely read.*

In addition to short stories, and serialized novels, it also ran many articles. To be well-informed, one read the Post. *It was sold everywhere; the covers by Norman Rockwell were especially featured. Each issue contained some articles, short fiction, and usually a series of stories concerning much the same cast, and it was the ambition of every short story writer to have one of these series going. Bonus rates were paid for such series.*

Selling the Post *was a boy's job, and boys would go from door to door*

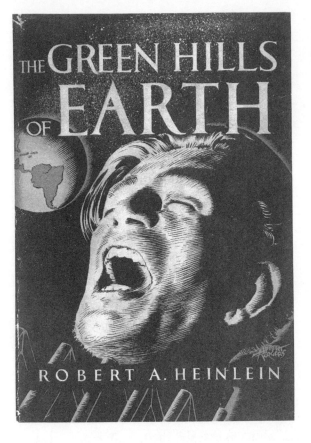

The Green Hills of Earth book
cover—a story first serialized in
the Saturday Evening Post,
February 8, 1947.

selling the Post, *with two companion magazines,* The Ladies Home Journal, *and* Country Gentleman. *One of Robert's first jobs as a child was being a P-J-G boy.*

The Saturday Evening Post *carried a column about the authors who appeared in each issue. The column was called "Keeping Posted," and Robert was asked for material about himself and a picture. Because it was his first appearance in the* Post *with "The Green Hills of Earth" he was included in that column.*

. . . sending you on Monday another interplanetary short, intended for slick (the *Post,* I hope)—the domestic troubles of a space pilot, titled either "For Men Must Work" or "Space Pilot" ["Space Jockey"]. It took me a week to write it and three weeks to cut it from 12,000 to 6,000 [words]—but I am beginning to understand the im-

Heinlein choosing a magazine in Ojai (north of Ventura) around 1947.

provement in style that comes from economy in words. (I set it at 6,000 because a careful count of the stories in recent issues of the *Post* shows that the shorts average a little over 6,000 and are rarely as short as 5,000.)

EDITOR'S NOTE: Robert's ambition to write for higher paying and wider markets than pulp magazines caused him to look around for an agent who had good connections with other markets. For this purpose, he consulted L. Ron Hubbard, who introduced him to Lurton Blassingame.

Lurton had come to New York ambitious to write, but discovered that he could not make the grade. So he remained in the publishing center and became one of the most highly respected agents there. His brother, Wyatt Blassingame, sold regularly, if infrequently, to the Saturday Evening Post.

Robert became, eventually, Lurton's star client, but he was preoccupied with "world saving" after the atomic bombs were dropped. The articles he wrote did not sell. He then began the juvenile series of books with Scribner's—starting with Rocket Ship Galileo *(working title:* Young Atomic Engineers*). For some years, he wrote one juvenile per year.*

The two men met on one of our trips to New York, and Robert urged Lurton to come to visit us in Colorado. Robert would accompany Lurton on a hunting trip, for elk and antelope and other game. I was asked to join them on fishing trips.

Although Robert neither hunted nor fished, he went on such trips with Lurton. During their trip to Gunnison, Colorado, where they went after elk, Robert "kept camp" while Lurton hunted through the mountains, along with a group of other hunters. Lurton bagged an enormous elk, and we were left with a freezer full of elk meat. It was my impression that Robert went along on such trips for Lurton's company.

Robert's next conquest, assisted by Lurton, was the Saturday Evening Post, *with "The Green Hills of Earth," followed by three other stories for that magazine.*

The friendship flourished, despite Robert's distaste for doing business with friends. It lasted until Lurton in the late 1970s, thinking of retirement, took on some younger associates. Robert's books are still handled by the Blassingame–Spectrum Agency in New York.

November 12, 1946: Robert A. Heinlein to Lurton Blassingame

. . . and I shall get back to work, probably on a story called "It's Great to Be Back!" A couple living in Luna City are about to return to

Earth, their contracts completed after three years. They have been homesick the whole time and are always talking about it. They return to Earth and discover that they had forgotten the disadvantages of living on Earth—uncontrolled weather, dirt, colds-in-the-head, provincial attitudes, stupid and ignorant people (the residents of Luna City are of course exceptionally intelligent and civilized because of selection for those qualities—only persons of high IQs and social compatibility would pay the cost of sending them to the Moon and keeping them there), etc., etc. At the end of the story they are more homesick than ever—for Luna City!—and are straining a gut to get back there. The story will be used also to give a picture of Luna City and the conditions of life on the Moon, social and economic, for background and color.

EDITOR'S NOTE: *Between 1947 and 1949, at least ten of Robert A. Heinlein's "slicks" were published; four appeared in the* Post *and two in* Argosy. *This was a remarkable achievement, but it was soon eclipsed by the success of his juvenile novels.*

ROCKET SHIP GALILEO

February 19, 1946: Robert A. Heinlein to Lurton Blassingame

I am going to write the juvenile outlined in my last [letter], starting two days hence. You will receive takes and a synopsis, and the finished manuscript should be in your hands about 15 March. [Two friends] convinced me that my own propaganda purposes will be served best by writing a series of boys' books in addition to the adult items previously described. I have purchased several of the popular boys' series novels and feel confident that I can produce salable copy—copy which can be sold to one of these markets: Westminster, Grosset and Dunlap, Crown, or Random House.

March 16, 1946: Robert A. Heinlein to Lurton Blassingame

I think his [the editor who turned down *Young Atomic Engineers*] conception of a story of the atomic era is inappropriate. We have entered a period of extreme change. I see two major possibilities—either a disastrous atomic war which will destroy for a long time the present technological structure, followed by a renaissance, the nature of which I am unable to predict, or a period of peace in which technical progress will be so enormously accelerated that only short range predictions can hope to be reasonably accurate. *Young Atomic Engineers* [*Rocket Ship Galileo*] is based on the latter of the two assumptions, i.e., a period of peace and unchecked technical progress.

❖ ❖ ❖

In doing fiction about the future, I regard myself as a professional prophet—a man who makes an honest attempt to evaluate the probabilities and to write stories setting forth patterns inherent in those probabilities. If I am to be honest, I must prophesy what *I* think will (or

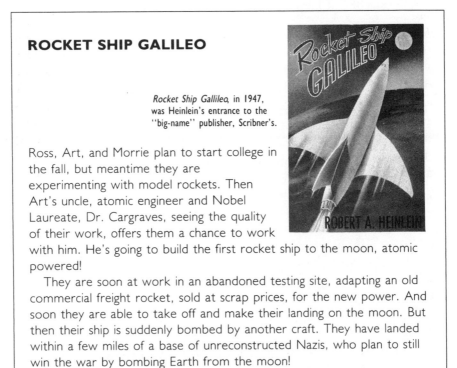

ROCKET SHIP GALILEO

Rocket Ship Gallileo, in 1947, was Heinlein's entrance to the "big-name" publisher, Scribner's.

Ross, Art, and Morrie plan to start college in the fall, but meantime they are experimenting with model rockets. Then Art's uncle, atomic engineer and Nobel Laureate, Dr. Cargraves, seeing the quality of their work, offers them a chance to work with him. He's going to build the first rocket ship to the moon, atomic powered!

They are soon at work in an abandoned testing site, adapting an old commercial freight rocket, sold at scrap prices, for the new power. And soon they are able to take off and make their landing on the moon. But then their ship is suddenly bombed by another craft. They have landed within a few miles of a base of unreconstructed Nazis, who plan to still win the war by bombing Earth from the moon!

Overcoming the Nazis and getting their ship is quite a problem!

could) happen, not what someone else thinks will happen. If Mr. ——— does not see my concept of the possibilities, he had better write it himself or get a hack writer who is willing to write another man's plot. That should be easy for him to do and I do not disapprove of such hack work—but it is almost impossible for me to do it, and I won't do it unless I'm hungry, which I'm not.

(*Young Atomic Engineers* contains two conventional deviations from what I believe to be reasonably possible; I have condensed the preparation time for the trip and I have assumed that four people can do work which should require more nearly forty. Otherwise, I regard the techniques used in the story, and even the incidents, to be possible, albeit romantic and in some respects not too likely in detail. But I *do* expect space travel and I expect it soon. The counterplot is more than a possibility, it is a distinct menace—though it may not turn out to hinge on a base located on the Moon.)

. . . I suppose you are used to the method of having a writer send in a few chapters and a synopsis. I will do that when requested to, but, unfortunately, once I have gone that far with a novel, that novel will be finished about ten days later, or at least with such speed that only the fastest possible response from the publisher can affect the outcome very much. I am sorry, but it is a concomitant of how I work. I work slowly on a novel for the first few chapters only. As soon as I can hear the characters talk, it then becomes a race to see whether I put down their actions fast enough not to miss any of them. It is more economical in time and money and it results in a better story for me to work straight through to a conclusion, rather than wait for an editor to make up his mind whether or not he likes it. Editors are not likely to like my advance synopses in any case, for it is simply impossible for me to give the flavor of a story not yet written in a synopsis.

[(The additional books proposed for this series are:
The Young Atomic Engineers on Mars, or *Secret of the Moon Corridors*
The Young Atomic Engineers in the Asteroids, or *The Mystery of the Broken Planet*
The Young Atomic Engineers in Business, or *The Solar System Mining Corporation*
And at least two more.)]

EDITOR'S NOTE *September 24, 1946. Letter of this date says that editor at Scribner's liked* Young Atomic Engineers.

September 27, 1946: Robert A. Heinlein to Lurton Blassingame

Young Atomic Engineers—I am delighted to hear that Alice Dalgliesh [editor at Scribner's] likes this ms. In my letter of 16 March 46 you will find a list of titles for a proposed series of sequels and considerable discussion of what I would like to do in re juveniles, as well as what I think might be done further to exploit this story. I expect to be guided by you in all those matters—my opinions are not final. I certainly would be willing to rewrite to editorial order and to plan stories to fit editorial desires in order to have my book brought out by so distinguished a house as Scribner's.

February 1, 1947: Robert A. Heinlein to Lurton Blassingame

I have signed the contract as you advised, but I am returning the contract to Scribner's through you in order that you may reconsider whether or not to ask them to make any changes in the contract . . . The manuscript has been revised and is now being retyped. It will be delivered to Scribner's by the tenth of February.

SPACE CADET

July 18, 1947: Robert A. Heinlein to Lurton Blassingame

Miss Dalgliesh and I agree with you on *Space Cadet*, but I won't write it until later this year.

February 17, 1948: Lurton Blassingame to Robert A. Heinlein

No danger of Scribner's turning down *Space Cadet*.

August 1, 1949: Robert A. Heinlein to Lurton Blassingame

There is a correction to be made in *Space Cadet*, which I have already given Scribner's for the second edition; it occurs to me that it should be made in the Norwegian, Italian, and Dutch editions. Will you relay it for me? It is quite simple: on the very last page there is a line of dialog: "Never lead with your left." It should, of course, read, "Never lead with your right."

EDITOR'S NOTE This mistake resulted from the manuscript's having been

SPACE CADET

Space Cadet, Scribner's, 1950.
Cover art by Clifford N. Geary.

The training of cadets for the Interplanetary Patrol takes place in Colorado, in space, and on actual patrol. Following some violent physical tests to see whether an aspirant is able to undergo the rigorous environment of space, the cadets go to training in the school ship.

They learn how to handle themselves in free fall in addition to the required academic subjects. Senior cadets take the younger ones in hand to teach them the traditions of the Patrol.

As a part of their training, they go as very junior officers on a patrol ship, and Matt and Tex run into an adventure in Venus jungles . . .

read by me, Lurton (who was left-handed), and several editors at Scribner's (none of us knew anything about boxing).

January 5, 1951: Robert A. Heinlein to Lurton Blassingame

I have written Miss Dalgliesh about the TV scripts [*Tom Corbett, Space Cadet*]. Did you read them? If so, you know how bad they are; I don't want an air credit on that show (much as I appreciate the royalty checks!) and I am reasonably sure that a staid, dignified house like Scribner's will feel the same way. It has the high moral standards of soap opera.

RED PLANET

November 18, 1948: Robert A. Heinlein to Lurton Blassingame

Enclosed is a copy of notes for a new novel [*Red Planet*] for Miss Dalgliesh, plus a copy of the letter to her . . . Read the letters, read

RED PLANET

Red Planet, Heinlein's 1949 juvenile for Scribner's, began the conflict between Heinlein and his editor Alice Dalgliesh.

Jim Marlowe, a teenaged Martian colonist, takes his pet Willis, a Martian bouncer, away to school with him. The headmaster impounds Willis, since pets are not allowed at school. Jim rescues the bouncer, and he and his friend Frank run away from school, taking Willis with them.

A COLONIAL BOY ON MARS

   After a wild cross-country trek which includes a visit to a Martian building, the three are able to thwart a plot to prevent the colonists from making their annual migration. Thanks to Willis's ability to record exactly voices and words that he has heard, the colonists revolt against the plan, not wishing to live through an extremely cold Martian winter in high latitudes.

the notes as well, if you have time. Advice is welcomed.

   The decision to postpone the ocean-rancher yarn [*Ocean Rancher* was supposed to be the third book in the Scribner's series, but it was never written.] called for a revision of my writing schedule. These are my present intentions: while Miss Dalgliesh is making up her mind, I intend to do one short story, 4,000 words, intended for adult, slick, general market, with *Post, Colliers, Town and Country, This Week,* and *Argosy* in mind. I should be able to show this to you by the middle of December.

   If Miss Dalgliesh says yes, I will write the boys' novel next, planning to complete it before January 31. While she is looking it over, I expect to do another 4,000-word slick, following which I will revise the novel for Miss Dalgliesh. That should take me up to the end of February.

March 4, 1949: Robert A. Heinlein to Lurton Blassingame

   There is actually no need for you to read this letter at all. It will not inform you on any important point, it will contain nothing calling for action on your part, and it probably will not even entertain you. I may not send it. I have a number of points to beef about, particularly Miss Dalgliesh; if Bill Corson [a friend who lived in Los Angeles] were here, I'd beef to him. He not being here, I take advantage of your good nature. I have come to think of you as a friend whom I know well enough to ask to listen to my gripes.

If Miss D. had said *Red Planet* was dull, I would have had no comeback. We clowns either make the audience laugh or we don't; if we entertain, we are successes; if we don't, we are failures. If she had said, "The book is entertaining but I want certain changes. Cut out the egg-laying and the disappearances. Change the explanation for the Old Martians," I would have kept my griping to myself and worked on the basis that the Customer Is Always Right.

She did neither. In effect she said, "The book is gripping, but for reasons I cannot or will not define I don't want to publish it."

I consider this situation very different from that with the publisher in Philadelphia who first instigated the writing of *Rocket Ship Galileo*. He and I parted amicably; he wanted a book of a clearly defined sort which I did not want to write. But, from my point of view, Miss Dalgliesh ordered this particular book; to wit, she had a standing arrangement for one book a year from me; she received a *very* detailed outline which she approved. She got a book to that outline, in my usual style. To my mind that constitutes an order and I know that other writers have been paid their advance under similar circumstances. I think Scribner's owes us, in equity, $500 even if they return the manuscript. A client can't take up the time of a doctor, a lawyer, or an architect, under similar circumstances without paying for it. If you call in an architect, discuss with him a proposed house, he works up a floor plan and a treatment; then you decide not to go further with him, he goes straight back to his office and bills you for professional services, whether you have signed a contract or not.

My case is parallel, save that Miss Dalgliesh let me go ahead and "build the house," so to speak.

I think I know why she bounced the book—I use "bounced" intentionally; I hope that you do not work out some sort of a revision scheme with her because I do not think she will take this book, no matter what is done to it.

I think she bounced the book from some ill-defined standards of literary snobbishness—it's not "Scribner's-type" material!! I think that point sticks out all through her letter to me. I know that such an attitude has been shown by her all through my relationship with her. She has spoken frequently of "cheap" books, "cheap" magazines. "Cheap," used in reference to a story, is not a defined evaluation; it is merely a sneer—usually a sneer at the format from a snob.

She asked me to suggest an artist for *Rocket Ship Galileo*; I suggested Hubert Rogers. She looked into the matter, then wrote me that Mr. Rogers' name "was too closely associated with a rather cheap magazine"—meaning John Campbell's *Astounding S-F*. To prove her point, she sent me tear sheets from the magazine. It so happened that the story she picked to send was one of my "Anson MacDonald" stories, "By His Bootstraps"—which at that time was again in print in Crown's *Best in Science Fiction*!

I chuckled and said nothing. If she could not spot my style and was

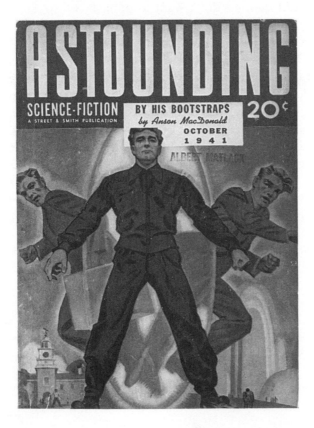

Dalgliesh's infamous example of Hubert Rogers' cover for the "cheap" magazine, John W. Campbell's *Astounding*, featuring "By His Bootstraps" by Heinlein's own alias, Anson MacDonald.

Impressed only by the fact that the stuff was printed on pulpwood paper, it was not my place to educate her. I wondered if she knew that my reputation had been gained in that same "cheap" magazine and concluded that she probably did not know and might not have been willing to publish my stuff had she known.

Rogers is a very fine artist. As an illustrator he did the trade editions of John Buchan's books. I am happy to have one of his paintings hanging in my home. In place of him she obtained someone else. Take a look at the copy of *Galileo* in your office—and don't confuse it in your mind with the fine work done by [Clifford N.] Geary for *Space Cadet*. The man she picked is a fairly adequate draftsman, but with no ability to turn an illustration into an artistically satisfying composition. However, he had worked for Scribner's before; he was "respectable."

I think I know what is eating her about *Red Planet*. It is not any objection on her part to fantasy or fairy tales as such; she is very proud of having published *The Wind in the Willows*. Nor does she object to my pulp-trained style; she accepted it in two other books. No, it is this: She has fixed firmly in her mind a conception of what a "science fiction" book should be, though she can't define it and the notion is nebulous—she has neither the technical training nor the acquaintance with the body of literature in the field to have a clearly defined criterion. But it's there, just the same, and it reads something like this: "Science has to do with machines and machinery and laboratories. Science fiction consists of stories about the wonderful machines of the future which will go striding around the universe, as in Jules Verne."

Her definition is all right as far as it goes, but it fails to include most of the field and includes only that portion of the field which has been heavily overworked and now contains only low-grade ore. Speculative fiction (I prefer that term to science fiction) is also concerned with sociology, psychology, esoteric aspects of biology, impact of terrestrial culture on the other cultures we may encounter when we conquer space, etc., without end. However, speculative fiction is *not* fantasy fiction, as it rules out the use of anything as material which violates established scientific fact, laws of nature, call it what you will, i.e., it must [be] possible to the universe as we know it. Thus, *Wind in the Willows* is fantasy, but the much more incredible extravaganzas of Dr. Olaf Stapledon are speculative fiction—*science fiction*.

I gave Miss Dalgliesh a story which was strictly science fiction by all the accepted standards—but it did not fit into the narrow niche to which she has assigned the term, and it scared her—she was scared that some other person, critic, librarian, or whatever, a literary snob like herself—would think that she had published comic-book type of material. She is not sufficiently educated in science to distinguish between Mars as I portrayed it and the wonderful planet that Flash Gordon infests, nor would she be able to defend herself from the charge if brought.

As a piece of *science* fiction, *Red Planet* is a much more difficult and much more carefully handled job than either of the two books before it. Those books contained a little straightforward descriptive astronomy, junior high school level, and some faked-up mechanical engineering which I could make sound authoritative because I am a mechanical engineer and know the patter. This book, on the other hand, has a planetary matrix most carefully worked out from a dozen different sciences all more complicated and esoteric than descriptive astronomy and reaction engines. Take that one little point about how the desert cabbage stopped crowding in on the boys when Jim turned on the light. A heliotropic plant would do just that—but I'll bet she doesn't know heliotropism from second base. I did not attempt to rub the reader's nose in the mechanics of heliotropism or why it would develop on Mars because she had been so insistent on not being "too technical."

I worked out in figures the amount of chlorophyll surface necessary to permit those boys to live overnight in the heart of a plant and how much radiant energy would be required before I included the incident. But I'll bet she thought of that incident as being "fantasy."

I'll bet that, if she has ever heard of heliotropism at all, she thinks of it as a plant "reaching for the light." It's not; it's a plant spreading for light, a difference of ninety degrees in the mechanism and the point that makes the incident work.

Between ourselves there is one error deliberately introduced into the book, a too-low figure on the heat of crystallization of water. I needed it for dramatic reasons. I wrote around it, concealed it, I believe, from any but a trained physicist looking for discrepancies, and I'll bet ten bucks she never spotted it!—she hasn't the knowledge to spot it.

Enough of beating that dead horse! It's a better piece of *science* fiction than the other two, but she'll never know it and it's useless to try to tell her. Lurton, I'm fed up with trying to work for her. She keeps poking her nose into things she doesn't understand and which are my business, not hers. I'm tired of trying to spoon-feed her, I'm tired of trying to educate her diplomatically. From my point of view she should judge my work by these rules and these only: (a) will it amuse and hold the attention of *boys*? (b) is it grammatical and as literate as my earlier stuff? (c) are the moral attitudes shown by the author and his protagonists—not his villains—such as to make it suitable to place in the hands of minors?

Actually, the first criterion is the only one she need worry about; I won't offend on the other two points—and she knows it. She shouldn't attempt to judge science-versus-fantasy; she's not qualified. Even if she were and even if my stuff were fantasy, why such a criterion anyhow? Has she withdrawn *Wind in the Willows* from the market? If she thinks *Red Planet* is a fairy tale, or a fantasy, but gripping (as she says) to read, let her label it as such and peddle it as such. I don't give a damn. She should concern herself with whether or not boys will like it. As a matter of fact, I don't consider her any fit person to select books to suit the tastes of boys. I've had to fight like hell to keep her from gutting my first two books; the fact that boys *did* like them is a tribute to my taste, not to hers. I've read a couple of the books she wrote for girls—have you tried them? They're dull as ditch water. Maybe girls will hold still for that sort of things; boys *won't*.

I hope this works out so that we are through with her. I prefer pocketing the loss, at least for now, to coping with her further.

And I don't like her dirty-minded attitude over the Willis business. Willis is one of the closest of my imaginary friends; I loved that little tyke, and her raised eyebrows infuriate me. [Willis is the young Martian adopted as a pet by the hero; it's Willis who often gets him out of trouble.]

March 15, 1949: Robert A. Heinlein to Lurton Blassingame

First, your letter: the only part that needs comment is Miss D's remark about getting a good Freudian to interpret the Willis business. There is no point in answering her, but let me sputter a little. A "good Freudian" will find sexual connotations in *anything*—that's the basis of the theory. In answer I insist that without the aid of a "good Freudian" *boys* will see nothing in the scene but considerable humor. In *Space Cadet* a "good Freudian" would find the rockets "thrusting up against the sky" definite phallic symbols. Perhaps he would be right; the ways of the subconscious are obscure and not easily read. But I still make the point that *boys are not psychoanalysts*—nor will anyone with a normal healthy sex orientation make anything out of that scene. I think my wife, Ginny, summed it up when she said, "She's got a dirty mind!"

Somebody around this controversy does need a psychoanalyst—and it ain't you and it ain't me and it ain't Willis.

March 18, 1949: Lurton Blassingame to Robert A. Heinlein

Book will have to be changed before it can go on the recommended library list. There is a certain amount of censorship in the juvenile field. Publishers must sign an affidavit when asking for books to be purchased by libraries, saying there is nothing in them which will offend either youngsters or parents. Dalgliesh is sending list of changes needed in *Red Planet*. Once those changes recommended by the juvenile librarian are made, Scribner's will take book. Scribner's is a respected house and excellent connection for RAH.

EDITOR'S NOTE: *Around this time, Robert was looking for an idea for the story "Gulf," which he had promised to John W. Campbell, Jr. for the special November 1949 issue of* Astounding. *We approached this task in a fashion today known as brainstorming. I would put up an idea and Robert would knock it down.*

The title, "Gulf," was the hitch. Eventually I suggested that it might be possible to do something like the Mowgli story—a human infant raised by a foreign race, kept apart from humans until he reached maturity. "Too big an idea for a short story," said Robert, but he made a note about it.

Further brainstorming resulted in the notion Robert wanted to do a superman story for "Gulf." What did supermen do better than their peers? "They think better," I replied. So another note was made.

Then Robert disappeared into his study and wrote eighteen pages, single spaced, of notes on ideas which the Mowgli suggestion had started rolling in his brain. He worked on those pages the whole night, and came out with a batch of papers titled The Man from Mars [Stranger in a Strange Land].

The Man from Mars was then set aside, and "Gulf" was written to meet JWC's deadline, as it must be sent off to New York before we departed for Hollywood. We planned to drive to California at the end of May, and had no idea just when we would return to Colorado.

March 24, 1949: Robert A. Heinlein to Lurton Blassingame

I agree to all changes [on *Red Planet*]. Let's go ahead with the contract. Please ask her to send me the original manuscript. Please ask her to make her instructions for revision as detailed and as specific as possible. She should bear in mind that, since these revisions are being made to suit her taste and her special knowledge of requirements of the market, *my* taste and *my* limited knowledge of them cannot be a guide to me in making revisions—else I would have submitted a manuscript satisfactory to her in the first place.

❖ ❖ ❖

I note with wry amusement that she no longer speaks of the book as "fairy tale quality," "not *our* sort of science fiction," "lack of controlled imagination," "strange shaped Martians," etc. The only point she still makes which she originally made is about Willis and (pardon my blushes!) s-x. Okeh, s-x comes out; it was probably a mistake on the part of the Almighty to have invented s-x in the first place.

I capitulate, horse and foot. I'll bowdlerize the goddamn thing any way she says. But I hope you can keep needling her to be specific, however, and to follow up the plot changes when she demands the removal of a specific factor. I'm not just being difficult, Lurton; several of the things she objects to have strong plot significance . . . if she takes them out, the story ceases to be. Removing the details objected to about Willis is a much simpler matter; it's offstage stuff and does not affect the story line until the last chapter.

If she forces me to it, I'll take out what she objects to and then let her look at the cadaver remaining—then perhaps she will revise her opinion that it "—doesn't affect the main body of the story—" (direct quote).

I concede your remarks about the respect given to the Scribner imprint, the respect in which she is held, and the fact that she is narrowly limited by a heavily censorship-ridden market. I still don't think she is a good editor; she can't read an outline or a manuscript with constructive imagination.

I expect this to be my last venture in this field; 'tain't worth the grief.

April 18, 1949: Robert A. Heinlein to Lurton Blassingame

The revised version of *Red Planet* will be in your hands by the end of the month and you may tell Miss Dalgliesh so. I am complying with *all* her instructions and suggestions.

April 19, 1949: Robert A. Heinlein to Alice Dalgliesh

The manuscript of *Red Planet* is being returned, through Mr. Blassingame. You will find that I have meticulously followed all of your directions, from your letter, from your written notes, and from your notations on the manuscript, whether I agreed with them or not. I have made a wholehearted attempt to make the changes smoothly and acceptably and thereby to make the story hang together. I am not satisfied with the result, but you are free to make any additional changes you wish wherever you see an opportunity to accomplish your purposes more smoothly than I have been able to do.

Most of the changes have been made by excising what you objected to, or by minor inclusions and variations in dialog. However, on the matter of guns, I have written in a subscene in which the matter of gun licensing is referred to in sufficient explanatory detail to satisfy you, I think.

❖ ❖ ❖

The balance of this letter is side discussion and is in no sense an attempt to get you to change your mind about any of your decisions concerning the book. I simply want to state my point of view on one matter and to correct a couple of points.

At several different times you have made the point that this book was different from my earlier books, specifically with respect to colloquial language used by characters, with respect to firearms, and with respect to aggressiveness on the part of the boys. I have just checked through *Rocket Ship Galileo* and *Space Cadet*—as published—and I do not find any of these allegations substantiated. In both books I made free use of such expressions as "Yeah," "Nope," "Huh", "Stinker," and similar sloppy speech. In both books the boys are inclined to be aggressive in the typical, male-adolescent fashion. See pages 8, 23, 42, 107, 200, and 241 of *Space Cadet* and all of *Rocket Ship Galileo* from page 160 to the end—not to mention a couple of minor brushes earlier. In re guns, *Space Cadet* cannot be compared with the other two books as all the characters are part of a military organization from one end to the other, but *Rocket Ship Galileo* can be compared with *Red Planet*. In *Rocket Ship Galileo* they are handling dangerous explosives in chapter one. From page 62 to the end they are all heavily armed at all times—*and no mention is ever made of licensing them.* On pages 165–6 Art and

Ross each kill a man, a few pages later Morrie kills about eighty men. On page 167 dialog makes clear that they are long used to guns. I bring up these points to correct matters of fact; I do not like being accused of having switched the mixture on you.

Now, as to matters of opinion—You and I have strongly different evaluations as to the best way in which to handle the problem of deadly weapons in a society. We do not seem to disagree in any important fashion as to the legitimate ways in which deadly weapons may be used, but we disagree strongly as to socially useful regulations concerning deadly weapons. I will first cite two points which sharply illustrate the disagreement. I have one of my characters say that the right to bear arms is the basis of all human freedom. I strongly believe that, but you required me to blue-pencil it. The second point concerns licensing guns. I had such licensing in the story, but I had one character strongly object to it as a piece of buttinsky bureaucracy, subversive of liberty— and I had no one defending it. You required me to remove the protest, then build up the licensing into a complicated ritual, involving codes, oaths, etc.—a complete reversal of evaluation. I have made great effort to remove my viewpoint from the book and to incorporate yours, convincingly—but in so doing I have been writing from reasons of economic necessity something that I do not believe. I do not like having to do that.

Let me say that your viewpoint and evaluation in this matter is quite orthodox; you will find many to agree with you. But there is another and older orthodoxy imbedded in the history of this country and to which I hold. I have no intention nor any expectation of changing your mind, but I do want to make you aware that there is another viewpoint that is held by a great many respectable people, and that it is quite old. It is summed up in the statement that I am opposed to all attempts to license or restrict the arming of individuals, such as the Sullivan Act of the State of New York. I consider such laws a violation of civil liberty, subversive of democratic political institutions, and self-defeating in their purpose. You will find that the American Rifle Association has the same policy and has had [it] for many years.

France had Sullivan-type laws. When the Nazis came, the invaders had only to consult the registration lists at the local gendarmerie in order to round up all the weapons in a district. Whether the authorities be invaders or merely local tyrants, the effect of such laws is to place the individual at the mercy of the state, unable to resist. In the story

Heinlein's Expert Rifleman medal, from his naval days.

Red Planet it would be all too easy for the type of licensing you insist on to make the revolution of the colonists not simply unsuccessful, but impossible.

As to such laws being self-defeating, the avowed purpose of such laws as the Sullivan Act is to keep weapons out of the hands of potential criminals. You are surely aware that the Sullivan Act and similar acts have never accomplished anything of the sort? That gangsterism ruled New York while this act was already in force? That "Murder, Inc." flourished under this act? Criminals are never materially handicapped by such rules; the only effect is to disarm the peaceful citizen and put him fully at the mercy of the lawless. Such rules look very pretty on paper; in practice they are as foolish and footless as the attempt of the mice to bell the cat.

Such is my thesis, that the licensing of weapons is subversive of liberty and self-defeating in its pious purpose. I could elaborate the arguments suggested above at great length, but my intention is not to convince, but merely to show that there is another viewpoint. I am aware, too, that even if I did by some chance convince you, there remains the unanswerable argument that you have to sell to librarians and schoolteachers who believe the contrary.

I am not inexperienced with guns. I have coached rifle and pistol teams and conducted the firing of millions of rounds from pistols to turret guns. I am aware of the dangers of guns, but I do not agree that

those dangers can be eliminated nor even ameliorated by coercive leg-
islation—and I think my experience entitles me to my opinion at least
as much as schoolteachers and librarians are entitled to theirs.

❖ ❖ ❖

I am sorry to say in answer to your inquiry that I do not expect to be
able to come east soon. If Miss Fowler passes this way, we shall be very
glad to see her and to show her some of the sights if she wishes.

May 9, 1949: Robert A. Heinlein to Lurton Blassingame

As to the name on *Red Planet* ms., no, I'm not adamant; I'll
always listen to your advice and I'll lose a lot of sleep before I will go
directly against your advice. But I feel rather sticky about this point, as
I hate like the deuce to see anything go out under my own name,
without even sharing responsibility with Miss Dalgliesh, when said item
includes propositions in which I do not believe. The matter of style,
plot, and the effect on my literary reputation, if any, I am not adamant
about, even though I am not happy about the changes—if you say to
shut up and forget it, I'll shut up. It's the "Sullivan-Act-in-a-*Martian-
frontier-colony*" feature that I find hard to swallow; from my point of
view I am being required to support publicly a doctrine which I believe
to be subversive of human liberty and political freedom.

EDITOR'S NOTE: *Because of the necessity of editing* Red Planet *to suit the
sensibilities of librarians (who, at that time, were mostly elderly ladies),
Robert seriously made the suggestion that Miss Dalgliesh's name be added
to the book as an author. This suggestion might have been made over the
telephone—the files are incomplete on this point.*

But the storm blew over, and Red Planet, *firearms or no, Willis' sex or
no, became very popular. It was one of Robert's most popular books for
juveniles.*

May 17, 1949: Robert A. Heinlein to Lurton Blassingame

I'll have to give some thought to the Scribner's beef over the
name. I can't see why Alice Dalgliesh's name, tacked on, should be a
handicap. Maybe they would like to send the script back for reworking
to *my* ideas. It seems to me that if she insists on rewriting the story by
remote control, then she should expect to share the blame.

On the other hand, it is fairly evident that you feel that the story is just about as good now as it was before. I am sorry to say that I don't think so; maybe it's good but it ain't a Heinlein story; it's been denaturized, had its teeth pulled. But I am very reluctant to go against your advice. I think it will damage my reputation and I *know* that it includes ideas of which I violently disapprove. What do you think, Lurton? Lay it on the line.

FARMER IN THE SKY

September 8, 1949: Robert A. Heinlein to Lurton Blassingame

I am up to page 150 in the first draft of my current story ["Farmer in the Sky"], intended for *Boys' Life* and for juvenile book, and should have this draft finished in ten days. It will probably take another month to shape it up into a satisfactory serial version and book-length version.

September 24, 1949: Robert A. Heinlein to Lurton Blassingame

The first draft of the *Boys' Life* and juvenile trade book job is finished, but the motion picture [*Destination Moon*] has developed daily crises which will probably continue until the shooting is over, about the end of November. As there is a long, tedious job of cutting to do to turn the book into a 20,000-word serial, I don't know when I will be sending in the manuscript. You may tell Crump [editor of *Boys' Life*] if you like, that the story is finished, but it may be a month or six weeks until it is ready. My situation here is unclear; my contract is up next week, the movie not yet shot, and myself unwilling to extend the contract on its present terms.

We'll see.

EDITOR'S NOTE: *Robert had done the script for* Destination Moon *with Rip Van Ronkel in Hollywood in 1948. George Pal purchased the script, and Robert was to do technical direction on it.*

The normal delays ensued. We arrived in Hollywood in early June 1949—shooting was supposed to begin soon thereafter. However, with rewrites, preproduction, and all the things that go on in Hollywood, actual shooting did not start until around October or November.

FARMER IN THE SKY

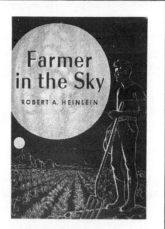

Heinlein wrote *Farmer in the Sky* for Scribner's in 1949 during the hold-ups of filming "Destination Moon."

Bill Lermer, a Boy Scout, and his widowed father decide to emigrate from Earth to Ganymede. In order to be eligible, the father must marry. This story tells about Bill's adjustment to his new step-mother and step-sister, their voyage to Ganymede, and how all four work to build a farm in an inhospitable environment.

The new home is built, a farm started amid the wonderful sight of Jupiter and its other moons, Io, Europa and Callisto. Bill finds that his scouting is universal—a troop is formed in the space ship *Mayflower*, continued on Ganymede, amid many adventures. Bill and his family learn survival.

While waiting for the film production to begin, Robert wrote Farmer in the Sky.

November 20, 1949: Robert A. Heinlein to Lurton Blassingame

. . . I'm working fifteen hours a day; the book-length version of *Farmer in the Sky* is now with the typist and the serial length for *Boys' Life* is being cut—slowly, because I have so little time. I've got it down under 40,000; there will be much tedious work before I can get it down to 20,000 and probably will not finish it until after the picture is finished. I'm working seven days a week and getting six hours of sleep, and I can't speed it up beyond that.

March 6, 1950: Lurton Blassingame to Robert A. Heinlein

Boys' Life found suspense problem. Scribner's very pleased with book.

April 24, 1950: Robert A. Heinlein to Lurton Blassingame

I am glad to hear that [*Boys' Life* editor] Crump is taking the serial [published in *Boy's Life* as "Satellite Scout"], since I need every cent I can scrape up for [house] building. Nevertheless, I would turn down his bid of $750 if I could afford to. It occurs to me, however, that, if he had me in a squeeze before. I have him in a squeeze now. He has scheduled it for the August issue; the makeup date must be staring him in the face, particularly as he is ordering a color painting for the cover from [Chesley] Bonestell.

❖ ❖ ❖

And *please be sure to tell him* that I am certainly entitled to as much time to make up my mind whether or not I like his offer as he is to make up his mind whether or not he likes a story that he ordered from me in the first place. And tell him that I am proud, mean, stiff-necked,

---

BETWEEN PLANETS

Between Planets was given a working title of *The Rolling Stones*. Heinlein soon after used *The Rolling Stones* as the title for another book. Art by Clifford Geary. Scribner's, 1951.

Don's parents suddenly order him to join them on Mars, bringing with him an odd, plastic ring of no apparent value. He leaves his school on Earth for the space station where he's to catch his ship. He meets and befriends a Venus "dragon," Sir Isaac Newton. But his ship is intercepted by Venus, no longer willing to be a mere property of Earth. Willy-nilly, Don is shipped to Venus.

There he finds work washing dishes. Several attempts are made to steal the ring. Then Earth armed forces land and ravage the town. Don joins the Venus army. Much later, he is ordered to report—to Sir Isaac. The dragon needs the ring, which contains the clue to a scientific discovery made secretly on Earth. With it, they can build an ultrafast ship and weapons to force Earth to relinquish control of the planets. Don gets to Mars on that ship—a hero!

and that you doubt very much if you can get me to accept a lowered word rate, since I have been known in the past to pass up sales rather than take a cut.

Don't quite let the sale get away from you—but if you can get him on the hook and keep him there, we may be able to squeeze a couple of hundred dollars' worth of blood out of this stone. I don't care whether he gets sore or not; this is my swan song with Crump; sales to him are not worth the trouble and worry.

Don't get yourself in bad with him; blame it all on me.

Even if you have cashed the check already, I hope you will call him up and twist his arm a bit.

April 21, 1951: Robert A. Heinlein to Lurton Blassingame

. . . The transformation from *Farmer in the Sky* to "Satellite Scout" [the *Boys' Life* version] took *five* drafts and consumed most of six weeks . . . whereupon I was left in suspense while [Crump] made up his mind whether or not he liked my condensation.

BETWEEN PLANETS

January 18, 1951: Robert A. Heinlein to Lurton Blassingame

I am 14,000 words into the new boys' book [*Between Planets*] and the villains are way ahead. The first part always goes slowly; I have to get acquainted with the characters.

March 15, 1951: Robert A. Heinlein to Lurton Blassingame

I've just answered a nite letter from Miss Dalgliesh asking for a synopsis of *Between Planets* (formerly *The Rolling Stones*). [*The Rolling Stones* was a working title, later used for another book.] She wants the finished manuscript by the first—I can't make it, by at least a week, but I am pushing night and day.

March 17, 1951: Robert A. Heinlein to Lurton Blassingame

Between Planets is rolling nicely; I expect to finish it by a week from today, or even sooner. However, the necessity of smooth-typing it will keep me from sending it on earlier than about the first week in April. I have told Miss Dalgliesh.

April 1, 1951: Robert A. Heinlein to Lurton Blassingame

Herewith two copies of *Between Planets*. In this same mail I have sent Miss Dalgliesh an airmail postcard telling her that the ms. will arrive in New York at the same time she receives the card (or should). Since they are so anxious to have it at the earliest possible date, will you please send the original over to her at once?

May 31, 1951: Lurton Blassingame to Robert A. Heinlein

Word from *Blue Book* taking *Between Planets*, paying $1,000.
Scribner will publish about 1 November, allowing *Blue Book* to schedule story for September or October issue.

June 3, 1951: Robert A. Heinlein to Lurton Blassingame

Good news indeed about the sale of *Between Planets* to *Blue Book*. Please tell Kennicott [Donald Kennicott, editor of *Blue Book*, who knew nothing of science fiction except H. G. Wells's title] that there is no resemblance at all between Wells's *War of the Worlds* and my *Between Planets*—also that he should read Wells's book; it's a dilly. The move-overs should resemble in appearance the mythological fauns or satyrs, the "goat-men," but should avoid too close a resemblance, i.e., avoid terrestrial musculature, articulation, and physiognomy, both of goats and men. Faunus veneris is a biped, horned, and smaller than a man, but its appearance merely suggests the faun of Greek mythology. It is not actually related to any earthian life form; there is plenty of elbow room for the artist to use his imagination.

June 28, 1951: Lurton Blassingame to Robert A. Heinlein (telegram)

Scribner's proofs on their way airmail special delivery.

THE ROLLING STONES

December 1, 1951: Robert A. Heinlein to Lurton Blassingame

The boys' novel *Rolling Stones* is about a quarter finished, smooth draft—and an unsatisfactory story line thereafter. The trouble is that I am trying to do domestic comedy this time with nothing much in the way of revolutions and blood—and I find comedy harder to write. Oh, I can keep up wisecracking dialog all too easily, but the characters have to do something too, something important. With space warfare and intrigue ruled out by the nature of the story I find that a problem. Story centers around twin boys and their eccentric family. Family goes to asteroids in family spaceship, get into various sorts of trouble, get out again.

January 5, 1952: Robert A. Heinlein to Lurton Blassingame

The new boys' novel, *The Rolling Stones*, is rolling along. I am hard at work seven days a week.

January 15, 1952: Robert A. Heinlein to Lurton Blassingame

I heard from Miss Dalgliesh about *Rolling Stones*; she is enthusiastic.

March 8, 1952: Robert A. Heinlein to Lurton Blassingame

I am sorry to say that I am again having "sex" trouble with Miss Dalgliesh—she has decided (from her Olympian heights as an amateur Freudian) that *The Rolling Stones* contains some really dangerously evil connotations. Her letter was rather horrid and I was quite offended. I am not asking you to front for me this time; I answered her myself. Since the business matters are all completed, it is strictly an author–editor matter and you have troubles enough without being put in the middle on this. But enough is enough and I do not intend to tolerate any more of this sort of thing. *The Rolling Stones* may be the last juvenile I will do, or, if I do another, perhaps we will offer it to ——— rather than to Miss Dalgliesh.

I consciously intend to write wholesome stories for boys and mean to leave out entirely the sophisticated matters which appear in my writings for adults. In addition, Mrs. Heinlein went over this one most carefully, trying to find things Miss Dalgliesh might object to. When we were both satisfied that it was as pure as Caesar's wife, we sent it off. I feel sure that you would have returned it to me for revision had you seen anything in it which could have been construed as dirty. So she liked it and signed a contract for it—and now decides that it is dirty. The anecdote about the Vermonter who made a pet of a cow, "—same as you might a good hunting dog—" Miss Dalgliesh says suggests "certain abnormal sex practices." Well, it doesn't suggest anything to me except that my wife has made a pet out of a horse next door, which was what it was based on—and I am dead certain it won't suggest anything horrid to my boys and girls. But I gave her a revision—because we decided that the anecdote was not dirty but *was* dull.

Her other objection was this: "Flat cats seem to me a trifle too Freudian in their pulsing love habits." Since I intentionally desexed them entirely, even to parthenogenesis, I found this a bit thick. I always called a flat cat "it" rather than "he" or "she" and gave the only named one a name with no sex connotation. These things I did because I knew she was hipped on the subject—but it was useless; she is capable of seeing phallic symbolism in Jack's beanstalk.

Another objection she made has nothing to do with sex, but I find it illustrative of how far afield she has gone to find trouble: she objected to my naming a prospector "Old Charlie" *because the first name of Mr. Scribner is Charles!* How silly can one get?

I don't expect you to do anything but wished to inform you because you may hear reverberations. I rapped her knuckles most sharply. There are types of behavior I won't tolerate for any amount of money. I re-

---

THE ROLLING STONES

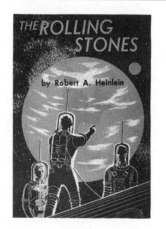

THE ROLLING STONES

by Robert A. Heinlein

Heinlein tried to make *The Rolling Stones* wholesome, but Dalgliesh saw some Freudian connotations in Heinlein's creation of "Flat Cats."

Castor and Pollux Stone, seventeen-year-old twins, go into space with their unusual family in a secondhand spaceship, called *The Rolling Stone*. They take along a cargo of battered bicycles to trade to settlers on Mars.

Grandmother Hazel and their father, Roger Stone, support the project by writing episodes for *The Scourge of the Spaceways*, one of whose characters is the Galactic Overlord. Three episodes a week is their normal output.

The twins buy a Martian flat cat, Fuzzy Britches, a creature most people enjoy petting. In transit they find that flat cats multiply with extreme rapidity, given sufficient food. They are forced to put the creatures into deep freeze.

In the asteroid belt, the twins create a demand for the flat cats, now thawed, selling them to lonely miners.

---

taliated in kind (which is why I left you out of it); I took one of her books for girls and subjected it to the sort of analysis she gave mine. I know quite as much Freudian, bogus "psychology" as she does; from the criteria she uses, her book was dirty as hell—and I told her so, citing passages. If she is going to leer and smirk at my perfectly nice kids' book, I can do the same to her girls' stories. Amateur psychoanalysts make me sick! That impressive charlatan, Dr. Freud, has done quite as much harm as Queen Victoria ever did.

March 7, 1952: Robert A. Heinlein to Alice Dalgliesh

1. If you are going to make changes, I prefer to see them in advance of proof.

2. "Old Charlie"—I happen to like the name Charlie better than the name Danny, but the issue raised strikes me as just plain silly. "Charlie" is a very common nickname; there is probably at least one character named Charles in over half of currently published novels. Are we to lay off the very common names "Bob" and "Alice" because you and I happen to have them? In any case, nine-tenths of my readers are quite unaware of the name of the publisher; children very rarely pay attention to the name of the publishing house. It would be just as reasonable to place a taboo on "Harry" and on "George" and on "Joe" because of the names of the President, the late King, and the Russian dictator.

3. Flat cats and Freud—no, I most emphatically do not agree to any changes of any sort in the flat cats or anything about them. I am considerably irked by the phrase "—a bit too Freudian in their pulsing love habits." *What* love habits? I remember all too clearly the advice you gave me about Willis in *Red Planet* and how I should "consult a good Freudian"—in consequence, I most carefully desexed the creatures completely. I used the pronoun "it" throughout (if you find a "he" or "she", it is a fault of my proofing); the circumstances make it clear that the first one, and by implication, all the others, reproduce by parthenogenesis. Do you object to the fact that they like to be petted? Good heavens, that *can't* come out; the whole sequence depends on it—so don't tamper with it. In any case, I set up a symbiosis theory to account for them being such affectionate pets.

If you choose to class the human response to the flat cats (the desire on the part of humans, particularly lonely humans, for a pet which can be fondled and which will show affection)—if you class this tendency (on which the sequence turns) as a form of sex sublimation, I will not argue the classification. By definition "sex" and "libido" may be extended to almost any human behavior—but I do not agree that there is necessarily anything unhealthy, nor queasily symbolic, in such secondary (sex?) behavior.

Following your theory, I really must point out that the treatment of Rusty in *Along Janet's Way* [written by Miss Dalgliesh] is extremely significant (to a good Freudian) and highly symbolic, both in secondary sex behavior and in sublimation phenomena—in fact, not the sort of book to put into the hands of a young girl. That business with the nightgown, for example. From the standpoint of a good Freudian, every writer (you and I among others) unconsciously uses symbols which are simply reeking with the poisonous sexual jungles of our early lives and our ancestries. What would a half-baked analyst make of that triangular scene between the girl, the young man, and the male dog—and the nightgown? Of the phallic symbolism and the fetishism in the dialog that followed? And all this in a book intended for young girls?

Honest, Alice Dalgliesh, I don't think that you write dirty books. But neither do I—and lay off my flat cats, will yuh? Your books and your characters are just as vulnerable to the sort of pseudoscientific criticism you have given mine as are mine. So lay off—before I haul Jinks into this argument.

About Freud: Look, Freud was not a scientist; he was simply a brilliant charlatan. He did not use scientific methodology, and his theories are largely unsubstantiated and are nowadays extremely suspect. From a practical standpoint the practitioners of his "psychoanalysis" have been notably unsuccessful in curing the mentally ill. Christian Science has done as well if not better—and is about as well grounded in scientific proof. I grant you that Freudian doctrine has had an aura of scientific respectability for the past generation, but that aura was unearned and more and more psychiatrists are turning away from Freud. I concede that, among other damages, Freud and his spectacular theories have helped to make the layman in our maladjusted culture extremely sensitive to sex symbols, real or false, and this situation must be taken into account by a writer. But we shouldn't go overboard in making concessions to this artificial situation, particularly because it is impossible to write any story in such a fashion that it will not bring a knowing leer to the face of a "good Freudian."

(Let's look at another aspect of the problem; it is to be hoped, I suppose, that the readers of your list of books will presently graduate to Scribner's trade books for adults. Let us suppose that I manage to keep my readers sealed in cellophane, sterile in vitro—then comes the day when they start reading other Scribner's books. I'll mention a few: Hemingway—with his painful reiteration of the emasculation theme—*From Here to Eternity*, which needs a glossary of taboo words to explain its taboo situations, *Europa* and *Europa Revisited*, which combine communist propaganda with pornography in a most curious fashion. I am not panning Scribner's adult list; my point is that the gradient from one list to the other can be ridiculously steep.)

STARMAN JONES

March 24, 1953: Lurton Blassingame to Robert A. Heinlein

[Scribner's] wants some minor changes in the novel [*Starman Jones*] and hopes you won't mind making them. These are limited to the first chapter and the last. In the first chapter, [Dalgliesh] says the stepfather sounds like the conventional pulp-paper villain, since he comes in and wants to beat the boy the first night he is married to the boy's mother. . . .

For the last chapter, she thinks that some of their readers wouldn't fully understand all that you are saying so briefly in the scene where the hero is back at the farm. How much time—earth time, that is—has elapsed? She also wants a bit more made of the fines, or whatever way the hero pays for the fact that he started out as a liar. It might help here if the powers that be keep the hero as an astrographer (sic) . . . because he had the moral fiber to admit his error and since then acted in every way as a man.

These aren't serious and I hope you won't mind making them.

March 25, 1953: Robert A. Heinlein to Lurton Blassingame

Now, about the changes Miss Dalgliesh wants: I think that it is necessary that [she] write directly to me, explaining in detail what changes she wants and why and specifically what she wants done to accomplish those changes. Offhand, she certainly has not asked for much; nevertheless, on the basis of what you have relayed to me, I am not convinced that the changes are either necessary or desirable.

. . . I don't say that I *won't* make this change [i.e., the "stepfather" change], but I *do* say that I am going to need a helluva lot of convinc-

STARMAN JONES

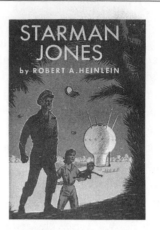

With *Starman Jones* in 1953, Heinlein and Dalgliesh had fewer conflicts, though she still asked for changes.

When Max finds living with his new stepfather impossible, he leaves for Earthport, taking the books of navigation tables left by his uncle, a former officer on the interstellar ships, hoping to find work on the ships. But the board refuses, taking the books from him, but giving him the deposit money on them. Sam, a former spaceman, persuades him to use the money to get them false papers as crewmen.

Aboard the *Asgard*, his relationship to his uncle is discovered, and he is bumped to chartsman trainee. There he reveals that, with his trick memory, he's memorized all the tables. Then a mistake leaves the ship lost. The nearest planet has a dangerous life-form. All higher officers are dead and the navigation books are lost. Only Max's memory is able to bring the *Asgard* back to known space.

The future of Max as a spaceman and officer is assured.

ing. . . In my opinion it would badly damage the dramatic timing of the story to make this change. What I have now accomplished in six pages would, with the proposed revision, require tacking on a couple of chapters, change the opening from fast to very slow, and in particular (this is what I hate most) change the crisis in the boy's life from a dramatic case of having the rug jerked out from under him in a matter of minutes into a situation in which he simply becomes increasingly annoyed with an unpleasant situation.

❖ ❖ ❖

The suggested revisions in the ending are not difficult, and the last chapter as I wrote it is certainly open to criticism. But (as usual!) I have comments. I kept that last chapter short because the story actually ends with the next to the last chapter, i.e., the character change is complete.

THE STAR BEAST

August 27, 1953: Robert A. Heinlein to Lurton Blassingame

. . . the new boys' book [*The Star Beast*] is, for the present, going nicely. I've gotten no farther than the first chapter, but that puts me over the worst hump. I had a pretty well worked out story with a juicy new extraterrestrial character but, while I thought it could be written and sold, I was not satisfied with the plot line. Things were in too low key, not enough action and not enough conflict. Ginny came up with a new way to start the story, which I believe has fixed that difficulty. In any case, I am writing it.

December 21, 1953: Lurton Blassingame to Robert A. Heinlein (Sent to Sydney, Australia)

Scribner's wants new title for book, *Lummox* (original title) still on stands as title of another book. Or a subtitle. Hopes this won't interfere with elbow-bending.

March 11, 1954: Lurton Blassingame to Robert A. Heinlein (Sent to Honolulu, Hawaii)

In conference with [Scribner's] about new book. Idea that children can divorce parents horrifies her. It would be bad for book club sales. But she loved book, and this is only complaint.

EDITOR'S NOTE: Blassingame allowed changes (see letter of October 8, 1954).

October 8, 1954: Robert A. Heinlein to Lurton Blassingame

As soon as I can get the travel book [*Tramp Royal*] out of the way I will start on a novel. It should be my annual boys' novel, but I may make it an adult novel instead. I am finding the nonsense connected with juveniles increasingly irksome. The latest is a hoorah over *Star Beast* which has occupied much too much of my time lately. It was not a business matter, so I did not bother you with it while it was going on—but it has left an extremely bad taste in my mouth and made me quite reluctant to continue the series with Scribner's. I have a full file on it but a brief summary will be enough to show my viewpoint: A Mr.

Learned T. Bulman, reviewing it for the *Library Journal*, wrote Miss Dalgliesh a letter saying that I had "destroyed" the book by including the notion that children might be "divorced" from unsatisfactory parents through court action and placed in the hands of guardians; Mr. Bulman in effect demanded that the book be withdrawn and revised, under pain of being lambasted in the *Library Journal*.

(The man did not even seem to realize that the procedure referred to in my story was a legal and accepted part of our own social structure; the *only* new element lay in calling such a court action a "divorce.")

You will remember that Miss Dalgliesh had qualms about this point and got permission from you to revise as she saw fit during my absence. The published version is as she revised it. But, instead of answering Mr. Bulman and standing up for the book as she edited and published it, she conceded his whole case and tossed it in my lap—this, from her point of view, constitutes "defending" me.

I concede that she is a nice person in many ways, that she is a good editor and highly respected, and that she sells books to libraries. I

THE STAR BEAST

The *Library Journal* threatened to lambaste Heinlein if he didn't withdraw *The Star Beast* because of its suggestion that children could divorce their parents.

The
STAR
BEAST

by ROBERT A.
HEINLEIN

John Thomas Stuart XI has a pet—Lummox—brought back from a space trip by an ancestor. "Lummie" began as a tiny pet, but over the generations (by earth standards) has grown huge, and is everlastingly in trouble. Lummie's race locates him, and demands his return.

Mr. Kiku, Under-Secretary for Spatial Affairs, finds that Lummox has no wish to leave for his home without his "pet," John Thomas to return to her ancestral home . . . she has been raising "John Thomases" for a long time, and wishes to continue doing so . . .

readily concede that I might be much worse off with another juveniles editor. But what irks me are the very conditions of writing for kids at the present time. My books do not cause juvenile delinquency; I consider it irrelevant that horror comics and crime television (may possibly) do so. Obviously, the juvenile delinquency in some New York City public schools is disgraceful and dangerous—but to tackle the matter by searching for minute flaws in teenage trade books strikes me as silly and as inappropriate as treating cancer with hair tonic.

Yet this fluff-picking goes on with unhumorous zeal. Mr. Bulman wrote to me that he did not object to the idea of "divorce" for unfortunate children in itself, but that one of the characters was "flippant." This epitomizes the nature of the objections; these watchful guardians of youthful morals do not want live characters, they want plaster saints who never do anything naughty and who are always respectful toward all the shibboleths and taboos of our present-day, Heaven-ordained tribal customs.

I could write such books, of course—but the kids would not read them.

I feel that I am caught in a squeeze between the really difficult job of being more entertaining than a comic book or a TV show and the impossible task of doing the first while pleasing a bunch of carping elders whose whims and prejudices I am unable to anticipate. I realize that there is no way to get rid of these pipsqueak arbiters of morals and good taste—but I would prefer to think that I had the backing of my editor once said editor approved the final form of a book. I do not feel that I have it from Miss Dalgliesh.

In the first place, she seems to me to be overpoweringly anxious to appease these knotheads, and for reasons pragmatic rather than moral, i.e., she has told me repeatedly that she did not herself do this and that [it was done] because of librarians and teachers. I always followed her advice, although often most reluctantly as it seemed to me that the censoring was often trivial and silly—like calling a leg a "limb" so as not to shock dear old Aunt Mamie. I *knew* that the changes meant nothing at all in re the protecting of the morals of children—but I went along with her in such matters because it was represented as pragmatic economic necessity.

But when appeasement goes so far as to disavow me and my works instead of standing up for me, I get really burned up! This Bulman wrote to her, not to me. I think she should have told him politely to go to hell, i.e., that we were doing the best we could and that if he did not like it, it was unfortunate but we could not please everyone all the time. I think, too, that she could have told him that Scribner's published the book, believed in it, and stood behind it. I do not expect from her Olympian aloofness when the fight starts; I expect her to be partisan—on *my* side. She's my editor—and this attack comes from the outside directed at our joint production.

Instead she seems to follow the policy that "the customer is always right"—she promptly agreed with Bulman in his criticism and claimed (quite incorrectly) that the stuff he objected to had stayed in the book over her protests at my insistence. Then she "defended" me by making a mild plea for freedom of expression.

I do not know as yet whether I will do another juvenile book or not. If I decide to do another one, I do not know that I wish it to be submitted to Scribner's. I have taken great pride in being a Scribner's author, but that pride is all gone now that I have discovered that they are not proud of me.

I've had bids from other editors for my juveniles, one from a major house only two weeks ago. In the past I have given these overtures a polite no. Possibly I could now find an editor who takes a strong stand against this sort of nonsense . . . or possibly not. Miss Dalgliesh tells me that I will find that she is more broad-minded than most of the other juveniles editors, and she may well be right. This knuckling under to petty minds may be a common practice in the trade.

I've taken great pride in these juveniles. It seemed to me a worthwhile accomplishment to write wholesome stories which were able to compete with the lurid excitements of comic books. But I am really very weary of being required to wipe my feet and straighten my tie before being allowed in the house by those who stand between me and my juvenile readers. I am rather strongly inclined to let Mr. Bulman and his ilk write their own adventure stories for boys, since they know exactly how it should be done—and Miss Dalgliesh can edit them.

I have neglected adult writing in order never to miss getting my annual boys' books in on time . . . which has possibly been a mistake. But the response to the boys' series has been so warm that I have given them priority. But right now I am undecided whether to go ahead with them, or to drop them and concentrate on adult novels, where I can say what I think and treat any subject I please without being harassed by captious chaperones.

October 15, 1954: Lurton Blassingame to Robert A. Heinlein

You're not in as much of a squeeze as you think. We'll have to see whether the *Library Journal* lambastes you, and sales. If sales stay up, the squeeze wasn't tight enough to hurt.

TUNNEL IN THE SKY

October 25, 1954: Robert A. Heinlein to Lurton Blassingame

I am starting a novel [*Tunnel in the Sky*] as soon as I finish this letter. That is to say, that I start walking up and down and swearing at the cat; I should start the first chapter any time between midnight tonight and two weeks from now.

Look, I *did* write to [Learned T.] Bulman just once and no more—I

TUNNEL IN THE SKY

Lurton Blassingame thought that *Tunnel in the Sky* had "slick" possibilities. Heinlein had cracked the tough slick market with "The Green Hills of Earth."

The class in "Advanced Survival" is taking their final exam, but Rod and his class fail to return to earth, as the "gate" through which they went for the test failed to work. This is the story of how the youngsters really survive on another planet, uninhabited except for strange life species.

Rod becomes the leader of the group, which sets up its own encampment. They meet strange beasts, odd vegetation, and see how pioneers live.

---

have not answered his answer and do not intend to. The thing that made writing to Bulman so extremely difficult and time wasting was that (Scribner's) had written to him also, *conceding all of his objections*, but telling him that she was writing to me and that I would explain where I stood. That is what made it so damn difficult—I have to write to him and refute his nonsense without calling her a prevaricator . . . or worse.

So far as I am concerned I have dropped the matter, do not intend to write to him again, and have not answered her last letter about it. But it is not out of my mind, as I feel equally strongly impelled to write another boys' book and not to write one. I like that series, am proud of it, and it has paid well, but I have a very sour taste about my relations with Scribner's. I agree that Miss Dalgliesh must sell books and should stay on as good terms with librarians as possible, but it does not strike me as good business to kowtow to everything that any librarian wants.

December 11, 1954: Robert A. Heinlein to Lurton Blassingame

Just a quick report—
I finished boys' book *Tunnel in the Sky* at 3 A.M. today. Must be cut and retyped; ms. should be in your hands by end of January.

December 31, 1954: Robert A. Heinlein to Lurton Blassingame

Schoolhouse in the Sky [*Tunnel in the Sky*] went out to be smooth-typed yesterday. I expect to have it in Miss Dalgliesh's hands by 26 January, as requested.

January 24, 1955: Robert A. Heinlein to Lurton Blassingame

Herewith are the table of contents and the word count on *Schoolhouse in the Sky* [*Tunnel in the Sky*]; they were squeezed out yesterday in catching an air express dispatch in order to put the first copy in Miss Dalgliesh's hands as early as possible. . . . It is not exactly a juvenile, although I've kept it cleaned up so that it can pass as a juvenile. It is not the ordinary run of science fiction, either. I don't know what it is . . . well, it's a story.

I hope this reaches you before you have read it, because I want your expert help on one feature. The story has quite a lot of hunting in it. As you know, I know very little about hunting—but I am strongly aware of how easily one can lose the reader through small mistakes that break empathy. If you find *anything* which you feel does not ring true, will you please point it out to me and I will rewrite as directed to correct the fault.

February 1, 1955: Robert A. Heinlein to Lurton Blassingame

I am surprised and pleased to hear that you think *Schoolhouse* [*Tunnel in the Sky*] may have slick possibilities. I am still more surprised that you passed the hunting scenes without suggesting changes. (I would be most happy to make such changes.) I did not use a central nonhuman character in this book because the book is filled with the killing of animals . . . all perfectly legitimate, of course, but I was afraid of questionable empathy if I let this story shift at any point to a nonhuman viewpoint in view of the necessity of showing them killing for meat. In my next one I will no doubt have a successor to Willis, Lummox, etc.

In the meantime, I have been hung up for a solid week on the new adult novel. It is the Man-from-Mars idea that I first talked about several years ago. It is an idea as difficult as it is strong and one I have had trouble with twice before. If I don't break the logjam soon I'll put it aside and write a different novel. I am not especially distressed about it; if I don't whip it this time, I will some other time, and I expect to deliver an adult novel some time early this year, either this one or another one.

TIME FOR THE STARS

December 13, 1955: Robert A. Heinlein to Lurton Blassingame

I have finished the new Scribner's book, *Time for the Stars*, and it is today being started by the typist. I expect to send you ms. in January, which should be plenty of time to try to sell serial rights.

Please do not tell Miss Dalgliesh I have finished it, or she will want to see it early—and I don't want her to have any more time to second-guess than her schedule requires. If she asks about it, please tell her that you understand I have it in process and that you are sure that I will be on time as usual . . . all of which is the literal truth.

TIME FOR THE STARS

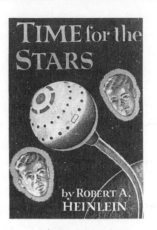

Time For the Stars, Scribner's, 1956. Cover art by Clifford N. Geary. Dalgliesh thought that the hero might be too old for a juvenile novel.

Tom and Pat are identical twins. When tested by the Long Range Foundation, they are found to be telepathically linked. Thus, eventually, Tom is chosen to go to the stars on a torch ship, reporting back to Pat, who remains on Earth (investing their combined incomes and building in time a financial empire). At almost light speed, time is slowed enormously—as Einstein showed—so Tom seems to stay young while Pat ages. Eventually, Tom can no longer contact his twin, but by then can contact Pat's daughter—and then granddaughter and finally, Vicki, Pat's great-granddaughter. The ship explores new worlds, but finally cannot go on. Then they are rescued by the first faster-than-light ship, made possible by what the ship has revealed of time. Back on Earth, Tom finds Pat is a very old man. But Vicki is just the right age!

March 9, 1956: Robert A. Heinlein to Lurton Blassingame

Now, about *Time for the Stars*. I don't feel strongly about it at all. If [Dalgliesh] wants to cut some of the opening, she is welcome to do so. If she prefers to have me cut it, tell her to send the chapters she wants cut back to me *with specific instructions as to just what parts she wants eliminated and just how many words she wants taken out.* Or she can do it herself, if she prefers.

I don't understand the criticism about age group appeal. She complained that I had lost them the Armed Services market in *Rolling Stones* by making the twins two years under draft age when the story opened, even though they were eighteen when the story closed. So in this story I very carefully made the boy just graduating from high school with an implied age of eighteen—and he is too old, she tells me.

Is *Stover at Yale* no good for high school kids just because the hero is old enough to be in college?

I can make my central character *any age she wants* at the opening of the story. But it can only be one age. If she will tell me what age she thinks is best for the market, I can tailor the central character of my next book to fit. But I can't make him simultaneously of draft age and of junior high school age. Nor can I keep him from growing up as the story progresses without limiting myself to a simple action story spanning not more than a few weeks. This is difficult to do in space-travel stories—but I can do it if she wants it.

CITIZEN OF THE GALAXY

December 11, 1956: Robert A. Heinlein to Lurton Blassingame

I have completed a draft of the next novel [*Citizen of the Galaxy*] intended for Scribner's. The present title is *The Chains and the Stars*. It

CITZEN OF THE GALAXY

Alice Dalgliesh considered *Citizen of the Galaxy* to be Heinlein's best book.

Thorby is a slave, abducted as an infant and suffering all a slave's mistreatment for years. Now he is sold again, this time on Sargon to Baslim, a beggar. But Baslim treats him well, frees him, adopts him, and teaches him all a beggar's tricks. Baslim, he slowly realizes, is really an intelligence agent in a war against slavery. Then Baslim's work is discovered and he is eliminated.

Thorby finds safety for two years among the Free Traders and learns their ways. Then he is taken to the Guard and enlisted. But then he is identified as the lost heir of one of Earth's most powerful families—one secretly supplying the slavers!

It takes more time to learn new ways. Then he forces out the crooked managers and takes over—to use his wealth and life fighting the slave trade.

Citizen of the Galaxy was also serialized in Astounding from September to December 1957, but there were some differences from the Scribner's book edition. Here, cover art by Van Dongen.

ran considerably too long, so I have two or three weeks of cutting to do on it. I hope to have the chewed-up copy in the hands of a typist by Christmas, which should enable me to place a copy of it for possible serial sale in your hands around the middle of January. The Scribner's copy will meet Miss Dalgliesh's deadline (what date this year?), but I will send it later, as I want to cut and slant the serial (adult) version slightly differently from the Scribner's (juvenile) version. As usual, it is an ambivalent story, actually adult in nature but concerning a boy and with no sex in it that even Great Aunt Agatha could object to. But I am going to try this time to improve it a little for each market with some changes in emphasis.

February 8, 1957: Lurton Blassingame to Robert A. Heinlein

Alice Dalgliesh says Citizen Robert's best story to date.

February 28, 1957: Lurton Blassingame to Robert A. Heinlein

No more cutting on *Citizen*—it's a tight story, more can't be taken out. Miss Dalgliesh wants one very small cut, about organized religion.

May 17, 1957: Robert A. Heinlein to Lurton Blassingame

Thanks for the suggestion about submitting plots for approval to Miss Dalgliesh, but we tried that once or twice and it just caused trouble; she approved the plots in outline but not when she saw the story, even though I had stuck to the plot line. This caused the biggest hassles I've had with her, over *Red Planet* . . . which has merely turned out to be her biggest seller of the list, even though I refused all of the changes she wanted where they differed from the approved plot. No, if I ever submit to her another story, it will be sight unseen till then and take it or leave it. I know I have not made clear why two changes, admittedly easy and unimportant, threw me into a spin and lost me ten days working time, cum much anguish. I don't know that I *can* explain it, but it is true. Part of the reason lies in that Chicago lecture of mine you read recently: [Mark Reinsberg arranged this as a seminar of four lectures, which were published as The Science Fiction Novel by Advent Publishers]. I necessarily write science fiction by one theory, the theory of extrapolation and change—but once it reaches the editor (in this case) it is tested by an older theory, the notion that this our culture is essentially perfect and I *must not* tinker with any part of it which is dear to any possible critic who may see the story. These things have now added up to the point where I feel unable to continue. I *may* write another. I don't know yet. I can't until some of the depression wears off. But I don't know how to tell her that I probably won't deliver the story she is expecting—I've tried six or eight times, wasted many days, and all the ways I can express it either sound rude or inadequate. I know this sounds silly, but it is true.

HAVE SPACE SUIT—WILL TRAVEL

November 8, 1957: Robert A. Heinlein to Lurton Blassingame

Here are three copies of my new novel for Scribner's *Have Space*

HAVE SPACE SUIT—
WILL TRAVEL

Have Spacesuit Will Travel,
Scribner's, 1958, became a
Heinlein classic.

While Kip Russell is trying out the repairs he
has made on the space suit he won in a soap
contest, he hears a voice over his radio:
"PeeWee to Junebug!" And he is off on an
adventure with PeeWee and the Mother
Thing to the stars.

   Set down on Pluto, the Mother Thing attempts to communicate with
her people, but fails, and Kip must go outside in blistering cold to rescue
her. They are then taken to the Lesser Magellanic Cloud where,
together with a Roman centurion, Iunio, PeeWee, and Kip are put on
trial to defend the human race before a tribunal of a highly civilized race.

Suit—Will Travel. They are intended (I hope) for trade book, American
serial, and British serial.

November 19, 1957: Lurton Blassingame to Robert A. Heinlein

   Have Space Suit—Will Travel is a fine story . . . enjoyed all of it.

December 6, 1957: Lurton Blassingame to Robert A. Heinlein

   Scribner's enthusiastic about the book.

CHAPTER IV

❖

THE LAST OF THE JUVENILES

❖

STARSHIP TROOPERS

November 22, 1958: Robert A. Heinlein to Lurton Blassingame

I finished a draft of a novel, working title *Sky Soldier*, at 5:20 this morning; I will start patching its solecisms and such on Monday. It won't have to be cut other than for dramatic reasons, as the draft runs about 60,000 words—proving that I *can* write a novel without forcing the publisher either to jack up the price or use smaller type . . . a point on which you may have entertained legitimate doubts.

You will receive the ms. some time after the first of the year; my typist will do it during her Christmas vacation. Miss Dalgliesh has inquired as to whether I intended to submit a book; I have admitted that I have—but I have *not* admitted that it has been written. I don't want her to see this until the last possible moment (I have given her only the title and theme: a boy serving his military service in the future). I want to give her the least possible time to have nervous-Nellie second thoughts about it . . . because I am not going to change it to suit her.

January 10, 1959: Robert A. Heinlein to Lurton Blassingame

Earlier today we mailed you two copies of *Starship Soldier* . . . since I anticipate that [Dalgliesh] is not going to like parts of this book,

STARSHIP TROOPERS

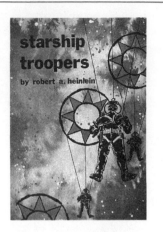

Alice Dalgliesh and the entire Scribner's editorial board turned *Starship Troopers* down. Putnam's eagerly picked up the title and Heinlein moved his career.

In this culture, the franchise or right to vote must be earned by volunteering for Federal Service. It is not necessary that this service be in the military—quite the opposite. Johnny's decision to enter the military is opposed by his father, but upheld by his instructor in history and moral philosophy. So Johnny goes into the Mobile Infantry. We first see him in a drop.

Equipment and training has changed since the twentieth century, and each trooper is as well equipped as a modern army. Johnny makes several drops, and gains in experience and rating, and eventually becomes an officer candidate.

I might as well get the row over with . . . It is not a juvenile; it is an adult novel about an eighteen-year-old boy. I have so written it, omitting all cleavage and bed games, such that Miss Dalgliesh can offer it in the same list in which she has my other books, but nevertheless it is not a juvenile adventure story. Instead I have followed my own theory that intelligent youngsters are in fact more interested in weighty matters than their parents usually are.

January 21, 1959: Lurton Blassingame to Robert A. Heinlein

Starship Soldier enjoyed. Except that there were places where action stopped and author went in for lecturing.

EDITOR'S NOTE: Starship Soldier, *later* Starship Troopers, *was turned down by the entire Scribner's editorial board.*
Lurton called and advised me; Robert was still asleep. I had to tell him.
As a matter of fact, Lurton was certain that he could place the book with another publisher. Walter Minton, president of G. P. Putnam's Sons, later said that one of his editors told him that there was a Heinlein juvenile

available. Walter instructed the editor, "Grab it."

Miss Dalgliesh made the following suggestions about the book:

1. *use it only as an adult serial*
2. *sell it elsewhere*
3. *put it away for a while*

The Scribner's connection had ended; with it, the annual quarrels over what was suitable for juvenile reading. After Starship Troopers *was published, Robert wrote only one more juvenile—Podkayne of Mars.*

February 19, 1959: Robert A. Heinlein to Lurton Blassingame

. . . I think I have handed you a less salable item than most in this ms. and I will be happy indeed to place it with Mills [Robert P., editor of *F&SF* magazine] and with any major trade book house—for which purpose I am willing to rewrite, revise, cut, or expand to *any* extent necessary. From a story standpoint, I am now convinced that this is not my best work; I intend to sweat and make it so. (But, privately to you, revision will be literary revision; I will not let even the ghost of Horace Greeley order me to revise my ideas to fit popular prejudice—I'll hike up the story but the ideas will remain intact.) *"Eppur si muove!"* I stand by my heresies. But I have no intention of saying this to an editor quite so bluntly; I'll simply improve the story as *story* until he will pass it.

March 23, 1959: Robert A. Heinlein to Lurton Blassingame

Now to the pièce de résistance, the Putnam contract for *Starship Soldier*:

First, my very warmest thanks to you for your unsparing efforts on this ms. I know that you thought it was weak (and so do I . . . and I intend to try to repair the weaknesses); nevertheless, you sold the serial rights to the leading specialty magazine and trade book right to a major trade house. My morale is greatly bucked up thereby.

I've been rather "shook up" over this ms. . . . The book should be better than it is; I think I can improve it. I certainly will try to, working closely with an editor. Who will be my editor at Putnam?

September 19, 1960: Robert A. Heinlein to Lurton Blassingame

. . . However, the Scribner's angle is a special case. Yes, I do know that Miss Dalgliesh is no longer there. But my irk is not alone at her; it includes Mr. Scribner himself. I feel that I was treated in a very

shabby fashion, and I regard him as in part responsible and do not
wish to place any more stories with his firm. Scribner's had published
twelve of my books and *every single one of them made a profit for them*
and each one is *still* making money for them. At one time Miss Dalgliesh told me that my books had kept her department out of the red.

So I offer a thirteenth book . . . and it is turned down with a brisk
little note which might as well have been a printed rejection slip, for
it was just as cold and just as informative.

I then found it necessary to write to [George McC] to find out what
the score was. He told me that it had been a joint action, in which
several of the editors had read my ms—*including Mr. Scribner*—and that
Scribner himself had joined in rejecting it.

Based on my royalty records I conjecture that my books have netted
for Mr. Scribner something between $50,000 and $100,000 (and grossed
a great deal more). They have been absolutely certain money-from-
home for his firm . . . and still are. Yet after years and years of a highly
profitable association, Mr. Scribner let me be "fired" with less ceremony
than he would use in firing his office boy . . . not a word out of him,
not even a hint that he gave a damn whether I stayed with them or

Heinlein with his Hugo Award for *Starship Troopers* at the Pittsburgh World Science Fiction Convention.

not. I submit that this is rudeness, unpardonable in view of the long association.

Writers hear a lot of prattle about how speculative the trade book business is and how prestige houses (such as Scribner's) will publish a book which might lose money because the author should be encouraged—and hope to make it up on the rest of their list. Well, I seem to be part of the "rest of their list," the part that makes up their losses—for I certainly did not appear to be a writer they were willing to take even a *little* chance on, when it came to scratch. I was simply dumped.

Furthermore, the ms. couldn't have been bad enough to justify dumping me in view of the fact that three other editors bought it . . . and then it went on to win the Hugo [Award] for [1959]. (Besides that, I notice that, despite ———'s earlier worries, the trade book sold 5,000 copies in the first two and a half months . . . and now he tells us that sales are picking up.)

It seems to me that, if the pious crap they hand out about "taking a chance" on authors actually meant anything, Mr. Scribner himself would have said to his editorial board: "Maybe this isn't the best book Mr. Heinlein has ever done—possibly it will even flop and we'll lose a little money on him this time. But his books have been steady sellers in the past and we'll have to give him the benefit of the doubt. Perhaps with a little revision it will be more acceptable; if you don't want to write to him about revisions, let me look over the ms. again and I will write to him . . . but we can't simply reject the book out of hand. Mr. Heinlein is part of the Scribner's family and has been for years."

Too goddamned much to expect, I suppose. At least that was *not* the way he handled it.

Lurton, it seems to me that, with any other successful writer on their list, Scribner's would have published that book—perhaps with revisions and perhaps not as a juvenile—but they would have published it. But if Mr. Scribner felt that he simply could *not* publish it, I think the circumstances called for a note, a letter, a measure of polite discussion, from the boss to me . . . a minimum of formal politeness.

I did not receive that minimum. I think Mr. Scribner treated me with extreme rudeness . . . so I don't want to work for him. Lurton, I have elaborated this matter because, in several letters lately, you have pointed out that the new juvenile editor at Scribner's is anxious "to welcome me back." So I have explained why I am not going back. I have nothing against the lady who now has that department—but the firm is still Mr. Scribner's. If the action had been taken by Miss Dalgliesh alone— But it was *not*; when I got tossed out, Mr. Scribner in person had me by the scruff of the neck and took part in the tossing, without even a formal word of regret.

PODKAYNE OF MARS

March 8, 1962: Lurton Blassingame to Robert A. Heinlein

Enjoyed all of *Podkayne Fries*—except ending. She was such a sweet kid that I hated for you to kill her. That is the Heinlein touch— tell Ginny to beware. It's a good story.

March 10, 1962: Robert A. Heinlein to Lurton Blassingame

Is *Poddy* a juvenile? I didn't think of it as such and I suggest that it violates numerous taboos for the juvenile market. It seems to me that it is what the Swedes call a "cadet" book—upper teenage, plus such adults and juveniles as may enjoy it—and the American trade book market does not recognize such a category. But possibly it might

PODKAYNE OF MARS

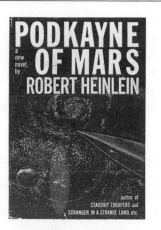

Podkayne of Mars, G.P. Putnam's Sons, 1963, was Heinlein's last juvenile novel. The cover art is by Irv Doktor.

As originally written *Podkayne* depicted the tragedy of a mother who was too busy with her career to supervise her children's upbringing. Podkayne turns out well enough, although something of a dreamer; her brother is another story, an asocial monster.

Podkayne has as her ambition to be a starship captain, later in life, but when Uncle Tom invites her and brother Clark to go on a cruise to Earth and Venus, ambition is temporarily abandoned. As the result of a political intrigue, Podkayne and Clark find themselves in much trouble on Venus . . .

be well to let [Putnam] have this story at once and see what happens.

Lurton, for several years now I have been writing just stories, with no eye on the market, and have been writing them with no criterion save the fixed belief that a story which interests me, and the solution of which satisfies me, will interest and satisfy a sufficient percentage of readers to make the story commercially usable. Maybe I'm wrong about this—maybe I should study the market and try like hell to tailor something which fits the current styles. But it seems to me that, if I am to turn out work of (fairly) permanent value, my own taste (checked by yours and by Ginny's) is what I must follow. Of course, this may result in my losing the market entirely—but I hope that it will result in better stories than if I tried to compound the "mixture as before."

I know that the ending of *Poddy* comes as rather a shock. However, that is the ending that seemed to fit—to me. The story follows a definite progression: a girl child with no worries at all and a preposterous ambition . . . then, step by step, she grows up and discovers that the real world is more complex and not nearly as sweet as she had thought . . . and that the only basic standard for an adult is the welfare of the young.

Oh, I could revise that last chapter to a "happy" ending in about two hours—let Poddy live through it, injured but promised a full recovery and with the implication that she will eventually marry this rich and handsome bloke who can take her with him to the stars . . . and still give her brat kid brother a comeuppance and his lumps (and it is possible that I will at least consider doing this if no editor will risk publishing it as it is). But I don't want to do this; I think it would ruin the story—something like revising *Romeo and Juliet* to let the young lovers "live happily ever after."

But it took the deaths of Romeo and Juliet to show the families Montague and Capulet what damned fools they were being. Poddy's death (it seems to me) is similarly indispensable to this story. The true tragedy in this story lies in the character of the mother, the highly successful career woman who wouldn't take time to raise her own kids— and thereby let her son grow up an infantile monster, no real part of the human race and indifferent to the wellbeing of others . . . until the death of his sister, under circumstances which lay on him a guilt he can never shake off, gives some prospect that he is now going to grow up.

I could state that the theme of the story is that death is the only destination for all of us and that the only long-range hope for any adult lies in the young—and that this double realization constitutes growing up, ceasing to be a child and putting away childish things. But I can't say it that baldly, not in fiction, and it seemed to me that I needed Poddy's death to say it at all. If Poddy gets to have her cake and eat it too (both marriage and star-roving), if that little monster, her brother, gets off unscathed to continue his clever but asocial career, if their mother gets away with neglecting her children's rearing without having it backfire on her—then the story is just a series of mildly adventurous incidents, strung together.

March 23, 1962: Robert A. Heinlein to Lurton Blassingame

I understand and appreciate, I think, your remarks about Cézanne and his black outlines—but this is an endless problem for me with no easy solution. If I preach overtly, I get complaints from Ginny, you, the editor, and in time the readers . . . and I'm all too prone to preach. In this book, *Poddy*, I'm limited by what Poddy herself would say—which is perhaps just as well!!!

May 9, 1962: Robert A. Heinlein to Lurton Blassingame

Please tell Peter Israel of Putnam's that I will tackle the revision he wants very shortly, say about the first of the week. I have one other job to finish first. I still have strong doubts about the artistic and dramatic necessity of a happy ending on this story—but I'll do my damndest.

May 20, 1962: Robert A. Heinlein to Lurton Blassingame

Neither editor liked my title and I did not [like] either of their suggestions. I have suggested to Pohl [Frederik Pohl, editor of *If*] *Podkayne of Mars*, which suits him. If it does not suit Mr. Israel I hope that he will suggest one which all three of us can agree on, as I prefer to have magazine version and book carry the same title if possible.

The new kittens are two weeks old and fat and healthy. A hawk or an owl got Ginny's ducks.

May 25, 1962: Lurton Blassingame to Robert A. Heinlein

Beautiful job on the revision.

CHAPTER V

❖

THE BEST LAID PLANS

❖

PUBLIC SPEAKING

August 15, 1968: Robert A. Heinlein to Lurton Blassingame

I have given both these bids considerable thought. As you know, I do not like speaking dates, but on the other hand, I realize that I must accept some of them, especially those from librarians. This time the matter is further complicated by the fact that both bids come via Scribner's (not my current publisher) and, while one group offers to pick up the tab, the other group asks Scribner's to do so—and Scribner's has agreed to do so.

I do not want Scribner's to pick up the tab. After long thought I have concluded that I do not want *any* publisher *ever* to pick up the tab when I make a trip to speak; I would much rather see a publisher spend money to advertise and distribute my books than to have promotion money spent on airfares and hotel bills for the author.

So I have finally arrived at this policy, which I now present to you for comment and (I hope) approval. From here on I will continue to avoid speaking dates when possible except speaking dates involving librarians. With respect to their bids, I will accept them if possible in such cases and *only* such cases as the group which wishes to have me appear wants me badly enough to pay my travel and hotel expenses plus a nominal fee of, let us say, fifty dollars.

WRITING PLANS

November 19, 1945: Robert A. Heinlein to Lurton Blassingame

. . . My particular talent is for the prophetic novel, i.e., the novel laid in the future, perhaps only a few years in the future but nevertheless in the future. I have no objection to doing contemporary fiction and am open to advice, but there is this one thing which I do especially well. There is a book market for it and at least a limited slick market for it. I believe that the slick market for it will be much greater than before the war, primarily because of atomics. I think people will want to be told what to expect in the coming atomic age. I have notes for many, many stories; do you want to discuss stories with me ahead of time, or shall I just go ahead and write?

I also write fantasy and would like to emulate Stephen Vincent Benét. The SEP [*Saturday Evening Post*] has been publishing quite a lot of fantasy since —— took over; I would like to do the sort of thing they publish.

January 1, 1946: Robert A. Heinlein to Lurton Blassingame

I am quite used to being considered too spectacular. My own brother, a colonel of engineers, thought my pre-war stories about the atomic bomb and atomic weapons to be sheer moonshine; he has since flown over Hiroshima and changed his mind.

April 20, 1947: Robert A. Heinlein to Lurton Blassingame

I am starting a short, Luna City series, slanted for *Post*, tomorrow. Like the hired man said, "We've had a lot of trouble around here," but you may expect regular copy for some time hence.

June 24, 1947: Robert A. Heinlein to Lurton Blassingame

To confirm my telegram of Tuesday, my new address is:

> Suite 210,
> 7904 Santa Monica Blvd.,
> Hollywood 46, Cal.

Letters or telegrams sent there will reach me promptly. My telephone has been disconnected. We have closed our house and in a few days—

as soon as I can get some chores cleaned up—I am going to light out for the desert and get back to work. Leslyn [Heinlein's first wife] is going to stay in town. . . .

EDITOR'S NOTE: While Robert was working at the Naval Air Experimental Station in Philadelphia, I was reassigned to duty there by the Navy. At that time, I was a lieutenant (jg.) in the WAVES. We worked together on some projects, chiefly on attachment of plexiglas canopies. Both of us had other, separate projects.

When World War II ended, Robert resigned his position as an engineer to return home to Los Angeles with his wife. As I had not accrued many points in the system that governed release from the service, I was required to remain on duty until March 1946. I had already decided to return to college for an advanced degree, and made arrangements for that. Robert suggested that I go to UCLA rather than Berkeley, as I had planned.

While the GI Bill paid for tuition and books, the stipend allowed was rather scanty, so I needed to work part-time, attending classes and studying in what free time I had. So my social life lapsed almost entirely. What I

Robert and Virginia about the time of their engagement.

did retain was devoted to the symphony and figure skating. I saw very little of Robert and his wife, Leslyn, although we lived not too far apart.

When finals were finished in 1947, I had a call from Robert—he asked my help in clearing his papers from his house. He was getting a divorce.

I took the summer off from my studies to work—my finances were in poor shape. Robert spent that summer in Ojai, writing.

We were married in October 1948.

1948: Robert A. Heinlein to Lurton Blassingame

I'm back to work. The honeymoon is over, except for weekends. I hope, Lurton, to turn over to you more and better copy than you have seen yet. During my entire association with you, everything I have written has been turned out under difficult circumstances, most of them under most excruciatingly difficult circumstances. I have had to force myself to work, with the major portion of my mind and attention centered on the things that were happening around me and to me. I am not seeking sympathy, but I do want you to know that there is at least a fair chance that I will give you better material and more of it from now on.

November 6, 1948: Robert A. Heinlein to Lurton Blassingame

It isn't necessary to get Ginny to chain me to my typewriter four hours a day. I am frantically anxious to spend more hours than that at work every day. If I am spared more domestic upheavals for the next several months I should turn out a lot of copy. Right now I am racking my brain trying to cook up another subject for a boys' novel for Scribner's. I am not going to be able to go to Florida this winter to complete the diving and research I must do before I write *Ocean Rancher*. Therefore I have got to find another story for ———. It would be easy enough to cook up another space opera, but I shall do my darnedest to find something else to write about before falling back on that.

November 18, 1948: Robert A. Heinlein to Lurton Blassingame

Your remark that you were sure that I would do an (adult) novel within the next twelve months has caused me considerable thought. Do you really think so? I have long wanted to do bookbound adult novels, preferably of the H. G. Wells sort, but have never tackled anything but pulp serials and these boys' books for Scribner's. Do you think I should take time off . . . and make a real try at cracking the adult book market? If so, should I drop the speculative stuff and try a contemporary novel—or should I stick to my specialty?

January 28, 1949: Robert A. Heinlein to Lurton Blassingame

. . . In the meantime, I am collecting notes on (Forgive me!) the Great American Novel. Yup, Lurton, I have fallen ill of the desire to turn out a "literary" job. Specifically, I would like to do a job somewhat like Ayn Rand did in *The Fountainhead*, but with modern art, especially pictorial art, as my target. It may be a year or two before I feel ready to tackle it, but I am working on it.

The first draft of the boys' novel [*Red Planet*] for Scribner's was finished at 11 P.M. last Monday. I have taken three days off to attend to chores and correspondence and intend to start revising tomorrow. The finished manuscript should be in your hands within a fortnight.

October 1, 1949: Robert A. Heinlein to Lurton Blassingame

I have two short stories that I am very hot to do, one a bobby-sox for *Calling All Girls* and one a sci-fi short which will probably sell to slick and is a sure sale for pulp. The first is "Mother and the Balanced Diet," using the same characters as [in] "Poor Daddy," as the editors requested. The other is "The Year of the Jackpot" based on cycles theory—1952, the year that *everything* happens at once. But gosh knows when I will find time to do them. I probably will, as I *want* to do them. But I'm working myself nutty. (Oh, yes—I've got to prepare some stuff for —— too; possible [motion picture] uses for my published stuff.)

About the *Boys' Life* job, see above. You'll get both versions in about a month. We have to move this week; I'll send you a new address.

HOLLYWOOD WRITING

September 3, 1957: Robert A. Heinlein to Lurton Blassingame

I want to hold up for a little while in changing Hollywood agents. I still think that MCA is not the place for me to get personal attention but a recent incident makes it polite, at least, to delay: at 1200 26 August, Hal Flanders of Ned Brown's office phoned me and

Robert and Virginia on the set of "Destination Moon," 1949. Heinlein wrote the script based on his story in *ShortStories* magazine, September 1950.

offered me a Hollywood writing job doing a screen treatment of Herman Wouk's *The Lomokome Papers*. I turned down the job—I don't really want to write screen stories of anyone's work but my own, and this particular story *cannot* be repaired into an honest science fiction story anyhow; it is a philosophical tract packaged as a fantasy. Furthermore, I hope my decision will not disappoint you when I point out that the source of the work is such that we could hardly expect MCA to split the fee—and I prefer to stay under your management and writing for the New York market rather than become a Hollywood trained seal. In any case, I could not finish the novel, do this job, and sail on 26 November. But I did find the offer pleasing. . . .

November 16, 1961: Robert A. Heinlein to Lurton Blassingame

There will be a veritable spate of new Heinlein stories before this winter is over. Our bomb shelter is completed and stocked—and the durn thing was enormously more expensive than I had figured on when I started it. Now I have a couple of weeks of chores to clean up, including a big backlog of correspondence, filing, record keeping, etc.; then I shall apply the nose to this grindstone and keep it there all winter.

August 10, 1963: Robert A. Heinlein to Lurton Blassingame

This fall I might do about 10,000 words for *Boys' Life* (query them if you like), or write the last story of the Future History [see *The Past Through Tomorrow* in Chapter XI, "Adult Novels"], *Da Capo* (piles of notes on it but it has never quite jelled)—or possibly a new novel. Or perhaps all three in the order named. But that is a good many weeks away.

Re Scribner's: We might offer —— something someday—but only if Putnam's turns down a book.

April 17, 1964: Robert A. Heinlein to Lurton Blassingame

I have spent the past month on (a) flu, (b) reading several hundred pounds of accumulated magazines and technical reports, and (c) correspondence. The latter two are things I am endlessly behind on, always. There is no solution to the problem of trying to keep up with the ever-expanding frontier of science and technology, plus the world in general; I simply do the best I can, falling further behind each year, especially in electronics, biochemistry, and space travel technology. But I have made, implemented, and am keeping a good resolution concerning correspondence: I now answer almost all letters simply with postcards—a letter has to be really important *to me* to cause me to answer it by a real letter. The saving in time is very marked.

I will probably not write another story or book until after I learn whether or not I will have to go back to Hollywood this summer. And there is endless maintenance work to be done around this place. Today I got back to pick and shovel for the first time: cleaning some tons of silt out of my middle irrigation pool . . . silt from a flood clear back in September or earlier. Monday I expect to start on concrete work, repairing the lowest dam, if the weather holds. This has been a cold, very late spring. Ginny has just started on her garden work; it has been too cold up to now. There is still some snow on the mountain above us and it snowed down here only eight days ago.

June 23, 1967: Robert A. Heinlein to Lurton Blassingame

I am very anxious to get back to writing, including new copy for the proposed boy scout book—and I've just had a very pleasant, long letter from ——— telling me that ——— has again raised their rates . . . and that he would expect to pay me a still higher bonus rate if I'll ever come through with copy. But, Lurton, I've never worked any harder in my life than right now and it is utterly impossible for me to turn out fiction until I get this [Santa Cruz] house finished. Every time I turn my back something goes wrong. The cabinet and finish work is slowly (and very expensively) being finished. After that we still have the floors, ceilings, and fireplaces to do, plus the driveway, the front steps, and some exterior painting. It feels like an endless nightmare and the costs are utterly unbelievable. But there is no way to stop—short of being forced to stop by running out of money. Which is possible, despite the way you have been digging gold for us.

Sorry—I'm simply very tired tonight, up to midnight last night on the drawing board, on it again today under pressure so that the cabinet-makers could take a bunch of detail drawings home over the weekend . . . and now writing this under pressure so as not to miss the next mail dispatch. But we *are* getting a beautiful house just the way Ginny wants it.

Heinlein working at his desk, at "Bonny Doon," the Santa Cruz house.

September 16, 1973: Robert A. Heinlein to Lurton Blassingame

... In the meantime, I am hotter than a $2 pistol on *three* books. One is fiction and will be a long time in writing, as I must do much research on the history and culture and manners of speech of several periods I do not as yet know enough about. It will be an episodic time-travel fantasy (with a new gimmick for time travel), each episode independent and available for sale as a short story as it is written, but the whole thing linked together by an overall plot which will make it a novel of book length—somewhat the way [Paul] Gallico's "Adventures of Hiram Holiday" make one book—but nothing at all like Gallico's fine job save in its episodic structure. (I am going to reread his in order to stay as far away from his ideas as possible in all ways.) I have several episodes well worked out but each needs careful research—probably after a draft on each, then a final form after research; this will take lots of work. (I may turn out a juvenile sci fi adventure of the sort I used to do long before this episodic fantasy is completed.)

The second book is a memoirs-autobiography job to be published posthumously—and left uncopyrighted till then (hence of zero cash value in probate)—as a little bonus to Ginny for all the years she has put up with my cantankerous ways. If published about a year after my death it should bring her some return . . . if I am still writing and my works are still known at the time of my death. If I get it in fair shape, you may possibly see a draft of it later—depends on events. I have been gathering notes for such a book for many years and have recently started shaping them up . . . especially since 1969, which caused me to realize that I didn't have forever if it were to be a vendable property. Working title: *Grumbles from the Grave by Robert A. Heinlein (deceased)*. (It's amazing how frank and how acidly funny one can be when one is certain it will never see print until the writer is safely out of reach. I'll name names—then Ginny will have to edit it with the advice of a good lawyer to insure that she is safe, too—then no doubt the publisher's lawyers will want some names deleted or changed, too. But I am going to write it as if with a Ouija board. It will be easy to write—lots of notes, lots of pack-rat-saved souvenirs, more than fifty years of letters, many things I have never discussed—e.g., the frontline seat I had in the crisis many years back with Japan, before World War II—a crisis involving a war ultimatum that never got into the news . . . plus a Secret Life of (Walter Mitty) Heinlein, etc. I'm working on it.

But the third book will be written and finished for publication as soon as I am free of taking care of Ginny through this long, long siege of oral surgery. I have it in shape to start writing this very minute but will have many, many more card notes by that time—shortly after the first of the year. Working title: *Writing for a Living (and How to Live Through It)—Being the Ungarnished Facts about the Writing Racket for People Too Lazy to Dig Ditches*. The first part—*Writing for a Living*—is for the cover and the half-title page, the entire title being for the full-title page—although the book jacket might read *Writing for a Living* in large letters, plus *The Ungarnished Facts* in much smaller letters, plus my name in quite large letters—same size as the short title, or even larger, if publisher's judgment in dust jackets of my last several books is a guide. Besides that, for use on the inner flap and on the back of the dust jacket, and as title of the preface Ginny has suggested and is preparing a Latin fake quotation: "De Natura Scribendi etc.," a free translation being "Concerning the Nature of the Writing Business and How Not to Get Screwed in It." Ginny's command of Latin grammar is good and she knows many Latin bawdy idioms . . . but she will write it, then enlist the help of a professor of Latin here at the campus to insure perfect grammar and exact idiom—and a choice of words as nearly self-translating as possible by selection of proper cognates of

English. I'm probably attribute it to Juvenal or Ovid, as interpreted by Lazarus Long.

(It could have a How to Write for Money title—but I think that "How to—" has been overworked of late years.)

A somewhat-laundered translation could be used in the dust jacket blurb (and possibly an exact translation supplied to reviewers), but the Latin itself must be idiomatically perfect. In truth it will be a most practical guide for inexperienced aspirants who are wild to do the— comparatively mild—and rather fun work that writing entails. I am going to make it extremely practical—more practical than Jack Woodford's *How to Write and Sell* (his only good book, his only bestseller, and the basis for 90%+ of his reputation)—but I intend to make it lively, hard to put down as a good novel by any of the millions of aspirant-writers-who-never-will-actually-write, plus the thousands who do write and could make a living at it if they knew certain rules of the game—rules that are not taught in so-called creative writing classes, nor in any book on how to write that I have ever seen.

I intend to lace it with illustrative true anecdotes, changing names and dates and places only when necessary to avoid being sued—and will say so. It will have many a chuckle in it, plus a few belly laughs. I *know* I can do it. This will be a timeless book and should make money for many years. It just might be a smash hit, like Helen Gurley's *Sex and the Single Girl*—as everyone wants to know how to make money with least effort and almost as many have at least a secret hope of seeing their names in print as "Authors"—much like the great curiosity that most respectable women have about prostitution . . . and a secret wonder as to whether or not they could have made the grade in the Oldest Profession—only of course they never actually *would*, perish the thought! Almost as many feel that way about the Second Oldest Profession, the Teller of Tales—I know, from endless direct experience, that a person who actually *writes* for a living . . . and clearly does well financially at it . . . is an object of curiosity to many—an exotic creature, not quite respectable, but very interesting. I'm buttonholed about it every time I appear in public—which used to be fun but has grown to be a nuisance. So I might as well turn this nuisance into cash.

EDITOR'S NOTE: *None of the three books outlined here were ever written; some notes were collected, but nothing ever went on paper.*

Lurton telephoned one day, saying that Robert had been asked to give one of the Forrestal Lectures at the Naval Academy. Normally, Lurton would have regretted the invitation, but this was from Robert's alma mater. So it was accepted, and many months went into preparation for the talk.

Then along came a request from the Britannica editors for Robert to do an article on Paul Dirac and antimatter for the Compton Yearbook. Robert viewed that as an opportunity to review the entire field of modern physics, and sciences in general. So, doing that article took one year. And it was followed by a request for another article on blood—another year consumed in the study of biological sciences, with one article to show for that year's work.

Then came the invitation to be Guest of Honor at MidAmeriCon, which took up most of the year of 1976, what with all the arrangements to be made.

The year 1977 was passed in getting blood drives going among science fiction fans—and I must heartily recommend them for their cooperation in this project. Donors still send me copies of their ten-gallon certificates . . .

Thus did time pass, and those books Robert was so hot to do were never written.

Robert never did tell me just what the crisis with Japan was, when his ship steamed full speed toward the Orient.

SLUMP

March 31, 1959: Robert A. Heinlein to Lurton Blassingame

If the market is in this bad shape, I had better do one of two things; either quit writing for the pulp SF magazines and concentrate on television and possible slick sales, or simply retire and do what I want to do with my time. I could retire very easily now, and Ginny and I could live very comfortably, simply by dispensing with foreign travel, emeralds, and similar unnecessary luxuries—and I certainly do not fancy knocking myself out, breeding insomnia, etc., for the privilege of receiving word rates that are actually less, after taxes, than those I got twenty years ago—and are effectively less than half that when I spend the money. It doesn't make sense.

July 28, 1959: Robert A. Heinlein to Lurton Blassingame

I am returning your clipping about the sad state of fiction. It is enough to drive a man back to engineering. However, I have always worked on the theory that there is always a market somewhere for a good story—a notion that Will Jenkins [the real name of science-fiction writer Murray Leinster] pounded into my head many years ago. When I started writing there were lots of pulp magazines, many slick fiction magazines—no pocketbooks and no television. I think I'll just go on writing stories that I would like to read and assume that they can be sold somewhere to some medium.

MOTION PICTURE CONTRACT

November 8, 1968: Robert A. Heinlein to Lurton Blassingame

We have just finished a hard three days with the literary appraiser—hard but very pleasant; he turns out to be muy simpatico. Today I am trying to turn my notes into a long letter to Ned [Brown] re the *Glory Road* [fantasy novel, see Chapter XI, "Adult Novels"] contract. Darn it, I opened that contract determined to sign it unchanged if at all possible to live with it. Ginny says they let a second cousin write this contract when they should have used at least a first cousin.

TELEVISION SERIES

October 12, 1963: Robert A. Heinlein to Lurton Blassingame

Ned told me by phone that the contract is all set for the TV series and for me to do the pilot film shooting script. He gave me a lot of details, none of which I wrote down, as I don't believe a durn thing out of Hollywood until I see a signed contract and a check . . . Ned seems to have gotten from them simply everything he asked for . . . I simply told him to go ahead and get the best deal he could and I would sign it as long as it did not commit me to work in Hollywood.

But Ned said that I really must come out to Hollywood for at least one day's conference with Dozier, the boss. This I flatly refused to do until I have a signed contract in hand. I was not just being stubborn.

EDITOR'S NOTE: *Robert was quite accustomed to receiving telephone calls from Hollywood producers; they would want him to do a script. Each time, the suggestion would be made, "Why don't you hop on a plane and come out here and discuss it?"*

So, when in 1963, Robert received a telephone call from a Hollywood producer, Howie Horwitz, Robert was ready with an answer. Howie wanted Robert to do a pilot script for a science fiction TV series for Screen Gems. Then came the inevitable line: "Why don't you hop a plane and come out and discuss it?"

Robert replied, "Why don't you hop a plane to Colorado and we can discuss it here?"

To our amazement, Howie did just that.

Robert had sworn a mighty oath not to get involved in such an enterprise again. But Howie's presence disarmed him. Robert set to work after Howie left and produced a script. Then he found that trying to work between Colorado and Hollywood just wasn't possible. So in early 1964 we went out there for Robert to do rewrites under Howie's direction.

When the work was finished, we returned home. It was at just this point that the bankers went out to Hollywood from New York, and fired Howie and his boss. The script was shelved at Screen Gems, and Howie and his boss went across the street, and produced "Batman."

For all practical purposes, the pilot script was dead, along with the series, "Century XXII." There is a faint hope that it may be produced someday. As this is being written, someone recalled the script and is setting about the difficult task of undertaking to produce the film.

January 20, 1964: Robert A. Heinlein to Lurton Blassingame

Will you get me off the hook on several things? There has been a death in my family—no close emotional involvement for me, but some duty matters—so I am unexpectedly catching a plane in about an hour (Ginny remains here), then on my return Thursday will be leaving immediately to drive to Hollywood (Ginny accompanying me) and arriving there possibly late for Screen Gems story conference Monday 27 January. . . . The [TV] thing is sourer than ever and I see no hopes of saving it, but I must go out and try my best.

But today I'm badly strapped for time and ask help on some unfinished business (this damned screenplay has put me behind on *every-thing*)—and this funeral puts the topper on it—despite the fact that I answered sixty-three letters in the last three days, trying to catch up.

April 8, 1964: Robert A. Heinlein to Lurton Blassingame

I have many other things to acknowledge. We have been home three weeks now, two of them eaten by illness, the rest of the time used futilely in attempting to cope with an avalanche of accumulated low-priority paperwork, several hundred periodicals, etc., piled up not only while we were away, but left undone clear back from last August when (TV producer) first entered my life. This last Hollywood experi-ence has simply confirmed my earlier opinion that, while Hollywood rates are high, what a writer goes through to earn those rates makes it a losing game in the long run. I hope that you and I and Ned [Brown] make some money out of this—but if the series is never produced, I hope to have sense enough to stay home and write books in the future and leave the movie never-never land to those who enjoy that rat race.

CHAPTER VI

❖

ABOUT WRITING
METHODS AND
CUTTING

❖

October 25, 1946: Robert A. Heinlein to Lurton Blassingame

    . . . then write another short. This one is tentatively titled "Homesickness" ["It's Great to Be Back"] and is another Luna City and so forth yarn. If possible, I want to build up a background, as I did in *Astounding*, for a series of interplanetary shorts, laid in the near future (the coming century, to about A.D. 2050). The series will follow the formula, somewhat modified, of the SEP [*Saturday Evening Post*] series such as Earthworm Tractor, Tugboat Annie, Gunsmith Pyne, Blue Chip Haggerty, etc.—stories laid against a particular occupation or industry. My series will be laid against the background of *commercial* (not exploration nor adventure) interplanetary travel. Continuity will be maintained by names of places—Luna City, Drywater, Venusburg, New Brisbane, New Chicago, How-Far?, Leyburg, Marsopolis, Supra-New York, etc., and by consistent use of techniques, cultural changes, and speech changes. Characters will shift for each story, but a major character in one story may show up in a bit part in another.

    The science and engineering will be held to a minimum but will be authentic. An editor may be sure that I will respect facts of astronomy, atomics, ballistics, rocketry, etc. For example, the piloting in the story you are about to receive is as authentic as it can be at this date—if it is not as it *will* be, then it is at least as it *could* be; it is practical, with respect to time intervals, speeds, accelerations, and instruments used. When, in that story, I mention falling 700 feet on the Moon in forty seconds and thereby picking up speeds up to 140 miles per hour, and, thereafter, killing the speed with a one-second-plus blast at five-gravities, I know what I am talking about—I am a mechanical engineer, a ballistician, a student of reaction engines, and an amateur astronomer. I mention these things because they may help you sell my stuff—I won't give an editor any Buck Rogers nonsense. A great deal of study and research goes into the background of my stories.

May 16, 1947: Robert A. Heinlein to Lurton Blassingame

. . . As for formal coaching from Uzzell [a well-known "story doctor" and coach of the time] or anyone, I'm getting just the coaching I want from you . . . I'm afraid of coaching, of writers' classes, of writers' magazines, of books on how to write. They give me centipede trouble— you know the yarn about the centipede who was asked how he managed all his feet? He tried to answer, stopped to think about it, and was never able to walk another step. Articles and books on how to write have that effect on me. The author seems so persuasive, so sure that he knows what he is talking about, that I start having doubts about my own technique. It usually turns out that the author is urging the reader to do something quite unsuited to me—fine for him probably, but not my pidgin. If I try to imitate him, follow his directions, I usually fail to accomplish his methods and lose my own in the process . . .

I do get a great deal of help from studying other writers' stories, particularly in the respects in which I see that they have accomplished an effect that I do not as yet know how to accomplish. I find such study of what they have *done* more use to me than their discussions of *how* they do it.

Winslow says I don't understand plotting and probably I don't—I have been congratulated many times on the skill shown in my plotting when I knew damn well that the story in question had not been plotted in advance at all. My notion of a story is an interesting situation in which a human being has to cope with a problem, does so, and thereby changes his personality, character, or evaluations in some measure be-

Heinlein working at his desk, at "Bonny Doon," the Santa Cruz house.

cause the coping has forced him to revise his thinking. How he copes with it I can't plot in advance because that depends on his character, and I don't know what his character is until I get acquainted with him. When I can "hear the character talk" then I'm all right—he works out his own salvation.

January 31, 1948: Robert A. Heinlein to Lurton Blassingame

I certainly am sorry to have worried you and will try not to let it happen again—when I get into the final chapters of a novel it is sometimes almost impossible to attract my attention.

January 2, 1950: Robert A. Heinlein to Lurton Blassingame

My method of work is such that I always have a dozen or more stories being worked on.

March 20, 1953: Robert A. Heinlein to Peter Hamilton (editor of *Nebula Science Fiction*)

The problem of building up convincing background in a science fiction story becomes extremely difficult in the shorter lengths. In ordinary fiction, background may be assumed or most briefly indicated, but it is a most unusual science fiction idea which may safely be so treated. In all the years I have been writing science fiction I have done only one story under 2,500 words, that story being "Columbus Was a Dope" . . .

October 9, 1956: Robert A. Heinlein to Lurton Blassingame

. . . However, I have been fiddling with experimental methods of storytelling (none of which you have seen) and I am beginning to think that I may be developing a new method which might turn out to be important. It is a multiple first-person technique, but not the one used by John Masters in *Bowhani Junction*. Mine calls for using camera cuts and shifts as rapid as those in the movies; the idea is to give the speed of movies, the sense of immediacy of the legitimate stage, and the empathy obtained by stream of consciousness—a nice trick if I can bring it off! The greatest hitch seems to lie in the problem of shifting viewpoints, both without confusing the reader and without losing empathy through cumbersome devices. But I think I am learning how to do it.

I don't want to use this technique on commercial copy until I am sure I can force the reader to go along with a novel technique. James Joyce introduced into writing an important new technique, but he did it so clumsily that his so-called novels are virtually unreadable; if I do have here a usable new technique I want to polish it to the point where it can stand up in the open market in competition with the usual wares whose values are established and recognized.

Ginny suggests that I not use it in science fiction in any case, but save it for a lit'rary novel. She has a point, I think, as it would not be seriously reviewed in an S-F novel. We'll see.

ATTENTION

November 8, 1968: Robert A. Heinlein to Lurton Blassingame

Sure I signed the Gollancz [a British publisher] contract; and not in invisible ink, either. Then I stuck it into file and sent you the copy I had *not* signed—convinced that I had signed both of them. Ginny says that whenever she finds my shoes in the icebox, she knows I'm coming down with a story.

So here is the other copy—now signed.

WORKING HABITS

August 31, 1956: Robert A. Heinlein to Lurton Blassingame

. . . In the meantime, I have turned out no salable copy. Part of my trouble is that I have undertaken to do something which does not fit my working habits, i.e., agreed to produce a story outline. Outlines never have any reality to me, no vividness. Oh, I use what I call an outline but a sort that no editor would accept; it's actually simply musing on paper—then when the idea begins to take fire, I start at once to write the story itself and become acquainted with the problem and the characters as I go along. Sometimes this results in blind alleys and surplusage which has to be removed (*Door Into Summer* had Martians in it for half a day, then I chucked a few pages and got back on the track)—but by the time I am well into the story I am writing with sureness, hearing the characters, seeing their surroundings, and having the same trouble coping with their problems that they have. As you can see, this is not a method [that] lends itself to a formal outline, from which I can promise to derive an acceptable story. But it is the method I have taught myself and it works for me.

Trying to force myself into the more conventional method has not worked; it has simply resulted in my snapping at my wife for a couple of months and getting no other work done either. So I am going to devote the next week to an attempt to start a story suitable for *Boys' Life* on spec—no outline. Probably it will work and probably they will buy it. But if I can't click in about a week I shall have to tell them that I have nothing to offer them at this time—I shall have to cut my losses and get busy on something I can do.

September 13, 1956: Robert A. Heinlein to Lurton Blassingame

I've been wanting to write to you ever since I spoke with you on Sunday, but I have been busy on a draft of a novelette for *Boy's Life*. I finished it last night and will now try to clear my desk—starting with your letter.

I think I finally have a story that *Boys' Life* can use, provided I can now sweat it down to an acceptable length without bleeding it to death. The title is "Tenderfoot on Venus" and is about a Scout and his dog and his chum in a Boy Scout troop on Venus—no sex, no firearms, no fighting between the boys, knives used only for things that a Scout legitimately uses knives for, no villains other than the hazards of nature. I have no real doubts about the story; while it isn't immortal literature, it is a good, decent, adventure story. But I do want to use as much wordage as possible in the final draft because of the always present problem of building up a convincingly detailed background in a science fiction story laid in the future in a strange scene. Could you phone their editor and ask him for his absolute top word length? The more space I have, the better the story will be.

Final copy should be in New York about one month from now. They can count on that.

EMOTIONAL DISTURBANCES

August 27, 1953: Robert A. Heinlein to Lurton Blassingame

I greatly sympathize with her [Peggy Blassingame] emotional difficulty, being subject to it myself, although from different causes. When I am working on a book, any commitment at all other than the book itself is almost unbearable. A dinner date four days away will get between me and the typewriter and make it very hard to work. . . . very hard to keep and hold that out-of-the-world reverie that seems (for me) to be almost indispensable to empathic fiction. This neurotic peculiarity of mine is quite inconvenient to Ginny, as I am quite reluctant to take part in any social activity arranged earlier than about 5 P.M. on the day it takes place—I don't mind socializing during a story as long as I don't know about it ahead of time, but that limitation is very awkward for a hostess.

STORY CHANGES

March 28, 1957: Robert A. Heinlein to Lurton Blassingame

. . . delay on *Methuselah's Children.* Both Ginny and I have been over it carefully since I last wrote. She thinks it needs a complete rewrite from beginning to end; I am certainly convinced that it should

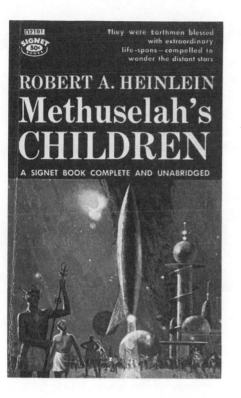

Methuselah's Children, Signet
(The New American Library),
1960. An earlier, shorter version
of the book was published by
Astounding in 1941.

not go on the market until I have worked on it a bit and perhaps completely rewritten it. I greet this task with the delight with which I change a tire in the rain at night, but it has to be done, I am afraid. Worst of all, it uses time I had intended to put onto new copy. With luck I should forward it to you not too late in April . . .

. . . My strongest misgiving about a release through Doubleday is on other grounds, however: I am afraid that *Methuselah* simply does not stand up to the quality of *Puppet Masters* and *The Door into Summer*; I am afraid it would look like a slump. It was written sixteen years ago; I have learned something of storytelling techniques in that time, I think.

EXCERPTS

February 16, 1968: Robert A. Heinlein to Lurton Blassingame

And I have another letter from —— concerning that request to use an excerpt from "Logic of Empire." This time he tells me approximately (not exactly) what he wants to excerpt but says that he cannot tell me how much I would be paid. Well, from what I know of British prices, I doubt if he contemplates paying more than ten to twenty dollars for a thousand words. But I can't see why he expects me to sell for an unstated price. I'm tempted to tell him that short excerpts call for short-short story rates—say about a shilling a word.

But I'm going to tell him no again. (a) I don't like to see my stories chopped up, in any case; each is meant to be read as a whole. (b) I have a dirty suspicion that he wants my name on the dust jacket at a cost of about ten bucks. (c) The controlling point: I don't like his action in bypassing my agent. If he wanted a rehearing he should have submitted his second proposal to *you*—he certainly knows who you are and where you are.

Damn it, on second thought I am not going to answer him now; I'll enclose his letter instead. If you want to answer it, do so. If not, send it back and I will do so. But I certainly do not like his unprofessional behavior in intentionally trying to bypass my agent.

INTRODUCTION

January 14, 1963: Robert A. Heinlein to Robert Mills

Lurton tells me that you and he have reached an agreement on the use of "Zombies" ["All You Zombies"] and that you now want an introduction to the story from me, telling why it is "one of my favorites."

At that point it suddenly lost status with me. The prospect of writing a blurb for one of my own stories I find almost as filled with grue as is attending an autographing party or writing for a fanzine. Why don't you write it? You seemed to like this story better than I did and your blurb in FSF [*The Magazine of Fantasy and Science Fiction*] was okay.

But, if you must have it, how about this:

"Mark Twain invented the time travel story; six years later H.G. Wells perfected it and revealed its paradoxes. Between them they left little for latecomers to do. But they are still fun to write. Some stories are chores, some are fun—this is one I enjoyed writing."

But I would still prefer for you to blurb it. If an author writes his own blurb, he is caught between the horns of conceit and false modesty.

FREE OPTION

January 27, 1961: Robert A. Heinlein to Lurton Blassingame

My whorish instincts protest the idea of a free option even for six months—but I'm willing to go along, pursuant to your advice. He [a would-be producer] would be a lot better off (safer) and I would be happier if there were some minor cash involved, with the deal spelled out. The option money needn't be much and it could have renewable dates by small payments. However, I suspect that he does not want to sign a formal option now because that necessitates spelling out the deal which is being optioned—and he probably hasn't any clear idea what the deal might be until he has a treatment to show financial backers.

CHAPTER VII

❖

BUILDING

❖

COLORADO SPRINGS

EDITOR'S NOTE: When Robert and I were first married, we lived in Colorado Springs. After the motion picture script sold, it was necessary to move to Hollywood, as Robert was to be technical director for what became Destination Moon.

After the shooting on the film was completed, Robert's contract was up, so we returned to Colorado to build our house there. While we were building, the Korean War began—although it was called a "police action," it was a full-fledged war; the draft was still in place, and prices on everything began to soar. Robert might be called back to do engineering, and although I was on inactive duty, there was the ever-present possibility that I might be called back to active duty. Neither of those things happened, but we went through a period of not knowing whether we would have to leave our house half-built and go off to war.

In one of these letters there is mention of the quickly rising costs of lumber; Camp Carson nearby Colorado Springs had been renamed Fort Carson, and an enormous building program had begun there. We were caught by the rising prices on everything needed to complete the house.

Before Robert began writing, he had some interest in planning single-family houses. He had several plans of his own. However, those were for a flat area, and the lot we purchased was on a hillside. Neither one of us was prepared, though, for the intricacies of the actual building of a house.

1776 Colorado Springs Street. The Heinleins got to pick their own house number for their Colorado Springs house. They moved in in 1950.

I was required to read Mr. Blandings Builds His Dream House. *We both avoided the mistakes in that story, but we made a brand new set of our own.*

July 9, 1950: Robert A. Heinlein to Lurton Blassingame

. . . We are going ahead with building and have the foundation in, the services in, and the septic tank built, but I shall have to shut down the job again and wait if monies do not come in. Yes, I know I could remedy that by giving you new copy and I wish to Heaven I could—but I am so fouled up with . . . handling payroll and purchases, and trying to be an architect that I can't write stories. I continue to have much trouble with the contractor.

August 13, 1950: Robert A. Heinlein to Lurton Blassingame

. . . I am sorry to get tough with him, but I've got to have the money. The checks you sent me got me past this week's payroll—but I had a serious disappointment on another matter this week and I am more strapped than ever. In the meantime, the army is reactivating a base here with a million dollar construction program and all local lumberyards immediately boosted their prices. Lumber has gone up 60% around here in the last six weeks. Nevertheless, the roof is being framed up now; we'll have it closed in by the end of this week—and we'll move in around Labor Day, if my nerves hold out. Then I intend to stop everything and start turning out new copy.

August 14, 1950: Robert A. Heinlein to Lurton Blassingame

Your letter of 11 August arrived today and caused us much jubilation . . . an advance check on the NAL contract twice the size we had expected, news that you had sold "Roads" ["The Roads Must Roll"] for TV, and news of the Kellogg show [*Tom Corbett, Space Cadet*] for *Space Cadet*. Ginny and I are agreed that you are the original miracle man. All this adds up to no more real money worries for Robert and assurance that we can finish our house in an orderly fashion without a mortgage.

EDITOR'S NOTE: We moved into the house Labor Day weekend. It was closed in, glazed, but the clerestory needed to have the glass bricks installed, so we spent the weekend pushing oakum into the spaces around the glass bricks, "floating" them. I obtained a large roll of brown paper and stapled it to the wall studs. At least we had a place to live in. The subfloor was laid, but it would be a long time before the house was finished. And Robert sat down and wrote The Puppet Masters.

September 13, 1950: Robert A. Heinlein to Lurton Blassingame

We finally managed to get moved into our new house. It is far from finished; while the outer shell is closed in solid, the interior is a forest of studs and butcher paper temporary partitions. We do have

The Heinleins' house at Colorado Springs. They had the house built themselves and ran into many difficulties—not the least being a shortage of building materials due to the war in Korea!

plumbing and we do have kitchen fixtures and we do have heating; we'll make out.

I am still much badgered by bills, mechanics, unavoidable chores, and such, but I have a place to write and should now be able to continue at it fairly steadily.

February 11, 1951: Robert A. Heinlein to Lurton Blassingame

. . . We managed to spend $6,000 in six days—which turns out to be awfully hard work. I have been trying to buy and get onto the job every bit of metal, every last stick of wood, needed to complete this house.

Incidentally, it just nicely cleaned us out again. The laughable price freeze [because of the wartime economy] came much too late to do a man who is building any good. But, with the material on hand, I now know that I can and will finish.

May 13, 1951: Robert A. Heinlein to Lurton Blassingame

We put up the ceiling this past week; tomorrow we paint it and start putting up wall paneling. The house looks like an Okie camp. Sunday is the only day I can do paperwork as I have mechanics working both days and evenings. I put in about a fourteen-hour day each day and am gradually losing my bay window. Housebuilding is most impractical, but we are slowly getting results.

June 10, 1951: Robert A. Heinlein to Lurton Blassingame

It is ten-thirty and I must be up around six. Today being Sunday I worked all day alone on the house. It continues to be an unending headache, but we are beginning to see the end—about another month if we don't run into more trouble. The biggest headache, now that the bank account is refreshed, is finding and keeping mechanics. This town is in a war building boom and every mechanic has his pick of many jobs. I should have four or five working; I have two, plus myself. I work at any trade which is missing at the moment. Fortunately, I can do most of the building trades myself, after a fashion. I have a stone mason doing cabinet work, which will give you some idea of the difficulties of getting help. Often I think of your comment, more than a year ago, that you hoped I would not have trouble but never knew of a case of a person building his own home who did not have lots of trouble. Well, we surely have had it, but the end is in sight—if I don't go off my rocker first.

What am I saying? I *am* off my rocker!

April 17, 1961: Robert A. Heinlein to Lurton Blassingame

Actually, I am not studying Arabic very much nor am I writing; I am moving massive boulders with pick and shovel and crowbar and block and tackle, building an irrigation dam—a project slightly smaller than the Great Pyramid but equal to Stonehenge. I no longer have any

"Project Stonehenge." The creation of a decorative pool was undertaken by the Heinleins alone—and made them a two-wheelbarrow family.

fat on my tummy at all but have a fine new collection of aches, pains, bruises, and scratches.

May 15, 1961: Robert A. Heinlein to Lurton Blassingame

We are now a two-wheelbarrow family. That accounts for the delay.

Don't brush it off. Are *you* a two-wheelbarrow family? How many two-wheelbarrow families do you know? I mean to say: two-Cadillac families are common; there are at least twenty in our neighborhood, not counting Texans. But *we* are the only two-wheelbarrow family I know of.

It came about like this: I started building Ginny's irrigation dam. Simultaneously Ginny was spreading sheep manure, peat moss, gravel, etc., and it quickly appeared that every time she wanted the wheelbarrow I had it down in the arroyo—and vice versa. A crisis developed, which we resolved by going whole hog and phoning Sears for a second one. Now we are both happily round-shouldered all day long, each with his (her) own wheelbarrow.

(Live a little! Buy yourself a second one. You don't know what luxury is until you have a wheelbarrow all your own, not constantly being borrowed by your spouse.)

This dam thing (or damn' thing) I call (with justification) *Project Stonehenge*; it is the biggest civil engineering feat since the Great Pyramid. The basis of it is boulders, big ones, up to two or three tons each—and I move them into place with block and tackle, crowbar, pick and shovel, sweat, and clean Boy Scout living. Put a manila sling around a big baby, put one tackle to a tree, another to another tree, take up hard and tight with all my weight on each and lock them—then pry at the beast with a ninety-pound crowbar of the sort used to move freight cars by hand, gaining an inch at a time.

Then, when at last you have it tilted up, balanced, and ready to fall forward, the sling slips and it falls back where it was. This has been very good for my soul.

(And my waist line—I am carrying no fat at all and am hard all over. Well, moderately hard.)

EDITOR'S NOTE: *Robert enjoyed doing rock work, and the grounds were greatly improved by three decorative pools and revetments done with rocks.*

SANTA CRUZ COUNTY

EDITOR'S NOTE: We loved our home in Colorado Springs—Robert had done so much in the way of rock work outside, and we had lavished our care on it for some years.

But there were two reasons why we had to leave. One was my health. For some years, it had become increasingly evident that I could not stand the altitude—I had "mountain sickness." The other reason was that the house was too small for our files of papers and books. We left Colorado on the seventeenth anniversary of our marriage, to look on the West Coast for land for building. Three months were spent on this quest before we bought the land in Santa Cruz.

We remained in that house until 1987, at which time we found that it was too far from medical services, which Robert needed quickly at times. So we looked in Carmel, and found a suitable house, although it had all the drawbacks of the ones we had decided against in Santa Cruz.

February 1, 1966: Robert A. Heinlein to Lurton Blassingame

We moved into this house because it is twenty miles closer to the land we finally bought than is the apartment in Watsonville and is the closest rental we could find to our new land—not very close at that: nine miles in a straight line, fourteen by road, twenty-six minutes by car. But the house, besides being nearer, is a vast improvement on the apartment. It is all on one floor, has three bedrooms (which gives me a separate room for my study), two full baths, a dishwasher, a garbage grinder, a double garage, and a gas furnace with forced air instead of electric strip heaters. It is an atrocity in other respects—such as a large view window which has an enchanting view solely of a blank wall ten feet away—but we will be comfortable in it and reasonably efficient until we get our new house built.

The dismal saga of how we almost-not-quite bought another parcel of land is too complex to tell in detail. Those forty-three acres of redwoods located spang on the San Andreas Fault—Ginny thought I had my heart set on them, I thought she had her heart set on them . . . and in fact both of us were much taken by them. It is an utterly grand piece of land—very mountainous, two rushing, gushing mountain streams with many waterfalls, thousands of redwoods up to two hundred feet tall. But in fact it was better suited to playing Götterdämmerung than it was to building a year-round home. Most of the acreage was so dense as to be of no possible use, and the forest was so dense that the one site for a house would receive sunlight perhaps three hours each day. Mail delivery would be a mile away . . .

❖　❖　❖

I agreed but insisted that we shop first for houses . . . as designing and building a house would cost me, at a minimum, the time to write at least one book as a hidden expense. So we did—but it took me only a couple of days to admit that it was impossible to buy a house ready built which would suit me, much less Ginny. Firetraps built for flash, with other people's uncorrectable mistakes built into them! (Such as a lovely free-form swimming pool so located as to be overlooked by neighbors' windows! Such as Romex wiring, good for only five years, concealed in the wooden walls of a house . . .)

The new property has none of the hazards of the property we backed away from buying. It is on a well-paved county road and has 220-volt power and telephone right at the property line. It does not have gas (we expect to use butane for cooking, fuel oil for heating), does not have sewer, does not have municipal water. So we'll use a septic tank and a spread field. It has its own spring, which delivers a steady flow at present of 6,000 gallons per day. We had a very heavy rainstorm over this last weekend, so I went up and checked the flow again and was pleased to find that it had not increased at all—i.e., it apparently comes from deep enough that one storm does not affect it. I'll keep on checking it during the coming dry season but we were assured by a neighbor (not the owner) that the spring had not failed in the past seventy-five years. I plan to try to develop it still farther and plan to install not only a swimming pool but two or three ornamental pools and ponds of large capacity against the chance that we might run short of water in the dry season. But I'm not worried about it; it is redwood country and where there are redwoods there is water.

The land is a gentle, rolling slope, with the maximum pitch being around one in ten and the house site level and about forty feet higher than the road. The parcel is clear but it has on it some eight or nine clumps of redwoods, plus a few big, old live oaks which look like pygmies alongside the sequoias. These are sequoia sempervirens, the coastal redwood, and ours are second growth, about a hundred feet tall,

Heinlein surveying at Bonny Doon. The Heinleins moved to Santa Cruz in the mid-sixties.

up a yard thick, and around ninety years old. There are also a few other conifers, ponderosa, fir, cypress, etc., but they hardly show up among the redwoods. I have not yet conducted a tree census, but we seem to have something in excess of a hundred of the very big trees, plus younger ones of various sizes. Each redwood clump is associated with the cut stumps of the first growth, six or eight feet thick and eight or ten feet high. Since redwood does not decay, they are still there, great silvery free-form sculptures. Ginny is planning one garden designed around a group of them.

I am very busy designing the house. I am anxious to start building as soon as possible as I really can't expect to get any writing done, at least until this new house is designed and fully specified. Building becomes a compulsive fever with me; it drives everything else out of my mind.

April 6, 1966: Robert A. Heinlein to Lurton Blassingame

. . . I'm still bending over a hot drawing board—I'm very slow, for I am *not* an architect and have to look up almost every detail. But the end is in sight. As soon as I can get a water system hooked onto our spring and a driveway bulldozed, we will probably buy a thirdhand trailer and move onto the place during building—Ginny is now willing to do this in order to move our cat here. There has been a rabies scare in Colorado Springs; all animals are under a quarantine and we are having to keep him in a kennel with our vet.

June 22, 1966: Virginia Heinlein to Lurton Blassingame

[Robert] is still relaxing, since when he spends too much time out of bed, he tires very easily . . .

Every once in a while I hear some sounds which seem to indicate that our cat is trying to despoil a bird's nest nearby . . . He seems to like it here, hasn't started that hike back to Colorado which I predicted.

July 1, 1966: Robert A. Heinlein to Lurton Blassingame

I have received, but not yet read, *The Psychology of Sleep*—but will read it as soon as I can stay awake that long; I want to find out why I am so sleepy. I seem to be practically well now, save that I am sleepy all the time; I'm sleeping twelve and fourteen hours a day. I get up late, have breakfast, and can barely stay awake long enough to go back to bed—get up again, get a couple hours of paperwork done (with great effort), then take a nap. Resolve to get something done after dinner but find myself going to bed again. It is not unpleasant save that I am totally useless and the work piles up. The incision seems to have healed perfectly and my surgeon says that after the 15th of July I can do anything I wish—lift 200 lbs . . . which will be remarkable as I never could in the past. (Oh, off the floor, yes—but not a clean press up into the air.)

*E*DITOR's NOTE *Robert's health was somewhat fragile. From time to time he would be required to have various major and minor surgery. Although he was able to do extremely heavy work at times, illnesses such as influenza hit him hard, and it might take weeks for him to recover.*

These illnesses fell into major and minor groupings. In his early days he had TB; recovery took about a year. In 1970, he had a perforated diverticulum, undiscovered for seventeen days; it took a long recovery period. Because of the shock to his system, he followed that with herpes Zoster. Because the doctors were afraid to remove his gall bladder at the time they operated for peritonitis, that operation had to be deferred until 1971, when he had recovered from shingles.

In 1978 in Moorea, he had a TIA [Transient Ischemic Attack, a tempo-

rary interference of blood to the brain], which resulted in his undergoing a carotid-bypass operation.

August 15, 1966: Robert A. Heinlein to Lurton Blassingame

Ginny is fretted and frustrated because she does not yet have water at the building site—badly needed to stabilize a very dusty excavation and to permit her to start ground cover for great, raw cuts that will wash away if not planted before the heavy rains. Someone warned us when we came here that Santa Cruz was very much a mañana place, with the leisurely attitude affecting even the gringos—and that person was so very right. We were promised a pumping system in two weeks; it has now been more than a month—if we don't have water in a few days, I am going to have to get very nasty with that subcontractor. Which I dread.

We can't pour concrete for the house until we have [a building] permit, but there are lots of other things to be done. I still hope and expect that we will be closed in by the rains and able to move in, even though the interior will still have to be finished—if Ginny and I both don't wind up in straitjackets before then.

Heinlein with Elf of Bonny Doon.

❖

Building

❖

September 4, 1966: Robert A. Heinlein to Lurton Blassingame

We have (a) started the house, (b) acquired an unhousebroken kitten, and (c) had a houseguest on our hands for three days when we literally have no room nor facilities for an ill houseguest—so we are running in circles...

The kitten is a fine little girl cat who buzzes all the time . . . and craps right under this typewriter with healthy regularity . . . and gets herself lost under the house . . . and insists on sleeping *under* Ginny's head . . . and throws our tomcat into a bad state of nerves most of the time. Apparently she isn't old enough to smell like a girl cat to him; she is simply a monster who has invaded his home and who takes up entirely too much of Mama's and Papa's time. But she is another lame duck; Ginny rescued her when she was about to be sent to the pound. Oh, me. Once we get her housebroken and once she comes into heat I think she will turn out to be a most welcome addition to the household—right now she's a burr under the saddle.

I finally fired our silly architect and took over the job myself . . .

❖ ❖ ❖

We have water now, on a temporary pump hookup from a temporary tank . . . The site is no longer the horrible dust desert that it was; [Ginny] has it watered down (endless shifting of the single sprinkler the temporary hookup will run) and little green shoots coming up to hold the soil against the coming rains. Between times she keeps coffee and lemonade and candy bars on the job and passes them around (very good for morale), and makes trips down to Santa Cruz as needed for almost anything—and keeps house and cooks and keeps books, and falls into bed dead beat each night. (But the extreme effort is going to get us into our house by the rainy season—we can hardly wait.)

❖ ❖ ❖

. . . asking me to lecture. The fee is satisfactory and I have in mind an outline for an appropriate lecture. Will you take over from here and accept subject to the following conditions? Mr. Heinlein's terribly busy schedule (i.e., mixing concrete, carrying block, and pushing a shovel, which is none of his business) will not permit him to accept a date to lecture earlier than the first of the year, and also I would expect transportation, to wit, round trip by air from San Francisco to Chicago.

. . . I guess that is about all, and I've still got to do some electrical work tonight—calculate the maximum working loads for the whole house and try to see if I can use a four-wire, three-phase cable underground . . . This is just one of the hairy little jobs the architect left undone.

The new cat is out again and again under the house—no way to get under, but she manages. Ginny has just gone out in the dark with a dish of cat food and a flashlight, to try to lure her out. Never a dull moment around here—

November 21, 1966: Robert A. Heinlein to Lurton Blassingame

I enclose a picture taken last week of the state of the job. As you can see, the masonry walls are almost complete. Four courses of "bond beam" now go around the top of what you see (looks like all the other courses but has buried in it four half-inch steel bars, poured in place—this building is for all practical purposes a steel-reinforced monolith; there are hundreds and hundreds of pounds of steel concealed in it).

But we are having trouble: (a) the winter rains have started; (b) our mason is being childishly temperamental. The contractor is quite disgusted with him, and I have refrained from telling him off simply because I did not wish to joggle the contractor's elbow—he being a number one conscientious and mature person.

December 4, 1966: Robert A. Heinlein to Lurton Blassingame

We are now building between raindrops, but thank God the masonry on the house is at last all finished. We still have two little masonry outbuildings to put up, a pump house and an electrical service housing, but these won't take long and are neither urgent nor difficult— even I could lay them up. We need about two weeks of dry weather to frame the roof and put on the roofing—but the winter rains have set in unusually early and unusually hard and it could very well be some time in January before we get the roof on. The contractor has decided that the job will work every dry day from now on, including Saturdays and Sundays. But dry days are scarce. There have been only two fairly dry days this week, it is storming right now and is supposed to rain even harder tomorrow. But I am not dismayed, as carpentry is not nearly as affected by weather as is masonry. Our worst problem is to get a long enough dry spell to permit us to put in the septic tank and to dig a 200-foot ditch for the services, water, electricity, telephone, and low-voltage messenger lines. This soil is getting very soggy for backhoe operations.

February 3, 1967: Robert A. Heinlein to Lurton Blassingame

At the moment, [Ginny] is over at the house site swinging a paint brush . . . The job is still moving but very slowly; it looks from the outside much as it did in the last picture I sent you, but quite a lot has been accomplished inside. We are stalled by the glazing—still no firm date as to when our double-glazing units will arrive. It is not only a strain on us—Ginny in particular, since she has to put up with the primitive housekeeping and cooking facilities of this summer cabin— but also it has had a very bad effect on our general contractor; he's become moody and tempery, and unable to supervise other mechanics without chewing them out—which in my opinion is not the way to get the most out of a man.

Robert and Virginia tree planting at Bonny Doon.

February 17, 1967: Robert A. Heinlein to Lurton Blassingame

Building—we seem to be frozen in a nightmare. The glazing units still have not arrived—the manager won't even promise a firm date. The water closets and hand basins which were supposed to be in stock in San Jose (it now appears) do not even exist and we must wait until the factory again makes a run of that color. One of the soi-disant "mechanics" who loused up our water system is now suing us for "wages"—trial on the 24th. We have developed a great big bog of quicksand in our driveway, so it must now be rebuilt at God knows what expense. In the meantime, the wiring progresses at painful slowness . . .

But our house in Colorado is sold at last and at not too great a loss—not much immediate cash out of the deal after closing costs and commission, but nevertheless I am much relieved. Ginny continues to swing a paint brush daily while I am slowly getting back to the drawing board to finish the detailing of the cabinet work. We are in good health, we don't owe any bills we can't pay, and Ginny says we can stay out of the red despite all these problems. The weather is beautiful, the rainy season is almost over, and things don't look too bad.

June 27, 1967: Robert A. Heinlein to Lurton Blassingame

Nothing else of any real importance today. Ginny is working herself silly everyday on the woodwork finishing—bleaching and sanding and varnishing the mahogany; I'm still sweating over a hot drawing board on the last of the finish details; today I'm designing Ginny's office. The cabinetwork and paneling is about 80% finished now; then we have the floors, ceilings, fireplaces, permanent lighting fixtures, front steps, driveway, and some exterior painting to do—still lots but the end is a faint gleam in the distance.

July 10, 1967: Robert A. Heinlein to Lurton Blassingame

This should be the last letter I'll have to write on a card table; Ginny has almost finished the bleaching and varnishing in my study. And today about half the cabinetwork arrived for her office; soon we will both be properly equipped for the first time in almost two years. Hallelujah! We'll be able at last to get our files straight and get caught up on correspondence and paperwork . . . and I am itching to reach the point where I can start in on new fiction.

Heinlein with the newly completed Bonny Doon.

Our soil is black loam on top of sand on top of hard pan. I think
we can control this driveway situation simply by treating it as a permanent watercourse, accepting that and installing a slaunchwise steel-
reinforced concrete ditch alongside. But I dunno. Yesterday my brother
Rex told me of a friend of his, a professional soil engineer, who has a
similar driveway problem and has not been able to solve it. (But I don't
think ours is that bad.)

We stayed home on the Fourth of July and worked—did not even
get to fire our cannon—can't get at it until the cabinetwork is finished
and I can unpack the dining room. But we did go away to Palo Alto
this weekend—heard some good music and saw a football game on
television, wild excitement for the life we have been leading. In truth
we had ourselves an awfully nice time and enjoyed getting away from
here. (All but the cat, who thinks it is utterly unfair to cats to put him
in a cage and take him to a kennel. But he needed the rest, too; he has
been losing fights. I wish I could teach him to fight only smaller cats,
or else Arabs—as the general with the eye patch says, it helps if you
can arrange to fight Arabs.)

We are both in good health and in quite good spirits. It is still a long
haul, but we can now see daylight at the end of the tunnel.

October 26, 1967: Robert A. Heinlein to Lurton Blassingame

. . . Then your check arrived and all was sunshine. That check almost exactly pays for the driveway—quite a complex and expensive structure because of underground drains for that quicksand problem— and leaves money on hand and November and December royalties for taxes, finish work inside (ceilings and recessed light fixtures), and this and that. No sweat. Utter solvency. Joy. So we declared a holiday, went downtown and bought Ginny a new dress, got hold of friends, and had dinner out, avec mucho alcohol and joviality. Today I have a mild hangover but my morale has never been better.

October 14, 1968: Robert A. Heinlein to Lurton Blassingame

After a delay of ca. 5,000 years I have formulated a basic natural law and named it, not for myself, but for the man who first noticed it: Cheops' Law—No building is ever finished on schedule. The guest house has been 90% finished for the past month. It is now 91% finished.

I am working hard every day at my desk. Deus volent, I will yet get some fiction written.

Virginia Heinlein landscaping at Bonny Doon, late sixties.

CHAPTER VIII

❖

FAN MAIL AND OTHER TIME WASTERS

❖

March 13, 1947: Robert A. Heinlein to *Saturday Evening Post*

"Green Hills of Earth" has brought me in such a flood of mail that it has almost ruined me as a writer—I don't have time to write. None of it appears to be from crackpots; about half of it comes from technical men. All of it shows that the United States is still made up of believers and hopers, for they echo the brave words I heard last summer, while standing in the shadow of a V-2 rocket: "—anything we want to do if we want to do it badly enough."

March 17, 1961: Robert A. Heinlein to Lurton Blassingame

. . . The rest of my time has been taken up playing scrabble (Ginny wins about 60–40: she has a better vocabulary than I have) and the endless load of correspondence. I've got about a dozen letters on hand from high school and college kids, asking me to help them on term papers—in recent years teachers all over the country have been giving kids assignments which result in me (and, I'm sure, many other writers) receiving letters accompanied by long lists of questions . . . which they want answered last Wednesday . . . and each letter, properly answered, takes a couple of hours of time. Hell, one college boy even phoned me from West Virginia, wanted to read me the questions over

Robert A. Heinlein with his shelf of his own fiction and awards at Bonny Doon.

the phone and have me answer them airmail special—otherwise he was going to flunk his English course. This was while I was working sixteen hours a day to cut that ms. for Putnam's, so I told him to go right ahead and flunk his course because I was not going to stop work against a deadline to meet a commitment I had not assumed.

March 9, 1963: Robert A. Heinlein to Lurton Blassingame

. . . I am clearing my desk of mail (pounds of fan mail and I'm tempted to burn it!—they all want quick answers, and only one in fifty encloses a stamped and addressed reply envelope)—and when I have that out of the way I will cut this new book, *Grand Slam* [*Farnham's Freehold*] or whatever we call it, and try to be free about April Fool's Day.

February 4, 1969: Robert A. Heinlein to Lurton Blassingame

(Speaking of the time burned up by overhead work such as that—poor Ginny! Fan mail has gotten utterly out of hand, and about a month ago, in a frantic attempt to get back to writing ms., I dumped it all on her. This morning in came about the 500th letter from still another young man who had read *Stranger* and wanted to discuss his soul with me. He had been "meditating" and taking courses in "sensativity" (sic). So I passed it over to Ginny, my surrogate chela in the guru business. She read it, looked tired, and said wistfully, "You know, I wish I had all the time to meditate that these kids seem to have.")

June 4, 1969: Robert A. Heinlein to Lurton Blassingame

What would be your opinion if I simply stopped answering mail from strangers?

I ask because the fan mail situation has gotten out of hand. In the past five years the volume has tripled, or more. Unless I keep it answered each day, the accumulation gets out of hand and it takes me forever to catch up. Yet I cannot answer it daily—even if I were never to write another story, there are still interruptions: trips out of town, houseguests, illnesses, etc.

This may seem trivial; it is not—unsolicited letters from strangers, fan mail plus endless requests for me to go here, speak there, donate mss., advise a beginning writer, these things add up to the major reason why I have not been able to turn out any pay copy in the period since we finished building. Secretarial help does not seem to be the answer. I can't use a full-time secretary and I have never been able to find a satisfactory moonlighter—tried again just this past month and thought I had one, an ex-Navy yeoman. Result: It cost two dollars per letter in wages with the answers to those letters limited to postcards in most cases and never longer than one sheet of the small-size notepaper, plus postage and materials—and *did not save me one minute of time.* In fact, it took more of my time than it would had I simply answered them myself.

Form letters won't serve; there is simply too much variety in the incoming mail—I must either draft or dictate each answer. Either Ginny or I must write the answers. Ginny has offered to do all of it (and frequently has coped with a logjam). But I don't want Ginny to do it as it is not fair to her to tie her to a typewriter when she wants and needs to spend every possible minute on landscaping this place (and I want her to landscape—no point in having a lovely place if it is allowed to look moth-eaten). Besides, she cooks, cleans, does all the shopping, and does the not-inconsiderable record keeping and tax work and bill paying and money handling.

So it is either do it myself—or quit answering mail from strangers.

I have been thinking about the following expedient: A form printed on a U.S. postal card reading something like this—"Thank you for your letter, which Mr. Heinlein has read and appreciated. We have no secretary and the volume of mail makes it impossible for me to answer each letter as it deserves. If your letter requires an answer other than this acknowledgment, please send a stamped and self-addressed envelope and refer to file number . . . In the meantime your letter will be held for thirty days in the pending file.

"We regret having to use this expedient, but the alternative is for Mr. Heinlein to give up writing stories in favor of answering letters.

"Sincerely,

"Virginia Heinlein

"(Mrs. Robert A. Heinlein)."

The above, with the surplus words sweated out of it and printed in smaller type, would go on a postcard—and each letter could be acknowledged each day simply by cutting the address off the letter and scotch-taping it to a card. Plus using one of those automatic serial-number stampers.

But it strikes me as an almost certain way to lose friends and antagonize people. Despite the fact that well over half the letters contain the phrase "—while I know you are a very busy man—" the truth is that ach writer-reader is so important in his own eyes that he feels sure .hat *his* letter is so different, so interesting, so important, that I will happily stop whatever I am doing and answer his letter in full. When he gets one of these printed forms, his reaction will be: "Why, that snotty son of a bitch!"

So what do you think I should do? Quit answering at all? Use this printed acknowledgment? Keep on trying to answer them all? Or some other course I haven't thought of?

June 13, 1969: Robert A. Heinlein to Lurton Blassingame

Thank you for your long and thoughtful comments about fan mail. I am glad to have your confirmation that the printed postcard method is a bad idea; I will not use it. But I am much afraid that there is no solution to the problem short of not answering it at all.

In the first place I am not "too conscientious" about it as I do *not* spend a couple of pages in answering silly questions; Ginny and I have long since cut it to the bone—the normal answer is done on a postcard. If an enclosure is required (such as a list of my books, the commonest enclosure request), we use the smallest note paper. True, I used to write careful answers to intelligent letters—but we gave that up over five years back; we had to.

Let's assume I could get a college student to answer letters satisfactorily at a dollar a letter (I can't, but let's stipulate it for the moment). That would still cost me a couple of thousand dollars a year—which I think is too much to pay for the questionable privilege of unsolicited mail from strangers. Most of my fan mail does not go through your office; the bulk of it is forwarded from publishers directly or has been addressed to Colorado Springs and forwarded from there (as every public library in the country has that C.S. address). Plus quite a chunk that is addressed to Santa Cruz. It adds up—it usually takes about a half hour each day just to *read* the fan mail. I can answer it usually, faster than I can read it, if a postcard will suffice. But Ginny is the *only* other person who can answer it quickly, as she is the only one sophisticated enough in what to answer and what to ignore to be able to do it.

But I do have to read it. Several times, when Ginny and I were especially busy, we have let what appeared to be fan mail pile up unread—and this is a mistake as again and again there has turned out to be one or more actual business letters buried in the fan mail simply because the external appearance (one or two forwardings, with nothing in the return address to tip me) led me to assume that it was fan mail.

As near as I can find out from inquiries made to other colleagues, I get far more mail than any of my colleagues—for none of the others seems to find fan mail any problem. (I recall a plaint published by James Blish asking readers to *please* write to him—he needed feedback!)

This morning at breakfast we were reading the mail, which included your nice letter—and Ginny sez to me: "Send this one back to L. and let him *see* how difficult the stuff is to answer." Well, I'm not sending it back but it was from a man and wife in New York who wanted to come out here on his vacation to talk with me. I must turn it down as man who travels a long distance to talk is affronted (reasonably? unreasonably?—either way, his feelings are hurt) if asked to leave in twenty minutes. What he asked for was an "afternoon or evening"—and what he will expect is a full day and late that night. I know, it has happened too many times. For this sort of letter is not at all uncommon; I got one from two students at Oxford University, England, earlier this spring, who wanted to come here this summer and stay an indefinite time; I got one from six students at Temple University who wanted to drive here on their Christmas vacation, camp on the beach, and see me every day. And we told you about the young man from Arizona who drove first to C.S., then here just last week. . . . sweet-talked his way past Ginny, then stayed until I chucked him out four hours later. Plus many others. So now we turn down *all* requests to come see us . . . but such turn-downs must be gentle.

. . . Surely, I could load all the answering onto Ginny; she would hold still for it. But as long as we aren't missing meals I see no reason why she should give up what she wants to do for this purpose—she's carrying her full load anyhow . . .

November 20, 1970: Virginia Heinlein to Lurton Blassingame

Yes, sir. We will be careful with graduate students. We answer all letters except those which go into the "screwball" file, the ones from people who are more or less obviously crazy.

E DITOR'S NOTE We went over to the use of form letters, a checkoff list. There were several different form letters. But I found myself adding handwritten P.S.'s to make them more personal, which consumed even more time. Arthur Clarke was shocked when we told him we were using form letters, but not too much later, he was using them, too.

E DITOR'S NOTE Lurton saw little of the fan mail, but occasionally a letter arrived addressed to him. In this case, he saw some merit, more than usual, in a letter from a graduate student in English. So he counseled caution in dealing with those.

❖ ❖ ❖

There is no copy extant of the checkoff letters, but when letters were answered on computers, here is how they ran:

❖ ❖ ❖

An ever-increasing flood of mail has forced Mr. Heinlein to choose between writing letters and writing fiction. I have taken over for him, but he reads each letter sent to him and checks the answer.

Four or five requests come in each week for help in class assignments, term papers, theses, or dissertations. We can't cope with so many and have quit trying.

Sincerely,

Virginia Heinlein
[Mrs. Robert A. Heinlein]
Even since Robert's death, fan mail still comes in asking me to answer questions about his work.

TIME WASTERS

November 3, 1951: Robert A. Heinlein to Lurton Blassingame

. . . In addition to the above, I've let myself be roped into going to Denver to speak to the Colorado Authors' League. I find myself in a running fight to keep my time from being nibbled away by such secondary activities. I avoid such things as much as possible, but too often I get backed into a corner.

January 27, 1952: Robert A. Heinlein to Lurton Blassingame

I have been asked to be a guest speaker on Edward R. Murrow's CBS program, "This I Believe." I'm flattered but am thinking of turning it down; I don't relish getting on a national hookup and doing an emotional striptease. Furthermore, such things take me away from my regular work by distracting my mind, sometimes for days, from story. No mention was made of a fee and I think it's a sustaining program with the guest speakers appearing just for glory. I mention this because you may think the "glory" important enough that I should do it anyhow. I won't give them an answer until I hear from you.

August 21, 1952: Robert A. Heinlein to Lurton Blassingame

. . . This entire year of '52 I have found frustrating. Today I tried to figure out exactly where the time had gone, since I have no copy to show for it. I can account for every day and don't see how, in most cases, I could have done anything about it, but that fact writes no stories. Believe me, Lurton, I have not loafed this year, but my time has been eaten away . . . operation, convalescence . . . cutting *Rolling Stones*, skating nationals, mechanics in the house three times wasting a month and a half, two unpaid writing jobs, two unpaid radio appearances, some unpaid speaking engagements, Arthur C. Clarke—one week, the George O. Smiths—two weeks, other houseguests totaling perhaps a week, shopping for a new automobile . . . death of a close friend—one week, two weddings where I was involved and could not refuse my time without being a heel, innumerable visits from readers who were polite enough to write and ask to see me, a novel started and aborted, same for a short, the damned telephone ringing and ringing and ringing and myself the only person in the house . . . and finally a trip to Yellowstone and the Utah parks. That last I could have skipped but Ginny deserved a rest and I needed one, even if I hadn't been accomplishing anything. All of the above adds up to about time enough to answer mail and read proofs. Some of these things you may feel I could have avoided—well, close up to them, they could *not* have been avoided. The telephone situation we have finally licked by putting a bell in the garage where I can't hear it and a cutoff switch in the house, thereby evading the company's rules.

Most of my troubles seem to arise from the difficulty I have in refusing to give my time to other people. Should I refuse to entertain the chairman of the British Interplanetary Society? Can I refuse to see a classmate who shows up in town with an engineer from my hometown in tow? A physicist from Johns Hopkins who is a fan of mine shows up and wants to meet me—can I refuse? Same for an air force intelligence officer who writes politely? Or the head of the Flying Saucer project? Today I was invited to address the southwest division of the Rocket Society and attend a night firing of a V-2 rocket—that one I turned down as it involved flying to White Sands—but it was a highly desirable date and one that I would have kept had I had the time. I don't know the answer but I am beginning to see why so many writers hire hotel rooms—I am entirely too well known for comfort. Anyhow, I am about to try another story.

September 4, 1952: Robert A. Heinlein to Lurton Blassingame

Now, about writing time: since the war it has been one damn thing after another, poor health, domestic trouble, housebuilding, et al. I hope that the future will be quieter. If not, I will simply do the best I can under the circumstances. Getting an office away from the house is not a solution I want at all—I've just finished a house with an office built into it. One minor new circumstance should be a help—we finally have a cutoff switch for the telephone, after long wrangling with the phone company.

I wrote to you as extensively as I did simply to let you know that my lack of output this year has not been through laziness but through complications. One problem I have not yet found a satisfactory solution to is the demand on my time resulting from becoming better known. I answer all fan mail and it comes in stacks. That is almost necessary, isn't it? I limit the answers to postcards but it takes time. There are frequent requests for me to speak in public—one only last night. I have adopted a policy of refusing such invitations if possible—but what do I do when the Colorado *Librarians'* Association asks me? . . . Perhaps the greatest time waster is the person who reads my stuff, is coming to Colorado Springs, and wants to call on me—and an amazing number of them manage to find their way to Colorado Springs, remote as this place is. If they simply walk in on me I won't see them. . . . But if they write or telephone and are courteous, I find it hard to give them a cold brush-off. I see no good answer to this problem, but will have to handle it by expediency as I go along.

❖   ❖   ❖

. . . This is probably the very last of the V-2s and it will be one of the very few unclassified firings for a long time. There is nothing like watching one of the big ones climb for outer space—it will make a believer out of you, I warrant. I do not regard a trip to White Sands as lost time for me; it comes under the same head as research. Since I write about rockets, I need to know what they sound like, talk to rocket men. Besides that, I will have an opportunity to meet Clyde Tombaugh, the man who discovered the planet Pluto and, perhaps, to see the canals of Mars through his telescope. . . . This is almost a once-in-a-lifetime thing, as perfect seeing, the right telescope, and the right technique are a rare combination.

January 6, 1953: Lurton Blassingame to Robert A. Heinlein

The script for the "This I Believe" program just checked in. It is certainly splendid, the best I have come in contact with. I have been especially interested in this program because one of my boys [clients], Ed Morgan, has been associated with it since the beginning. I do think this material of yours was excellent, and I am very proud of you.

THIS I BELIEVE

I am not going to talk about religious beliefs but about matters so obvious that it has gone out of style to mention them. I believe in my neighbors. I know their faults, and I know that their virtues far outweigh their faults.

Take Father Michael down our road a piece. I'm not of his creed, but I know that goodness and charity and lovingkindness shine in his daily actions. I believe in Father Mike. If I'm in trouble, I'll go to him.

My next-door neighbor is a veterinary doctor. Doc will get out of bed after a hard day to help a stray cat. No fee—no prospect of a fee—I believe in Doc.

I believe in my townspeople. You can knock on any door in our town saying, "I'm hungry," and you will be fed. Our town is no exception. I've found the same ready charity everywhere. But for the one who says, "To heck with you—I got mine," there are a hundred, a thousand who will say, "Sure, pal, sit down."

I know that despite all warnings against hitchhikers I can step to the highway, thumb for a ride, and in a few minutes a car or a truck will stop and someone will say, "Climb in, Mac—how far you going?"

I believe in my fellow citizens. Our headlines are splashed with crime, yet for every criminal there are 10,000 honest, decent, kindly men. If it were not so, no child would live to grow up. Business

could not go on from day to day. Decency is not news. It is buried
in the obituaries, but it is a force stronger than crime. I believe in
the patient gallantry of nurses and the tedious sacrifices of teachers.
I believe in the unseen and unending fight against desperate odds
that goes on quietly in almost every home in the land.

I believe in the honest craft of workmen. Take a look around you.
There never were enough bosses to check up on all that work. From
Independence Hall to the Grand Coulee Dam, these things were built
level and square by craftsmen who were honest in their bones.

I believe that almost all politicians are honest . . . there are hundreds of politicians, low paid or not paid at all, doing their level best
without thanks or glory to make our system work. If this were not
true we would never have gotten past the thirteen colonies.

I believe in Rodger Young. You and I are free today because of
endless unnamed heroes from Valley Forge to the Yalu River. I believe in—I am proud to belong to—the United States. Despite shortcomings from lynchings to bad faith in high places, our nation has
had the most decent and kindly internal practices and foreign policies to be found anywhere in history.

And finally, I believe in my whole race. Yellow, white, black, red,
brown. In the honesty, courage, intelligence, durability, and *goodness*
of the overwhelming majority of my brothers and sisters everywhere
on this planet. I am proud to be a human being. I believe that we
have come this far by the skin of our teeth. That we *always* make it
just by the skin of our teeth, but that we will always make it. Survive.
Endure. I believe that this hairless embryo with the aching, oversize
brain case and the opposable thumb, this animal barely up from the
apes, will *endure*. Will *endure* longer than his home planet—will
spread out to the stars and beyond, carrying with him his honesty
and insatiable curiosity, his unlimited courage and his noble essential decency.

This I believe with all my heart.

June 6, 1962: Robert A. Heinlein to Lurton Blassingame

No other news save that the Silly Season has opened and we
have many visitors; this will continue until fall. One of my plebes
showed up this week—an admiral now and chief of research, a job I
would like to have had (and might have achieved) if I hadn't gotten TB
a long time ago. However, all in all, I like being a writer and don't really

miss not being an admiral. (Dan Gallery managed to be both, but he is exceptional!)

August 10, 1963: Robert A. Heinlein to Lurton Blassingame

We have been badly slowed down, too, by visitors, a steady flood of them all summer long, friends, relatives, and readers, plus some of the organized science fiction fans—and none of them invited, not even the relatives nor any of the friends. . . . This place being a resort, people simply pour through here in the summer and if I shut off the phone, they ring the doorbell. I don't ever intend to try to write a story in Colorado Springs again between June 1st and September 1st; it is too much like trying to write directly under a busy three-holer. Even if my relatives had stayed home (and, damn it, they all traveled this year), friends, acquaintances, and strangers were enough to keep us in a hooraw. Had I not.been interrupted so many, many times by visitors, the work I was doing would have been farther along and the flood damage would not have been nearly so severe.

May 6, 1964: Robert A. Heinlein to Lurton Blassingame

The letter you received from Kenneth Green (and so kindly answered) is much more typical of fan mail—pleasant but with the same old phrases over and over again, and I get as tired of answering them as an old whore gets of climbing those stairs. I'll drop young Green a card in this mail, however; I always answer them, all but the crackpot ones.

But I have instituted a New Public Relations Policy—one which makes me almost as hard-to-get as the mysterious Mr. B. Traven. Some years ago you sent to me a clipping of Art Buchwald's column with a long quotation from Thornton Wilder in which Wilder declared such a policy, one in which he resolved not to let strangers waste his time, not in *any* fashion. I have kept that clipping up over my typewriter ever since you sent it to me—but I have not emulated it very well.

But I am pushing sixty now myself and it gets harder and harder each year to turn out a decent amount of copy—largely because total strangers want such large chunks of my time. I am darn well going to quit it! In fact, I *have* quit it. The only concession I am making is that I will continue to answer politely worded fan mail—but only by post-cards . . . and usually picture postcards which have no return address and room only for a sentence or two. Even that response costs me a dime for materials and postage, plus (much more important) about fifty cents' worth of my working, professional time that should be put on story-writing.

Someday I may be so browned off and bored with it that I will answer only such letters as are accompanied by stamped and self-addressed envelopes (about one in twenty). I was taught in school *always* to enclose such in writing to a stranger; my present mail shows that most teachers do not teach this courtesy today, as a lot of my mail starts out: "Dear Mr. Heinlein, Our English class is writing to their favorite author—" but a reply envelope rarely is enclosed, although the letter usually demands a reply and asks endless questions—often with a deadline stated.

Mr. Wilder says, in that clipping you sent me: "I hereby serve notice on the school children of America . . . that I am going to dump all their letters—" I'm not going to go quite that far just yet, Lurton—but I am now ignoring all requests for pictures and for anything which requires me to stir out of my chair to answer—or which requires me to use an envelope rather than a postcard when said envelope has not been supplied by the petitioner.

No doubt this will lose me a certain amount of good will. But it will greatly increase my working time—on pay copy—and the problem had grown way out of hand. To supplement this greatly reduced program on fan mail I am resolved not to do *anything* I don't want to do. No more public speeches, not even for librarians. No more interviews given to school kids—other than by telephone. No more "Library Week" appearances. No more breaking off my work (whether writing or mixing cement) to visit with strangers who "just happened to be passing through town and have always wanted to meet" me—unless it suits *me* and they manage to make themselves sound interesting enough to warrant the time. No more messing around with books I don't want to read sent to me, unsolicited, in the mails—and this includes books sent to me by Putnam and its associated companies, as the promotion department seems to feel that any Putnam-published writer should be willing at any time to act as an unpaid reviewer and source of trained-seal favorable testimonials. (They put out a lot of good books, but they never send me those books; they send me little stinkers that should never have been published.)

No more acknowledgments of fan magazines sent to me—it simply results in more of them and requests for free copy.

In short, no more of *anything* unless it durn well suits me and adds to my own pleasure in life. More and more, over the years, strangers have been nibbling away at my time. It has reached the point where, if I would let them, *all* of my working time would be wasted on the demands of strangers. So I am lowering the boom on all of it—and if this makes me a rude son of a bitch, so be it. My present life expectancy is seventeen years; I'm damned if I will spend it answering silly questions about "Where do you get your ideas?" and "Why did you take up the writing of science fiction?" several thousand or more times. I hereby declare that an author has *no* responsibility of any sort to the public . . . other than the responsibility to write stories as well as he knows how.

If I can stick to this, I should get in quite a lot more writing, and quite a lot more healthy work with pick and shovel and trowel—and a judicious mixture of these two may enable me to stretch that life expectancy quite a bit. But I'm not going to let those remaining years be nibbled away and wasted by the trivia that some thousands of faceless strangers seem to feel is their right to demand from anyone in a semi-public occupation.

July 10, 1967: Robert A. Heinlein to Lurton Blassingame

Herewith is a curious letter from an instructor, ——, at the U. of Oregon. I was about to tell him that I could not stop him, but not to let me see the result—but I decided that I had better let you see this and get your advice and/or veto. If Mr. —— does this adaptation "just for fun," as he proposes, I suspect that he will then fall in love with his own efforts and get very itchy to produce it. Which could be embarrassing. Lurton, even though "Green Hills" is a short, I think it has possibilities—someday—as a musical motion picture. So I am hesitant to authorize anything which might cloud the MP or stage rights. What shall I tell him? Or do you prefer to write to him? (I'm not urging you to—not trying to shove it on you. But I do want your advice.)

October 12, 1967: Margo Fischer [secretary to] Lurton Blassingame to Robert A. Heinlein

A drunk began calling at 3:15 insisting on Heinlein's phone number . . . After telling him at least seven times that he would have to write a letter which would be forwarded airmail, he became sarcastic and went on and on. After 15 minutes I told him I was hanging up, and I did. He was incoherent and it was impossible to tell him he had to write a letter. He said he would wire. He wanted to know about "—We Also Walk Dogs." I told him it was in an anthology published by World. He'll probably call you and be abusive about me. Over and over he kept saying, "Mam, Mam"—long silence, then he'd say, "It's a hard world." Silence. Then, "We should all be courteous to one another." Etc.

February 28, 1968: Margo Fischer to Robert A. Heinlein

Here's a little ego boo for you.

The telephone just rang. A voice said, "I was told I could get some information from you. About one of your clients. About Robert Heinlein." Cagey Margo. "Who is this?" "I'm nobody—that is, nobody in the business," he said. "Just a Heinlein fan." Me again—"Well, what did you want to know?"

He wanted to know when Heinlein was going to have another book. "He hasn't written anything for some time," was the complaint. "I have two favorite authors. Michener and Heinlein. Michener just came out with one and I was hoping I could make it a double red-letter day."

Then he added, "Heinlein is the one bright spot in this whole fantasy-science-fiction world." A pause. "*Moon* is the last one he's written, right?" Then I said, "Have you read *Stranger*?" Answer: "Four times." Finally, "Just one more thing—how long does it usually take him to write a book?"

HOW CAN YOU DEPRIVE YOUR FANS A MINUTE LONGER, BOB?

CHAPTER IX

❖

MISCELLANY

❖

STUDY

April 10, 1961: Robert A. Heinlein to Lurton Blassingame

No, we are not contemplating any immediate ventures into Arabic-speaking lands; all of Africa and the Middle East are too unstable at the present time to be attractive—besides, we've been there a couple of times. Tackling Arabic is simply to keep my mind loosened up with something new. It could have been any language I don't know, but I picked it because it is one of the five "critical" languages as listed by the State Department—i.e., an important language which is known by too few Americans; they have plenty of people who know French, German, Spanish, and such. One of the five is Russian and I didn't want to duplicate what Ginny has already done (besides, Russian is *very* hard; Arabic is relatively simple, save for the odd alphabet) and two of the critical languages are tonal languages, and my ear for tones is not very good; I don't think I could learn them as an adult. But I must admit that I have made no real progress as yet; I've nothing to force me to a schedule and there are too many other things that demand attention.

But I would like to, in time, be able to be of some use to the country by knowing a language which is needed. But if it is never of any use that way, I find the study of strange languages rewarding per se; I always learn a lot about the people and the culture when I tackle one.

But I have a dozen subjects that I want to study. I would like to go back to school and take a formal course in electronics; it has changed so much since I studied it more than thirty years ago—and I may, some day soon. About twenty years ago I dropped out of a figure-drawing class because I needed to buckle down and pay off a mortgage—and that turned me into a writer and I haven't been back. But I want to go back, it is something I love doing—and I would like to add a wing to this house and get into sculpture again, too, but simply signing up for a figure sketching class is more likely. I am not a still-life artist. There are only five things really worth drawing; four of them are pretty girls and the fifth is cats.

PREDICTIONS

March 13, 1947: Robert A. Heinlein to *Saturday Evening Post*

. . . I could list many more variables—never mind. Swami Heinlein will now gaze into the crystal ball. First unmanned rocket to the

Robert Heinlein with Teense in the dining room at Bonny Boon.

Moon in five years. First manned rocket in ten years. Permanent base there in fifteen years. After that, anything! Several decades of exploring the solar system with everyone falling all over each other to do it first and stake out claims.

However, we may wake up some morning and find that the Russians have quietly beaten us to it, and that the Lunar S.S.R.—eight scientists and technicians, six men, two women—has petitioned the Kremlin for admission of the Moon to the USSR. That's another unknown variable.

And keep your eyes on the British—the British Interplanetary Society is determined to get there first.

The worst thing about this business of predicting technical advance is that there is an almost insuperable tendency to be too conservative. In almost every case, correct prophecy of the Jules Verne type has failed in the one respect of putting the predicted advance too far in the future. Based on past record, if the figures I gave above are wrong, they are almost certainly wrong in being too timid. Space flight may come even sooner. I *know* that, yet I have trouble believing it.

November 7, 1949: Robert A. Heinlein to Lurton Blassingame

. . . My real claim to being a student of the future, if I have a claim, lies in noting things going on now and then in examining speculatively what those trends could mean—particularly with respect to atomics, space travel, geriatrics, genetics, propaganda techniques, and food supply. To evaluate my success in such it would be necessary for a person to have some familiarity with my published writings. But I don't intend to dig through my writings and say, "Look, here in *Beyond This Horizon* I predicted the robot-secretary recording telephone and now it has been patented!" I *did*—and it *has*—but that doesn't mean anything. The short-term prediction of gimmicks isn't prophecy; it is merely a parlor trick.

PROPHECY

September 24, 1949: Robert A. Heinlein to Lurton Blassingame

EDITOR'S NOTE With the motion picture about to start shooting, and with Robert at work on the next juvenile for Scribner's, a request came in from

Cosmopolitan *for an article about prediction of what the U. S. would be like in the year 2000. In this letter Robert was asking for information about what sort of article the editors would like—he made some suggestions about it.*

When the article was finished, Cosmopolitan *turned it down. It sold to* Galaxy *and was published as "Pandora's Box." The article was periodically updated, and the most recent version can be found in* Expanded Universe.

. . . Under "treatment" come a couple of other questions: This article is to be prophetic. Fine—that's my business; I make my living as a professional prophet of what science will bring to us. But such an article—nonfiction—must consider and to some extent report the *present* status in various fields before the author can go out into the wild blue yonder with predictions. Therefore, I inquire how much reporting do they [*Cosmopolitan*] want of the sort which one finds in *Scientific American*, *Science News Letter*, *Nature*, etc., and how much speculation or prediction do they want? The two things are closely related, but are not the same thing. Also, how far in the future shall I go? (For example, everybody knows that the cancer men, radiation men, and biochemists stand an excellent chance of perfecting selective radiation treatment of certain types of cancer in the very near future by finding ways to bond short half-life isotopes to some compound which a particular type of cancer will pick up selectively.)

Or should I go well into the future and consider the necessary statistical effect of food supply, geriatrics, life-span research, public health, etc., in forcing the development of a brand-new art, planetary engineering, as it affects the growth of colonies on the planet Mars?

❖ ❖ ❖

The synthesizing prophet has another advantage over the specialist; he knows, from experience and by examining the efforts of other prophets *of his type* in the past that his "wildest" predictions are more likely to come true than the ones in which he lost his nerve and was cautious. This statement is hard to believe but can be checked by comparing past predictions with present facts. (Show me the man who honestly believed in the atom bomb twenty years ago—but H. G. Wells predicted it in 1911.) (The "wild fantasies" of Jules Verne turned out to be much too conservative.)

How can one spot a competent synthesizing prophet? Only by his batting average. If *Cosmopolitan* thinks my record of accomplished predictions is good enough to warrant it, then let's by all means go all out and I'll make some serious predictions that will make their hair stand on end. If they want to play safe, I'll do an Inquiring Reporter job and we'll limit it to what the specialists are willing to say. But I can tell them ahead of time that such an article will be more respectable today and quite unrespected ten years from now—for that is no way to whip up successful prophecy.

❖   ❖   ❖

. . . I would proceed as follows:

First, I would cut down the field by limiting myself to (a) subjects in which the changes would matter to the readers personally and not too remotely. A new principle in electronics I would ignore unless I saw an important tie into the lives of ordinary people, (b) subjects which are dramatic and entertaining either in themselves or in their effects. Space travel is such a subject, both ways. So is life-span research. On the other hand, a cure for hoof-and-mouth disease, while urgently needed, is much harder to dramatize, (c) subjects which can be explained. The connection between parapsychology and nuclear engineering is dramatic potentially but impossible to explain convincingly.

❖   ❖   ❖

Since the article is for popular consumption I would wish to hook it, if possible, with some startling piece of quoted dialog, use illustrative anecdote if possible, and end it with some dramatic prediction.

December 20, 1955: Robert A. Heinlein to Lurton Blassingame

Please tell Howard Browne [editor of *Amazing Stories* and *Fantastic*] that I accept his incredible offer and that ms. will arrive by 10 January—but that I expect a copy of that celebration issue, inscribed by him to me, or I shall go into the corner and stick pins in wax images.

I can't imagine what I could possibly say that would be worth $100 for two pages; that isn't even long enough for a horoscope. But if they want to throw away their money in my direction I will go along with the gag and do my damndest to entertain the cash customers. Fortunately, I shall be dead before my "prophecies" can be checked on.

January 5, 1956: Robert A. Heinlein to Lurton Blassingame

Here is the ms. for Howard Browne. I discovered that 500 words were too cramping for what I wanted to say, so I called him yesterday (I assumed that you were at Ilikite, it being Wednesday) and got his authorization to let it run to its present length. No increase in the fee, of course, as the added length was entirely for my convenience.

PUBLISHERS

July 5, 1963: Robert A. Heinlein to Lurton Blassingame

As to Scribner's and Doubleday, I intend to let each of them get away with it and not argue further. But my opinion has not changed. Each of them is deviating from the contract as written and in each case to my financial loss. They would not let *me* deviate from contract if it cost *them* sizable amounts of money. Doubleday talks as if the 50–50 split on pocketbook were a law of nature. Nuts and nonsense; it is merely an extortion that writers usually have to put up with. The entire history of the Authors' Guild and of divisible copyright is one of slowly getting rid of these grabs which publishers defend under the theory of "usual practice." If the "usual contract" did not contain these grabs, trade book publishers would have to work hard at selling the trade edition. Doubleday has never once done a decent job for me of selling the trade edition (take a look at your records)—no, not once. Instead they have signed a "sweetheart" contract with one of their own subsidiaries, printed a very cheap edition which they called a trade edition but which was in fact a book club edition—and the nominal royalty in the contract meant nothing; the extremely low royalty in the "sweetheart" contract was the one that counted. Then they had half of the NAL edition as well—except this one book and now they have grabbed that, too, without my consent. No, I do not like Doubleday. Okay, they get this few hundred dollars—but I will never sign another contract with them.

Scribner's is a different case; they have a real sales organization for selling the trade edition, they do sell it and make money on it, for themselves and for me—and I am sorry on that account that they ever dropped me. . . . But, nevertheless, their contract does not permit them to cut my royalty just because they choose to put out, under their own imprint, a softcover edition. Nor does it cut any ice with me that the percentage royalty is higher than it would be if they farmed it out to, say, NAL—because I am convinced that if they did farm it out to NAL, the dollar return would be much higher, even though the percentage was lower. I may be wrong and time will tell—but, so far, their venture into softcovers, at three times the price of an NAL softcover, seems to be going over like a lead balloon.

As may be—each of these publishers is rewriting a contract to suit himself and against my explicit objections . . . and I shall argue no further with them; life is too short. They can keep their grabs and be damned.

MAGAZINES

March 9, 1963: Robert A. Heinlein to Lurton Blassingame

I don't think *Fantasy and Science Fiction* is riding the edge; I think they are just stingy. They claim 56,000 paid circulation. In view of their rates and their cheap production, plus some revenue from France and Germany, they should be showing a clear profit each month. Back in December —— told me that the publisher would happily pay me in advance. As it is, they got a bargain—copy for $1,500 that they normally pay $1,800 for, to any writer, known name or not. Still, it is pleasanter than offering copy to John Campbell, having it bounced (he bounced both of my last two Hugo Award winners)—and then have to wade through ten pages of his arrogant insults, explaining to me why my story is no good.

April 15, 1963: Robert A. Heinlein to Lurton Blassingame

Re *Playboy* article: I have the material well worked out and am prepared to deliver it by 10 May.

But I shall not deliver it on the basis of a phone call. The last time

I accepted a job from them based on a firm agreement by phone call there was a lot of nonsense afterwards about whether or not I was being paid for the work, or paid for an option, and I had to do two rewrite jobs.

. . . Just refer him to my letter of 2 April (of which you have a copy): "Just address a letter to me, or preferably to Mr. Blassingame, offering me a firm assignment for so many thousands of words for so many dollars on such and such a subject to be delivered by such and such a date—and with the explicit condition that the manuscript will be paid for whether used or not and that any rewriting lies outside the agreement and must be negotiated at an additional fee."

I meant every word. The assignment must be in writing and the clause about rewriting must be spelled out, and all the terms must be explicit—and a phone call means *nothing!*

Otherwise I will not bother to come in out of my garden. It's nice out there and I'm sick of this machine. I don't need the money; I've already worked too much this year and will have too high a tax—and I am especially aware of it on income tax day.

Apparently —— thinks I'm a nice accommodating guy. Please explain to him that I am a son of a bitch.

DEFAULT

January 27, 1961: Robert A. Heinlein to Lurton Blassingame

Please tell —— that I am a kindly old gentleman and that the "A." in the middle of my name stands for "Ebenezer Scrooge" and that I am buying a new freezer with my ill-gotten wealth to make room for him.

CHAPTER X

❖

SALES AND REJECTIONS

❖

November 24, 1947: Robert A. Heinlein to Lurton Blassingame

The last couple of rejection letters you have sent me are rather disturbing. Miss Helen Grey of *Town and Country* is mistaken in thinking that my sales to the SEP [*Saturday Evening Post*] have gone to my head. It is simply that an idea as good as "The Green Hills of Earth" doesn't come to me every week. I have been in a slump and am afraid that I am still in it. I continue to work and to work very hard indeed, but a lot of the stuff I turn out doesn't seem too good to me. Stuart Rose's rejection of "Broken Wings" is decidedly a disappointment, for I had believed that "Broken Wings" was up to standard. Still more disappointing is his statement "These space ship stories didn't do too well, according to our readership surveys." I interpret this as meaning that the *Saturday Evening Post* is no longer interested in my interplanetary stories unless they are utterly terrific, superior in every way to a story with a customary contemporary down-to-earth background . . .

I may turn out quite a number of second-rate stories before I recover completely from the effects of my domestic breakup. For the past several months I have been able to continue writing only by the exercise of grim self-discipline. It occurs to me that you might find it desirable to sell or attempt to sell stories written during this period to secondary markets under a pen name. What do you think? Would it be good business to protect my reputation, such as it is, by keeping my own name off material which in your opinion is not as good as my best? . . .

... From now on I must devote my time exclusively to preparing the second juvenile novel [*Space Cadet*] for Charles Scribner's Sons. I have been working on this boys' novel off and on for several months. I rather dread sitting down and turning out the first draft on it because I simply am not in the sanguine mood which should obtain in any book intended for the young. I could knock off half a dozen tragedies right now easier than I could write one cheerful story.

March 4, 1949: Robert A. Heinlein to Lurton Blassingame

This has been a bad twelve months without very much real literary success. I wasted months on two collaborations which did not pay off. I wasted three months on *Red Planet* and it has not paid off. I've done three stories meant for slicks and they have not paid off. Aside from some reprint stuff and a sale to *Boys' Life* it has been a long string of failures.

I think I have analyzed in part what the trouble has been: I've been doing hack work, writing what some one else wanted me to write rather than what I wanted to write. In any case, the next year can't be any worse if I write what I *want* to write and have some fun out of it. It might even be better; acceptances might start coming in instead of rejections. So—I plan to write *my* stories instead of editor's stories. I don't intend to do any more juveniles unless I happen to have a juvenile story that I want to write. I am not going to promise Scribner's, nor anybody else, one book a year. I am not going to work against deadlines. I am not going to slant stories for slick—nor for pulp—I am going to write *my* stories, the very best stories I can, and then let them sell (or not sell) to whatever market fits them. I can't do any worse than I have been doing; I might do better. And I think you will see a lot more copy out of me. I'm a fast producer when I'm happy at it.

January 2, 1950: Robert A. Heinlein to Lurton Blassingame

I want to get home awfully badly and I am worn out, but I need the money for house building.

Thanks for the *SatRev of Lit*—I am now a lit'rary man, entitled to wear a pipe, a spaniel, and baggy tweeds.

EDITOR'S NOTE *Robert did a review of* The Conquest of Space *by Chesley Bonestell and Willy Ley for the* Saturday Review of Literature. *It was titled (by the editors) "A Baedecker of the Solar System," and ran as the lead article for the issue in which it appeared.*

SALES

December 5, 1958: Robert A. Heinlein to Lurton Blassingame

I mailed the contract for "All You Zombies" to Bob Mills, unchanged. Certainly, I would have preferred *Playboy*'s fancy rates, but it took me exactly one day to write it, so what the hell? . . . I *hope* that I have written in that story the Farthest South in time paradoxes.

. . . She [a romance writer] writes very well, and rather than have her run out of material, I would be glad to volunteer my services. I'm not as energetic as I was in the Coolidge administration, but I've learned a lot since then and that's what a writer needs: ideas.

FOREIGN SALES

February 19, 1959: Robert A. Heinlein to Lurton Blassingame

. . . Is it really true that my foreign sales have been "fabulous"? You see, I have no experience whatever on which to form an opinion. I know that I take warm, special pride in these translations and we both enjoy the regularity with which the money rolls in. But are my foreign sales numerous in comparison with other writers of comparable domestic success? I just thought I had been damned lucky in being in the hands of an agent who had formed such excellent connections abroad and used them so well. I am sure that part of it is true.

February 26, 1959: Lurton Blassingame to Robert A. Heinlein

There are very few writers who sell in as many countries as you do. I try to line up with the agent in each country who is most respected for results and I check on this through visiting publishers to New York, and through them try to help our representatives in these publishers' countries; but in other countries, as here, the quality of the story is the deciding factor. It's the high quality of your stories that makes them so popular. Fortunately, you are writing about a subject that is of interest everywhere; we'd have great difficulty in selling your stories, even of this quality, if you were writing about baseball and football.

CHECKS

December 2, 1961: Robert A. Heinlein to Lurton Blassingame

It seems certain that Ginny gets more fun out of these checks than I do. She always grabs a letter from you first and you should see her eyes light up when she sees one of those long yellow pieces enclosed. Cash has the same effect on her that Elvis Presley has on teenagers—for the past hour she has been sitting in the tub, talking dreamily about how she is going to spend the money that came in today—a new ball gown, setting some emeralds she just happens to have sitting in the bank vault getting rusty, etc. I am sure she regards you as the source of all blessings.

December 5, 1961: Lurton Blassingame to Robert A. Heinlein

The Scribner royalties roll on and on. Here is another nice check to help with your Christmas shopping. And we have received a big batch of marks for you from Germany, and the check for this will go to you before the end of the week.

Boxing Day 1961: Robert A. Heinlein to Lurton Blassingame

. . . and also for a nice check from Germany to make our Christmas green. You will be pleased to hear that Ginny has already spent quite a chunk of it; she bought five dresses and a coat before I was out of bed this morning.

SHORT SHORT

May 9, 1962: Robert A. Heinlein to Lurton Blassingame

Carson Roberts, Inc., the advertising firm which has been preparing these short-short science-fiction ads for Hoffman Electronics

Few writers sold in as many countries as did Robert A. Heinlein. Here are a few examples of foreign editions, including the British edition of *Stranger in a Strange Land.*

(which you may have seen in *Fortune*, *Scientific American*, or elsewhere) have been bothering me for months to do a 1,200-word story for them. I have not bothered you with this because it is my usual policy to refer to you *only* such business as is really business—and I had no intention of writing 1,200 words of SF for anybody at any price. Such length is poorly suited to the genre.

But they kept raising the price, from $250 to $500 and then to $750—and I tried to shut them up by outlining in one paragraph how feeble a SF story would have to be to be told in 1,200 words . . . whereupon they accepted the outline and asked me to go ahead. I may possibly do so. If I do, I will submit it through you. Otherwise this is just for your information. It's a silly business at best—sixty-two cents a word is more than it's worth, but 1,200 words is a silly length for science fiction.

CHAPTER XI

❖

ADULT NOVELS

❖

THE PUPPET MASTERS

November 4, 1950: Robert A. Heinlein to Lurton Blassingame

I have not written lately because I have been working seven days a week and far into the night on the new novel—75,000 words down on paper so far and all I need now is a smash ending. That is giving me trouble. I should be working on it at this moment (8:30 P.M., Sat. Eve.) but enough things have accumulated that I must write.

December 2, 1950: Robert A. Heinlein to Lurton Blassingame

Herewith the original and first carbon of *The Puppet Masters*.

❖ ❖ ❖

As the story stands, it is a bit long (about 90,000 words) for serialization and much too long for a single-shot, but I would much rather cut to an editor's specific requirements than to cut blindly ahead of time. I append hereto something which you may or may not see fit to send along with the copy submitted for serialization: a list of possible breaks. I don't know whether this is good salesmanship or not, but I thought it might help if an editor could see at once that the story was very flexible, serialwise. As you know, I can cut, bridge, write around, etc., to shorten anything they want shortened to any extent they wish . . .

THE PUPPET MASTERS

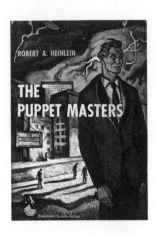

Doubleday published *The Puppet Masters*. *Galaxy* magazine had changed so much of it in the serialized version that Heinlein barely recognized his own style.

Aliens, in the form of slugs or parasites, suddenly appear on Earth and turn normal humans into zombies willing to do the invaders' will. A government agency sends agents to investigate, but those agents are lost. Two special agents, "Sam" and "Mary," are briefed and sent into the fray.

At different times, both "Sam" and "Mary" become the willing tools of the slugs, and there are horrifying scenes as they engage in war against their homeland. We see them completely committed to their masters. But as the U.S. comes close to being taken over by these aliens, fast action and all-out war eventually save the country.

I suspect, too, that a magazine editor will want the sex in this toned down; that's easy.

January 5, 1951: Robert A. Heinlein to Lurton Blassingame

Oh yes—Bradbury [Walter Bradbury, science fiction editor for Doubleday] wrote to me about *The Puppet Masters*; I wrote back agreeing to make all suggested cuts and changes, but nevertheless expressing some difference of opinion as to the advisability of the revisions. In my opinion a horror story—which this is—is not improved commercially by watering it down. Edgar Allan Poe wrote a great many things; I own and have read all his works—he is known for about 5% of his published writings, all sheer unadulterated horror, much of it *much* more grisly than mine. But I am going to do exactly what Bradbury says to do; he's paying for it and I need the money.

March 23, 1951: Lurton Blassingame to Robert A. Heinlein

Revision on *Puppet Masters* satisfied Doubleday. Sent word to Gold [H. L. Gold, editor of *Galaxy*].

April 3, 1951: Lurton Blassingame to Robert A. Heinlein

Talked with Gold today. The magazine is undergoing a policy change, and must wait before purchase. Controlled from abroad—France and Italy—will let LB know when there is definite word.

April 21, 1951: Robert A. Heinlein to Lurton Blassingame

You will recall that you advised me that Gold's original demands for revision for serial publication were outlandish in view of what he would pay—about $2,000.

June 3, 1951: Robert A. Heinlein to Lurton Blassingame

Galleys for *The Puppet Masters* have arrived; galleys for *Between Planets* are expected this week; Gold wants synopses for *The Puppet Masters*. I am still on a merry-go-round but will take care of these items without undue delay. I learn from the grapevine (but not from ——) that "Green Hills" is about to be published.

August 20, 1951: Robert A. Heinlein to Lurton Blassingame

I have been sitting on my hands this past week to keep from writing a stiff letter to Gold. He sent me an advance copy of the September *Galaxy* with the first installment of *The Puppet Masters*. Gold turns out to be a copy messer-upper; there is hardly a paragraph which he has not "improved"—and I am fit to be tied.

Now *Galaxy* is an excellent market and I do not wish to make your task any harder by antagonizing an editor to whom you may be offering more of my copy—but if I were free-lancing without an agent, I'd be quite willing to risk losing the market permanently in order to settle the matter. What I would like to say to him is: "Listen, you cheesehead, when we were both free-lance writers I had a *much* higher reputation than you had—in fact you never wrote a number-one science fiction story in your life—so who in hell do you think you are to be 'improving' my copy!"

Well, I didn't and I won't—but that is how I feel and it is the literal truth; Gold is turning out a good magazine, but as a writer he was never anything but a run-of-the-mill hack. This whole matter no doubt sounds like a tempest in a teapot, particularly as Gold did not change the story line but merely monkeyed with dialog, rephrased sentences and such—in short, edited the style. Look, Lurton, my plots are never novel, I am not an originator of brand-new and wonderful ideas the way H. G. Wells was; my reputation rests almost solely *on how I tell a story* . . . my individual style. It is almost my entire stock in trade.

Without changing the plot in the least, without changing the manuscript in any fashion that could be detected by someone else without side-by-side comparison, Gold has restyled the copy in hundreds of places from my style to his style. It would be very difficult to show how he has damaged the story, but in my opinion he has changed a story-with-a-moth-eaten-plot amusingly told into a story-with-a-moth-eaten-plot poorly told. This is my first serial appearance in a long time; his changes will not make it easier to get top rates for my next such appearance. The cash customers won't know what is wrong, but they will have the feeling of being let down—not quite "first-rate Heinlein."

I'll cite just one example out of hundreds: At one point I have a nurse say, "Eat it, or I'll rub it in your hair."

Gold changes this to, "Eat it, or you'll get it through a tube."

See the difference? My phrasing is mildly (very mildly) humorous. It conjures up a picture of a nurse who maintains discipline by cajolery, by the light touch, the joking remark. Gold's phrasing is as flatfooted and unsmiling as an order from a hard-boiled top sergeant.

There are both sorts of nurses, admitted. But the entire characterization of this nurse (Doris Marden) had been consistent as the sort of a person who kidded her patients into cooperation (modeled after a nurse who attended me at Jefferson Medical); with one phrase Gold louses up the characterization and turns her into the top-sergeant type.

In another place I describe the heroine as "lean"; Gold changes it to "slender"—good Lord, heroines have always been "slender"; it's a cliché. I used "lean" on purpose, to give her some reality, make her a touch different.

You see? All little things, but hundreds of them. I can't prove that the story is spoiled. Maybe it isn't, but I know that it is filled with stylisms that never would have come out of my typewriter. You might try the magazine version yourself without checking for the changes, but simply checking to see if it tastes the way it did the first time you read it.

All this is spilt milk except (a) the last installment may not yet be set in type, (b) it may be possible to prevent it from happening in the future. On the first point, the reader's impression of the story depends largely on how he feels when he finishes the story; if Gold can be

pushed into returning to the version he bought for the third installment, the louse-up of the first and second installments won't matter
too much. Could you talk tough to him, point out that it has been
repeatedly adjudicated that mere purchase of the right to publish does
not give to him the right to change copy under my byline and that he
must print as written, or run the risk of a lawsuit? Or could you kid
him out of it, convince him that he should do it to cater to my prima-
donna feelings? On point (b) you can either reach an understanding
now, or take it up whenever we again submit copy to him, but he must
clearly understand and (I think) agree in writing that *all* changes must
be made before the sale is completed; once sold the entire ms. is "stet"
and must remain so.

Hell's bells, I don't mind the few little changes that most editors
make and I don't mind a reasonable amount of revising done by me to
editorial order, but this guy has monkeyed with every page.

This is not artistic temperament talking, Lurton—had it been I would
simply have blasted at him in person. I am seriously concerned with
the business aspects—a strong belief that the property has been damaged commercially and that it will affect the market value of future
properties.

I've started fiddling with a new story.

September 24, 1951: Lurton Blassingame to Robert A. Heinlein

Gold tells me that he has written you a letter of apology for his
heavy hand on your story, and promises that, though he edits all material which comes his way, from now on yours will be inviolate.

THE DOOR INTO SUMMER

February 2, 1956: Robert A. Heinlein to Lurton Blassingame

I am 104 ms. pp. into a new novel, hopefully intended for the
so-called adult trade. It is giving me chronic headaches and chronic
insomnia and I wonder why I ever entered the silly business—but if I
hold up physically, *The Door into Summer* should be finished in draft
this month and finished in smooth around the end of March. Maybe.

We have a foot of snow on the ground, pheasants all over the place,
and Pixie hates it. He blames Ginny.

THE DOOR INTO SUMMER

Heinlein broke into Doubleday's adult market with *The Door Into Summer* in 1957. Cover art by Mel Hunter.

Dan is an inventor of a line of housekeeping robotlike devices. But his partners steal control of Hired Girl, Inc., from him, then place him in frozen sleep for thirty years into the future. There he learns that Hired Girl has a rival, Aladdin Corp. From the patents of Aladdin's devices, he discovers that the inventor is—himself!

Dan manages to use a discredited time machine to return several months before the time he was shanghaied. He now invents the devices of Aladdin Corp. He gives his shares of Hired Girl to an eleven-year-old girl, Ricky, who has a crush on him, telling her how to meet him when she is grown; then he and his cat, Pete, take frozen sleep for thirty years.

His partner in Aladdin Corp is honest, and Dan is now a rich man. When Ricky is awakened from the long sleep, he meets her. They go off together to be married.

May 31, 1956: Robert A. Heinlein to Lurton Blassingame

Re synopses for *Door into Summer*: I write my own synopses only when the editor twists my arm and demands it—which is usually. If Boucher [the editor of *The Magazine of Fantasy and Science Fiction*] is willing to do them himself, I'll be delighted; he's more literate than I am anyhow.

DOUBLE STAR

March 23, 1955: Robert A. Heinlein to Lurton Blassingame

I am aware that I should have written to you several days ago, but I trust you will forgive me when I say that I have completed the

DOUBLE STAR

Heinlein had considered selling *Double Star* elsewhere, as he disapproved of Doubleday's Book Club contracts.

Lorenzo Smythe is an actor—a good one, though now down on his luck. When a spaceman named Broadbent offers him a job, he is willing—until he learns it is to go to Mars. But Broadbent forces him by a secret way through Skyport and to the *Go for Broke*. Then he learns that he is to impersonate the great statesman Bonforte who has been kidnapped and who is due to deliver a major policy speech. Lorenzo is given tapes and films—and begins to "put on Bonaforte's head." But when Bonforte is found, he has been severely injured.

Lorenzo reluctantly carries on, meeting the press, entering a Martian "hive," even meeting Prince Willem, and learning more and more of Bonforte's manners and thoughts. Then Bonforte dies!

Broadbent and others finally persuade Lorenzo to carry on. He does, successfully for the rest of his life.

---

novel I was working on. Its present title is *Star Role* [*Double Star*], it runs about 55,000 words, and is intended for an adult audience. (No sexy scenes, however, and no taboo monosyllables—just an occasional damn or hell, and I may even take those out. The book should be suitable for the kids who will read it anyway.)

I held down the length in the belief that serial sale would be easier; I hope that this one will finally crack *Colliers*, the *Post*, or some other adult and not-SF-specialized market. I figure that, costs being what they are, a short length will make it more attractive for both trade book and pocket books as well.

❖ ❖ ❖

Double Star went on to win the Hugo Award for Best Novel of 1956 at the World Science Fiction Convention, New York, NY.

I don't know whether you should advise Doubleday or not. I like [Walter] Bradbury but I do not like the screwy "Science Fiction Book Club" aspect of their contract; they sold a lot of copies of my books with them and I got very little out of it—I do not regard two and a half cents per copy as a good royalty on a hardcover edition put close on the heels of the trade book. Since Bradbury turned down the travel book, we are no longer under option to Doubleday; perhaps this would be a good time to look into the Ballantine deal if it is still being offered.

In any case, I have an adult novel available for book and serial.

April 21, 1955: Lurton Blassingame to Robert A. Heinlein

Congratulations on a good novel. Enjoyed all of *Double Star*; wished it longer. No slow spots.

June 3, 1955: Lurton Blassingame to Robert A. Heinlein

The *Post* thought your novel was excellent and the only reason they did not buy it as a serial was that they do not want to devote that much space to science fiction. Campbell is buying it, to run in February, March, and April issues. Doubleday to bring it out in March.

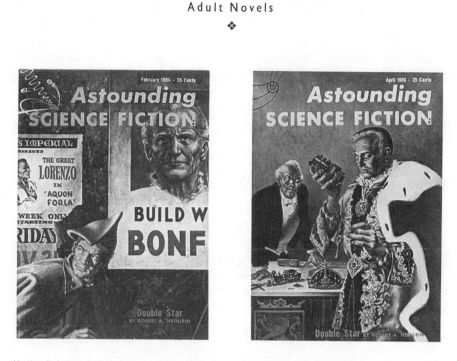

Heinlein had originally looked into a non-Science Fiction market for the serialized *Double Star* but eventually decided to publish in *Astounding* in three issues. Cover art by Kelly Freas.

GLORY ROAD

May 9, 1962: Robert A. Heinlein to Lurton Blassingame

I have not written for some time because I have been writing that new novel, now completed: *Glory Road*, 409 ms. pages, about 105,000 words. I am now revising it for my typist and will cut it a little but not much. You will have it not sooner than two months from now as my typist does my work as "moonlighting," as she has a daytime job. This is an adult market story with enough sex in it to give heart failure to those who complained about *Stranger*. It is fantasy verging on SF.

June 6, 1962: Robert A. Heinlein to Lurton Blassingame

. . . We intend to stay quietly at home all summer and I expect to spend the time hauling rocks and weeding and such. I do not expect to write until fall—after all, two novels in one year by the 1st of May

GLORY ROAD

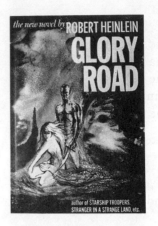

Glory Road was a departure for Heinlein, being more fantasy than science fiction.

Oscar Gordon, a Vietnam veteran, is vacationing by the sea in the South of France when he is approached by a beautiful woman. She needs his help. He agrees, and she gives him a sword and takes him to another world, where many dangers beset them. He has to defeat dragons, an ogre, and other monsters. Betweentimes, they make love.

She tells him she is Ishtar, Queen of Twenty Universes, but she is powerless without the Phoenix Egg, which he must recover. They reach the place where it is and Oscar now faces a series of truly horrible dangers. But he recovers the Egg.

She makes him her Prince and takes him to Center, her world. But he grows bored with all the privileges and protocol. He learns how to return to Earth and leaves.

---

is considerable copy, and I find I am tired and uninspired after finishing *Glory Road*.

August 6, 1962: Lurton Blassingame to Robert A. Heinlein

Glory Road is a departure, even for you. It is more fantasy than science fiction. It is an excellent adventure story, seasoned with sage thoughts, spiced with interesting sex. There were a number of spots where I wanted to stop reading and find an audience to share your ideas with. I do hope this will have a real success. I find it delightful.

September 30, 1962: Robert A. Heinlein to Lurton Blassingame

. . . I am not interested in his offer. Not the amount of the fee— a ms. is worth what you can get for it . . . sometimes zero. Nor do I object too much to the labor of cutting. What I do object to is that he wants me simply to chop off the last hundred pages.

If I do this, what is left is merely a sexed up fairy story, with no meaning and no explanations. I do not want this story published in such an amputated form. About thirty pages of that last hundred is indeed rather preachy, rather slow, and (if I were to cut) I would sweat that stretch down as much as possible—i.e., from the hero's arrival on the planet Center until his decision to leave—but I am quite unwilling simply to chop the story off at the point where they capture the Egg of the Phoenix. It leaves the story without meaning.

December 7, 1962: Lurton Blassingame to Robert A. Heinlein

Putnam likes *Glory Road*. There should be a little tightening in it, and "a few not very serious" suggestions for changes. Will mark ms. and send with detailed letter.

FARNHAM'S FREEHOLD

March 9, 1963: Robert A. Heinlein to Lurton Blassingame

The new novel ([*Farnham's Freehold*] working title: *Grand Slam*) I did in 25 intense days, 503 pages. Ginny seems to like it better than *Glory Road*, says it moves fast and can't be cut much. However, I intend to cut it a lot and get it to my typist about the end of this month. I haven't read it yet, but enjoyed it as I wrote.

March 21, 1963: Lurton Blassingame to Robert A. Heinlein

I don't know how you manage to produce a novel of 500 pages in 25 days, even a first draft.

July 8, 1963: Lurton Blassingame to Robert A. Heinlein

Good story in *Farnham's Freehold*, with enough adventure for some of the men's magazines.

August 21, 1963: Lurton Blassingame to Robert A. Heinlein

Peter [Israel] said he was writing you about cutting and revision ideas, and you probably have his letter by now.

FARNHAM'S FREEHOLD

By 1964 and *Farnham's Freehold*, Heinlein was firmly entrenched with Putnam as his publisher.

Hugh Farnham and his family are caught in the blast of an atom bomb, but are not killed. Instead, they are dumped into the far future, to a world none had envisaged. They are soon taken captive. Here the people who call themselves a master race are black, and they consider all other humans little more than animals, to be made slaves, tortured, or killed at will. Farnham is a slave now.

But eventually he interests the masters enough to gain a very limited freedom. He learns of the existence of a "time machine." With it, he manages to get his group back to a little before the time of the blast.

They take refuge in a cave in an enclave in the hills and prepare. The war comes, the nuclear blasts occur, and then plague strikes. But they survive.

October 4, 1963: Lurton Blassingame to Robert A. Heinlein

Peter Israel says, "Bob Heinlein is the boss. I'll express my opinions, but I have enough respect for his skill and judgment so that if he says a thing can't be done, I'll go along with the way Bob feels it has to be done. If he says the story cannot be cut below 100,000 words without seriously hurting it, I'll publish it at 100,000."

October 12, 1963: Robert A. Heinlein to Lurton Blassingame

Farnham's Freehold contract with Putnam's: On page two I have changed the wordage to "100,000" and struck out the delivery date and made it "to be arranged." I need to know [their] absolute rockbottom deadline for fall '64 publication. I know that he does not need the finished ms. by New Year's Day, that being what I struck out—nor could I deliver it by then in a smooth, retyped form; I've got too much to do to it, and my typist will need at least two months after I have finished cutting it. When you ask him for his absolute deadline, please point out to him that in twenty-five years I have never missed a deadline by even one day. I am quite sure that most editors stick at least a month of cushion into a deadline date since most writers are notoriously unpunctual in such matters. I want to know what his *real* date is. I will meet it.

THE MOON IS A HARSH MISTRESS

June 21, 1965: Robert A. Heinlein to Lurton Blassingame

The original of this letter goes with the original ms. of *The Brass Cannon* [*The Moon Is a Harsh Mistress*], the carbon goes with the carbon ms. Both will be sent to you tomorrow, original by airmail in the early

---

THE MOON IS A HARSH MISTRESS

The Moon Is a Harsh Mistress was originally titled *Brass Cannon* after the cannon the Heinleins bought on a trip to Louisiana.

While checking on "Mike," the computer that controls most functions on the Moon, Mannie finds that Mike has become conscious. Then Mannie finds himself heading the revolutionary movement with the Prof, the girl Wyoh, and Mike—who can assume many roles on the screen. The Moon was settled by convicts, but now enjoys a rich social life, though still badly exploited by Earth as master.

With the Prof's knowledge of history and Mike's powers, they plan a careful flight for freedom, using the catapults designed to sling their products to Earth to hurl rocks. Earth retaliates with nukes, but eventually surrenders. Mike, however, has been badly shaken by a nuclear strike. He still controls all electronics—but he no longer shows signs of consciousness.

The Moon Is a Harsh Mistress won the Hugo Award for Best Novel of 1966 at the World Science Fiction Convention, New York.

morning, carbon by air express in the late afternoon, in an attempt to have them go by different airplanes. As you probably know from the news, we are isolated other than by air—and the last I heard they were borrowing 1916 Curtiss pushers in order to move all the passengers, freight, mail, and food that is moving in and out of our small airport.

Anent ms.: Please send the original to Putnam; it has with it a form for their supercolossal prize contest. But would you please tell him that I really have no expectation of a science fiction novel winning. . . .

July 6, 1965: Lurton Blassingame to Robert A. Heinlein

Putnam's likes new book, same terms as last book. Don't like title; can you suggest another?

November 30, 1965: Robert A. Heinlein to Lurton Blassingame

You saw a copy of ——'s letter to me; I phoned him today. He had thrown me a curve in his proposals to edit a ms. which —— had approved in toto—but I tossed him another curve back saying okay and how quickly could he ship me the edited ms. for my approval?—and pointed out to him that I had *never* signed a contract in the past with Putnam's, nor accepted any advance, until the ms. was fully approved down to the least word. I think he was taken aback by this, but he quickly agreed to go over the ms. himself, see what the copy editor had done, and then either okay it the way I had submitted it, removing the copy editor's changes, or send it to me for my approval.

THE PAST THROUGH TOMORROW

March 9, 1963: Robert A. Heinlein to Lurton Blassingame

I am returning herewith Peter Israel's letter concerning the *Future History*. I don't know just what he wants. I had had in mind an omnibus reprint book, using the first three books of the *Future History*. We hold all rights to these *and we own the plates.*

❖   ❖   ❖

THE PAST THROUGH TOMORROW

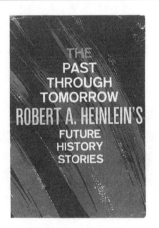

The Past Through Tomorrow collected Heinlein's "Future History" stories written for *Astounding* and the slicks.

This is a giant collection of the stories written for *Astounding* under the "Robert A. Heinlein" byline and many of the slicks. These stories all follow a consistent pattern of future history. When he began writing fiction, Heinlein laid out a big chart with the dates, major technical advances, political and sociological situation, and various remarks necessary for fuller understanding. There were also lines for the lifelines of major characters and for the beginning and duration of technical inventions. This came to be known as his "Future History" chart. The big chart was pinned to the wall, and stories, characters, and details were added to it as more stories were written or planned. It covered a period from about 1950 to the year 2200.

FUTURE HISTORY

DATES	STORIES	CHARACTERS	TECHNICAL

A.D.

Life Line

The Roads Must Roll
Blowups Happen

The Man Who Sold the Moon

Delilah & the Space Rigger
Space Jockey
Requiem
The Long Watch
Gentlemen, Be Seated
The Black Pits of Luna—
  It's Great to Be Back
  "—We Also Walk Dogs"
Searchlight

Ordeal in Space
The Green Hills of Earth

Logic of Empire

The Menace from Earth

2000

"If This Goes On—"

Coventry

2100

Misfit

Universe (prologue only)

Methuselah's Children

Universe
Commonsense

Characters: Pinero, Martin, Douglas, Gaines, Blekinsop, Harper, Erickson, King, Lentz, Harriman, McIntyre, Cummings, Wingate, Sam Jones, Satchel, Rhysling, Nehemiah Scudder, Novak, John Lyle, Zeb Jones, Master Peter, Magdelene, MacKinnon, "Fader" Randall, Persephone, The "Doctor", Lazarus Long, Ford, Libby, McCoy, Rhodes, Doyle

Technical: Douglas-Martin sun-power screens, Mechanized roads, Commercial rocket travel, Helicopters, Interplanetary travel, Growth of submolar mechanics, atomic cont. artificial radioactives, Uranium 235, (Hiatus), Developments in psychometrics and psychodynamics, Interplanetary travel resumed, Limited use of telepathy, Static submolar engineering (parastatics)

Chart of Future History from *The Past Through Tomorrow*.

DATA	SOCIOLOGICAL	REMARKS
Transatlantic rocket flight Antipodes rocket service	THE "CRAZY YEARS" Strike of '76 The "FALSE DAWN" First rocket to the Moon	Considerable technical advance during this period, accompanied by a gradual deterioration of mores, orientation and social institutions, terminating in mass psychoses in the sixth decade, and the Interregnum. The Interregnum was followed by a period of reconstruction in which the Voorhis financial proposals gave a temporary economic stability and chance for re-orientation. This was ended by the opening of new frontiers and a return to nineteenth-century economy.
Bacteriophage The Travel Unit and the Fighting Unit Commercial -stereoptics	Luna City founded Space Precautionary Act Harriman's Lunar Corporations PERIOD OF IMPERIAL EXPLOITATION Revolution in Little America Interplanetary exploration and exploitation American-Australasian anschluss Rise of religious fanaticism The "New Crusade" Rebellion and independence of Venusian colonists Religious dictatorship in U.S.	Three revolutions ended the short period of interplanetary imperialism: Antarctica, U.S., and Venus. Space travel ceased until 2072. Little research and only minor technical advances during this period. Extreme puritanism. Certain aspects of psychodynamics and psychometrics, mass psychology and social control developed by the priest class.
Booster guns Synthetic foods Weather control Wave mechanics The "Barrier"	THE FIRST HUMAN CIVILIZATION	Re-establishment of civil liberty. Renascence of scientific research. Resumption of space travel. Luna City refounded. Science of social relations, based on the negative basic statements of semantics. Rigor of epistemology. The Covenant.
Atomic "tailoring," Elements 98-416 Parastatic engineering Rigor of colloids Symbiotic research Longevity		Beginning of the consolidation of the Solar System. First attempt at interstellar exploration. Civil disorder, followed by the end of human adolescence, and beginning of first mature culture.

I suggest that we tell Israel that what we are offering is the first three volumes, for reprint, separately or as one jumbo volume—with plates furnished by us—and that if he does not want them, please tell us so in order that we may offer same to Doubleday's Science Fiction Book Club. I feel quite sure that they would take a chance on such an offer, with the plates laid in their laps. These three books are very famous in the field and they have not been available in hardcovers in years—and never from the S-F book club.

I WILL FEAR NO EVIL

August 21, 1969: Virginia Heinlein to Lurton Blassingame

Robert says that the new novel is as long as the Bible, but considering the number of authors of that, I doubt it. It is still in the process of completion. We'll send up a few rockets when it's done, and maybe you'll see one of them!

August 28, 1969: Virginia Heinlein to Lurton Blassingame

[Robert] left me a note saying, "Please tell him that I am anxious to learn what the new book is all about, too—especially the ending.
"I seem to be translating *Giles Goat Boy* into late Martian."

September 2, 1969: Virginia Heinlein to Lurton Blassingame

Robert's up to what he says is the last chapter. Then he added thoughtfully, "I hope it isn't like the short story." But I think this time he means it. He spent last night killing off someone; must have been a sort of Rasputin, from the length of time it's taken.

October 1, 1969: Virginia Heinlein to Lurton Blassingame

What word do you want about the novel? It's in the cutting stages—I thought that it dragged in spots. Don't you want to be surprised? All I can tell you is that it is quite different from anything I've ever read before, by Heinlein or anyone else. It will go to the typist before we leave here for the class reunion . . .

I WILL FEAR NO EVIL

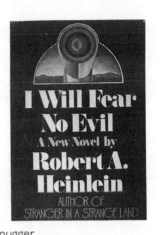

I Will Fear No Evil, G.P. Putnam's Sons, 1970, was also serialized in *Galaxy*.

Johann Sebastian Bach Smith, an extremely wealthy man, is being kept alive through the use of life support systems, until a suitable body donor can be found, at which point his brain will be transplanted into the young body. The body turns out to be that of his very capable secretary, who was killed by a mugger.

The two personalities now inhabit the same body and talk to each other. And Johann Smith learns to look around him with new eyes, as a female. He/she has experiences unknown to anyone else, having been of both sexes.

Eventually, using semen deposited earlier by Johann Smith in a sperm bank, Johann/Joan Eunice bears a child. It is his own child on both sides.

October 7, 1969: Virginia Heinlein to Lurton Blassingame

Re the new book, Robert has his doubts about Mac [Truman MacDonald Talley of NAL] liking it, pointing out that he turned down *Stranger*, but says he's been publishing some far-out stuff lately. My comment was that he can't sell the public Elsie Dinsmore anymore.

October 13, 1969: Virginia Heinlein to Lurton Blassingame

The cutting goes along slowly . . .

November 12, 1969: Robert A. Heinlein to Lurton Blassingame

While I was writing *I Will Fear No Evil* and you and Ginny and Margo were handling everything else, a lot of nonfrantic items accumulated in your box on my desk. It appears from the file that I have not acknowledged checks in writing since 22 June. I intend to acknowledge checks and books, so that you will have a written record.

December 4, 1969: Virginia Heinlein to Lurton Blassingame

I'm just afraid that I shall have to type *I Will Fear No Evil*, which will completely spoil my winter! I think the first draft was 689 pages.

January 19, 1970: Lurton Blassingame to Robert A. Heinlein

I spent more time reading *I Will Fear No Evil* than I've spent on a manuscript in years. This is only partly because of the book's length—I've gone through longer ones faster—but the novel has so many good lines in it that I gave myself time enough to enjoy and chuckle over them.

January 31, 1970: Virginia Heinlein to Lurton Blassingame

Today Bob will probably sign his "X" on two powers of attorney. One for you, one for me. Yours will be for conducting business affairs, mine a general one . . . and I suggest that we both keep them, not limited in time, for emergency use.

❖ ❖ ❖

Robert is in good spirits, but quite weak, with nurses around the clock. The incision looks huge to my inexperienced eyes, and it had a drain in it until yesterday . . .

February 12, 1970: Virginia Heinlein to Lurton Blassingame

This new novel is probably closer to mainstream than science fiction than any Robert has done . . . he wants to have some sort of mass distribution on it, either by early paperback or serial, or perhaps both. The paperback business doesn't seem to cut much into the trade edition sales, whereas the Doubleday Book Club does. If we can't get serial or early paperback publication, we'll reluctantly let it go into a book club edition. The sales on *The Moon Is a Harsh Mistress* proved my point on that.

February 26, 1970: Virginia Heinlein to Lurton Blassingame

Just returned from the hospital, and Bob was trying to eat lunch . . . he ate his whole egg for breakfast, and I don't know how much more, but he's still getting IV feeding, and is very unsteady on his feet. But at least we're away from the wheelchair, and he goes out into the corridors to walk. He'd refused to leave his room for about a month, and this is [a] considerable breakthrough. Also, I gave him *The Insult Dictionary*, and he started reading it, which is better than the detergent dramas and quiz shows, etc., he's been watching on TV.

❖   ❖   ❖

I am also sending a letter from Lady Gollancz. Robert read this letter, and said firmly, "No bowdlerization." So will you please tell [her] politely to go to hell? The passage referred to is the one in which the hero feels sorry for the victim rather than the criminal. She wanted to take it out.

EDITOR'S NOTE: By this time, publishers in many countries were putting out Robert's work, especially his juveniles.

Several British publishers had contracts for books, among them Gollancz. The chief of that firm had been knighted by the crown—Sir Victor Gollancz. When Sir Victor died, his wife took over the firm.

When they were about to publish one of the juveniles (and I am not sure now just which one·it was), Lady Gollancz asked whether she might omit several sentences dealing with punishment of a character for a crime he had committed. The law on this point is firm, both here and in the UK: no publisher of a reprint edition may make changes in copy once the sale is made, without the written consent of the author.

So Robert refused her request to make the change.

Yesterday, over in Santa Cruz, I ran across a note Robert had made about the new book. Sorry I can't quote it in full, but he said, "This may be my last novel. I am not going to let some editor cut it when he doesn't understand it completely." He's always said that this story couldn't be cut because of its complexity . . . although I thought it should be. It is possible that he's right. In any case, this is something that will have to be done cautiously rather than trying to fit it into a Procrustean bed. He did do some cutting before the final typing and Xeroxing. I read it and proofed and made changes, where the typist had made mistakes. And the cut version is a lot faster than the first one was!

March 7, 1970: Virginia Heinlein to Lurton Blassingame

I know that [Robert] has definite ideas about what he wants in the new book contract, but he just says, "You and Lurton handle it," so we'll have to stall a while longer.

March 31, 1970: Virginia Heinlein to Lurton Blassingame

Robert is pleased with the serial sale [of I Will Fear No Evil to If]. He had every intention of having serial publication on it, if possible.

❖   ❖   ❖

The doctors are very pleased with Bob's progress, but he still spends most of the time in bed, and is really not up to doing any work at all. Besides, sometimes his mind isn't as sharp as it usually is, and we hope that by the time this copy-editing is completed, he'll be up to looking at it . . . And having had the close brush with eternity he recently had, he's going to make some changes in his way of living. Just what those changes will be remains to be seen. It will probably include such things as no speeches (he finds them quite disturbing), no interviews, etc.

April 8, 1970: Lurton Blassingame to Virginia Heinlein

Rush me Xerox of your power of attorney. We need to attach it to the new Putnam contract.

November 20, 1970: Virginia Heinlein to Lurton Blassingame

The reviewers seem to be complaining about the lack of explicit sex in I Will Fear No Evil. One said, "The Victorian Mr. Heinlein—" Does any book ever please reviewers?

January 14, 1971: Virginia Heinlein to Lurton Blassingame

Thank you very much for the article from the New York Times. I will salaam to the Boss every morning from now on. How does one person get to be the hero of the New Right, Women's lib, and the hippie culture all in the same breath? We must all be schizophrenic!

CHAPTER XII

❖

TRAVEL

❖

August 6, 1952: Robert A. Heinlein to Lurton Blassingame

Back home to a bushel of mail and a constantly ringing phone—I wonder why we came back! But it was a fine trip—Jackson's Hole, Grand Tetons, Yellowstone Park, Craters of the Moon National Monument, Sun Valley, the "Days of '47" at Salt Lake City, Zion Park, North Rim of the Grand Canyon—where we rode mules down to the floor of the Canyon—then Bryce Canyon, thence through the main range to Aspen, and finally home.

AROUND THE WORLD I

August 17, 1953: Lurton Blassingame to Robert A. Heinlein

. . . very excited to hear plans for the round-the-world trip.

September 25, 1953: Robert A. Heinlein to Lurton Blassingame

We sail from New Orleans on 12 November and will leave here about 7 November. I am sorry to say that I will not be on the East Coast either coming or going, as we leave from the Gulf and return via San Francisco . . .

We have our trip about lined up, having each received permission from the Navy Department, having received passports, having booked passage for the two principal legs of the trip. We've been vaccinated, shot for cholera, typhoid and paratyphoid, tetanus; will be stuck for

Robert and Virginia in Sun Valley, during the 1952 tour of National Parks.

yellow fever on Wednesday. Ginny is down seeing about visas right now, but all the main hurdles are passed. I will supply exact times and places later but here is how it shapes up now: By freighter S.S. *Gulf Shipper* (U.S. registry) New Orleans, Panama Canal, half a dozen west S.A. ports to Valparaiso, fly over Andes to Buenos Aires, embark cargoliner (swimming pool and such) M.S. *Ruys* (Dutch), then Montevideo, Santos, and Rio de Janeiro, across South Atlantic to Cape Town, after which the ship hits half a dozen East African ports and Zanzibar, ending in Kenya before starting across Indian Ocean for Mauritius and Singapore. I want to leave the ship for a week at Cape Town to visit Kruger National Park, but Ginny insists that lions can open automobile doors—nevertheless, I want to make that motor trip and see lions, elephants, etc., in native habitat.

We leave the ship in Singapore and have booked no farther. I plan to visit Java and Bali at least and wind up at Darwin, Australia—we are trying to arrange booking for an island freighter now; if that doesn't work, we will visit the islands by airline and end up at Darwin anyway. Then we fly to Sydney, stay as long as we like in Australia, go to New

The Heinleins in Buenos Aires, a stop on their world tour of 1953.

Zealand, where we intend to visit both North and South Islands (there is an N.Z. airline that has a circle route), and eventually back home via the Fiji and Hawaiian Islands and San Francisco.

October 24, 1953: Robert A. Heinlein to Lurton Blassingame

As you can see, this is my "strike-out" letter—even though I may write again. You will see, too, that I have (with fantastic ingenuity and smug planning) placed all the real dope on page two, which you can now stick up on your bulletin board, or something. We'll send you postcards of calabozos and hippos and things. If I don't return on time, just forward my personal effects to Tahiti, fourth beachcomber from the left.

Wups! I forgot something—money. Don't send me any checks after about 7 November; just hold for me whatever comes in. It is possible that, after I am cleaned out by a gang of international gamblers headed by a beautiful blonde in sable, that I may ask you to cable me some dough—but it seems most unlikely, as I am taking plenty.

April 3, 1954: Robert A. Heinlein to Lurton Blassingame

We got home late Wednesday and spent Thursday and Friday unpacking and reading mail. I have answered none of the latter as yet and still can't find the top of my desk—and about two dozen bread-and-butter notes to write consequent to the trip as well. We are both okay save for head colds picked up in New Zealand and still with us. The trip back was okay until we were within ten minutes of Colorado Springs, whereupon the damned plane caught fire in its heating system, filled the cabin with smoke, and caused the skipper to turn back and make an emergency landing. This when I had about softened up Ginny to the notion of traveling by air in the future—

TRAVEL BOOK

EDITOR'S NOTE: In 1953 and 1954, Robert and I took a six-month trip around the world. When we returned, I suggested that Robert write a book about the trip. He wrote half of the book and sent it off to Lurton, to see whether there was or was not a market for it.

It turned out that there was no market for it.

Everyone who read this book loved it, but no one wanted to publish it.
Robert spent some months working on this book. It is too late to publish
it now—it's considerably outdated.

August 30, 1954: Robert A. Heinlein to Lurton Blassingame

I think you had better send the travel book manuscript back
and let me finish it. I have spent the whole summer expecting it back
in the next mail, frustrated by its half-finished condition, and unable
to get to work on anything else. I'll never send out an incomplete ms.
again—it is, for me, like having someone read over my shoulder; it
keeps me from concentrating on the work in the machine.

A long string of houseguests helped to wash out the summer, too.
The last of them are out of the house now and I should be able to
finish the travel book quickly. I want to start on my next novel in a
couple of weeks. I plan to do the next boys' book first, then an adult
serial novel.

EUROPE

January 24, 1955: Robert A. Heinlein to Lurton Blassingame

We have not yet been able to book our proposed trip, but we
still hope to leave about the 1st of May. Don't worry about the trips I
take cutting in on writing; in the long run they increase my output and
enhance its quality. Anything I do always winds up in a story eventually—and it is most unlikely that we will ever make another trip six
months long.

May 10, 1955: Robert A. Heinlein to Lurton Blassingame

We have luxurious quarters, the owner's cabin, about twice as
big as the other passenger staterooms. I don't know how we got it as
we did not ask for it, but it is very pleasant. For the first time in a ship
I have room enough to write and a comfortable setup for it. I might
even turn out a story . . . although this seems unlikely as my mind is
comfortably blank.

July 16, 1955: Robert A. Heinlein to Lurton Blassingame

How are you? Me, I'm a little confused. I've been in ten countries so far this trip, used nine languages, and thirteen sorts of money including U.S. MPC "funny money" in which $10 bills are printed in bright red and a nickel scrip looks like a cigar coupon. I've just finished calculating a trip into the Arctic Circle (which we start tomorrow morning) which involves marks, guilders, Belgian francs, and three sorts of kroner, all at different rates. I came out within about 10 percent of the right answer, which is better than I expected.

❖ ❖ ❖

Ginny has been spending money with joyful frenzy and everything costs six times what it should. I think I have money enough with us to cover everything, but I am no longer sure. Could you please send me a thousand dollars in American Express drafts (the only sort which is really easy to exchange everywhere) to the Heidelberg address above? Deus volent, I will still have them in my pocket when we reach New York, but I will feel easier if I have them. We will be back on the 6th of August; then we go to Bayreuth so that Ginny can sop up Wagner (the Ring Cycle) while I sop up beer—then home by easy stages. I estimate that we will be in New York about the 9th or 10th of September, but anything could happen between now and then.

LAS VEGAS

April 22, 1959: Robert A. Heinlein to Lurton Blassingame

We're back home and not quite broke—in fact, I didn't even manage to use up all of some traveller's cheques I bought in New York over a year ago, and now we have money running out of our ears, with all taxes paid. Ginny worked hard on the slot machines, did not manage to drop behind more than five dollars all week. I played the slots very little, craps one evening, and put a few chips on roulette *en passant* and broke about even—I wasn't there to gamble anyhow. One member of our party, a boy I went to Annapolis with, gambled all week, splurged on night clubs, etc., and returned to Colorado Springs with more money than he had started out with. I can't claim that, but I will say that they practically give you the joint free—provided you don't drop a lot of dough at the tables. Gourmet food is cheap, the most lavish night clubs in the entire world are very cheap, equivalent hotel rooms are about half what they would cost in New York. I understand that the taxis are expensive, but we hired a new Chevvie and never entered a taxi.

The Congress of Flight was almost the size of a World's Fair, with the most remarkable demonstrations and exhibits I have ever seen anywhere . . . The static exhibits included such things as the Atlas, Thor-Able, X-15, manned re-entry capsule for Project Mercury—and the 1911 Bleriot monoplane. The dynamic exhibits had everything, from several types of bombing to the most frightening precision flying I have ever seen—half a dozen nations each trying to bilge the others and the Chinese Nationalists stealing the show with a nine-plane diamond tight formation that did things I still don't believe. Nobody killed—although we in the audience almost had heart failure.

❖ ❖ ❖

Las Vegas is sort of an organized nervous breakdown. We are exhausted, sunburned, and euphoric . . . But the three largest bookstores in town do not sell science fiction—I looked for some of my own to give to friends—no dice.

To my great delight my name tag was read and recognized every few minutes all week long—a large percentage of the delegates read science fiction.

SOUTHWEST TRIP

March 9, 1956: Robert A. Heinlein to Lurton Blassingame

We are just back from an eight-day swing of Albuquerque, Las Cruces, and Portales, a very enjoyable time which included seeing friends at Sandia Weapons Center, the AEC [Atomic Energy Commission], a rocket society do at White Sands, seeing ——— ———'s new baby, photographing the gypsum sands, a real dust-bowl storm with the sun blacked out and silt up to the fence tops, a visit on a cattle ranch, lecturing at the University of New Mexico, getting stuck in the mud, and encountering quite a bit of sunshine and warm weather after a very hard winter. I am now trying to clear my desk.

USSR

August 15, 1960: Robert A. Heinlein to Lurton Blassingame

Well, I'm home and completely swamped by the volume of work in front of me. I've spent the past four days just trying to get enough stuff put away and thrown away so that I can get at my desk to write. As soon as I finish this letter I will get to work on an attempt to try to revise and extend the Intourist article along the lines you

The start of the May Day Parade, Soviet Union, 1960.

suggested—but, truthfully, trying to write humorously about the USSR won't be easy. Ginny and I laughed ourselves silly time and again, but it was hysterical laughter; there is not much that is really funny about the place.

E DITOR'S NOTE: Robert wrote two articles about this trip; they can be found in Expanded Universe.

ALMA

May 15, 1961: Robert A. Heinlein to Lurton Blassingame

We went to Alma, Oklahoma, on April 29th, using a chartered airplane and getting it all done in one day. "The Sequoyah Book Award" turns out to be a handsome plaque. I addressed the State Library Association and they had a book-signing afterwards—and durn if they hadn't sold almost two hundred copies of *Have Space Suit—Will Travel.*

Scribner's offered to pay for the trip, but I preferred not to be under obligations to them while there is such continuous pressure on me to quit Putnam's and go back to Scribner's. Anyhow, it cost less than two roundtrip commercial tickets and considerably less than it would have cost to drive it—and it's deductible. Anyhow, arriving by private plane added to the show.

SAN DIEGO

July 12, 1962: Robert A. Heinlein to Lurton Blassingame

My short trip to San Diego and to sea was terrific. A day under the sea in the submarine *Raton,* spent with destroyers hunting us and trying to (simulate) depth bombing—which they do with grenades, which make a terrible racket but, at most, break a light bulb—then we flew aboard the carrier *Lexington,* spent the night watching night operations, then day operations the next day, then flew back to Colorado Springs—elapsed time C.S. to C.S. fifty-four hours and almost no sleep. The night landings were made by supersonic fighters, Demons (F3H), and it was the most exciting—and the noisiest—thing I've ever seen.

GRUMBLES FROM THE GRAVE

She's an angle-deck carrier and landings and catapulting go on simultaneously, one of each about every thirty seconds—and they hit at about
130 miles per hour and roar away if they miss the wire. Besides that, I
was recognized repeatedly, which boosts my morale. The icing on the
cake was a birthday party in the air for me on the way home. Much
fun!

LAS VEGAS AGAIN

September 30, 1962: Robert A. Heinlein to Lurton Blassingame

I've got to bathe, shave, dress, and run—the Houston trip was
fast and frantic; the Las Vegas trip was long and delightful. Ginny hit
several nickel jackpots, I did not gamble at all but saw all the shows . . .
The space and aircraft exhibits were magnificent, there were many fine
parties and three open bars, and a fine firepower show—bombing,
Thunderbirds, refueling in the air, the new planes, and a joint AF and
Army Strike demonstration. And we saw many old friends. The Folies
Bérgère was as always, and the Lido de Paris show better and more
lavish than ever.

ANTARCTICA

December 28, 1963: Robert A. Heinlein to Lurton Blassingame

I think I told you by phone that *Popular Mechanics* wants me
to do another article, or several. Since then we have tentatively agreed
on a subject for the next one: the research going on at the South Pole.
I had in mind going there next year, but Stimson's last letter spoke in
terms of right away. Since summer has just started at the South Pole
this is reasonable—save that I am up to my ears in this Hollywood deal
with Screen Gems. The trip need not take long—ten days or two weeks—
but if I am to go at all this [Southern Hemisphere] summer, it must be
in the next few weeks, with conflict most probable with the Screen
Gems deal. . . .

It it does work out that I go now instead of about a year from now (anytime after Labor Day 1964, that is), this would solve the problem of what to use for a *Boys' Life* serial: Lay it at the South Pole and make it a mixture of science and adventure. And that would also solve the problem of my next juvenile for Putnam's—three novellas totaling about 50,000 words, *Nothing Ever Happens on the Moon*, *Tenderfoot on Venus*, and *Polar Scout*. [Putnam] has written me, twisting my arm a little to turn out another juvenile; this would satisfy [Putnam] for the '65 spring list, I think. If you see fit, you might ask *Boys' Life* if they would like a serial about Antarctica, one written from personal observation.

I should add that I told *Popular Mechanics* that, having given them a first article, I reserved the right to do other articles and fiction based on the trip. They want to pay only what they paid before . . . I could hitchhike the entire trip on military "space available," but I am more likely to go commercially to Auckland. But I can show a nice profit by writing other things on the same material.

EDITOR'S NOTE: This trip did not come off, but we did travel to Antarctica in 1983.

CARIBBEAN

December 11, 1964: Robert A. Heinlein to Lurton Blassingame

All the various checks sent registered in two mailings arrived, of course, and Ginny is again complaining that it is backing up on her. It is her own fault; spending is her province and she returned from this last trip with more than a thousand in cash—she didn't even really *try*. Her largest purchase was three "pans" (or drums) for a steel band, purchased in Trinidad, and they weren't expensive; they were simply hard to get home—one medium-sized, eighteenth-century brass cannon purchased in New Orleans (so now we are in business for ourselves). The cannon helped a little—$275—but when a guide offered to have a jewelry shop opened for her on a Sunday in Caracas she turned him down. We simply will have to buy some more stock after we pay the income tax; she has lost her touch.

Perhaps the most interesting part of the trip was visiting a Bush

Smorgasbord.

The 18th Century Brass Cannon
was the inspiration for the
original title of *The Moon Is a
Harsh Mistress.*

Negro village far up in the jungle in Suriname, formerly Dutch Guiana—
descendants of escaped slaves who continue to live Congo-style deep
in the rainforest, up a side river by launch. My principal reaction was
that bare breasts aren't necessarily sexy; the Zulus are much better
equipped in that region. We also visited an Amerindian settlement—
the Indians were polite and dirty, the Negroes were pushy and very
clean. As for other matters—well, a flying fish with a 12-inch fin wing-
spread flew into the lounge one evening through a port dogged open

only 4 inches without damaging the fin wings. I couldn't ask him how he did it; the landing killed him. We got a royal tour of the Boeing plant in Louisiana (guests of the chief engineer and chief counsel), and I beg to report that the Saturn is the most monstrous big brute imaginable and I do not believe that the Russians can do things on the scale of our Apollo project. I do believe we will have a man on the moon this decade; progress looks good. Ginny visited a Negro whorehouse in Jamaica, and behaved with such aplomb and savoir faire that one would think she had spent her whole life in one. We arrived in Denver late at night to find our flight did not run that day, so I chartered a 2-engine Aero-Commander and we landed in a snowstorm in Colo. Spgs. by GCA. I watched it from the co-pilot's seat—much like a carrier landing. The ground is covered with white stuff but it is good to be home.

EDITOR'S NOTE: *That brass cannon still stands in the living room. It served as the working title for* The Moon Is a Harsh Mistress; *of course, the title was changed as the editors did not think it was a suitable title for a science fiction novel.*

The cannon is a saluting gun from an eighteenth-century sailing vessel, but it still works. We used to fire it every Fourth of July.

December 28, 1964: Robert A. Heinlein to Lurton Blassingame

I behaved myself in Jamaica and all through the trip—first, because I was well chaperoned and, second, because I was never really tempted. The female passengers were all antiques and the chocolate items ashore were not tempting. No, I'm not racist about it—some of the Zulu gals I saw in South Africa were decidedly tempting. But not these. As for Ginny's savoir faire, here's how it came about: [someone from our ship] had a date with a mulatto gal, not bad looking but not too bright and quite notional. He . . . took Ginny and this gal and myself on a pub prowl through the lower depths of Kingston. About midnight this gal suddenly decided that we should all go to —— and gave the address to a cabdriver—instead of a night club, it turned out to be a cathouse complete with red light, eight or ten colored gals in the parlor, and a bar and jukebox in a room behind the parlor, where the madam (somewhat annoyed but polite) received us. [The gal's date] was terribly embarrassed and explained behind his hand to me that he had not had the slightest idea where we were going. But Ginny was not embarrassed, spotted what the place was at once, and was delighted to have had a chance to see inside one. We bought a couple of rounds of drinks, played the jukebox, and left—much to the madam's relief. (I strongly suspect that [the woman] had worked in that house.)

CLASS REUNION AND RETURN

November 12, 1969: Robert A. Heinlein to Lurton Blassingame

It was a wonderful trip for us, all the way through. I'm sorry that I arrived in New York so beaten down by my class reunion [in Annapolis] (some day we'll make a trip in which the *first* stop will be New York and arrive in prime condition)—I'm especially sorry that I missed the ballet in which the gals (did) (did not) wear body stockings . . . Jack Waite took an afternoon off to give us a personal tour of the Manned Spaceflight Center [in Houston]—high points: a view of Moon rock (swelp me, it looks to me like hundreds of little shiny golden spheroids embedded in a tannish gray matrix), a visit inside the mission control room during a computer-simulation of *Apollo 12* mission (the LEM was just "landing" on the Moon and you could follow it on the displays), and a long, detailed lecture on the Moon suits (for us alone) by the chief engineer of life support systems—who turned out to be Ted Hayes, whom I [had] hired as an undergraduate at U of Pittsburgh twenty-seven years ago to work at the Naval Aircraft Factory—and I lured him into signing with me rather than General Electric by promising him that he could help develop pressure suits for fighter planes and I kept my promise and it led directly to him developing the first suit used on the Moon.

❖　❖　❖

We stayed over an extra day in Houston at Patricia White's [the widow of Ed White, who died on Apollo I] request—"some people who wanted to meet us." Ginny told you a bit about that party by phone . . . It was a big party in a big house and I don't know what all Ginny did—but I was followed around all evening by three tall beautiful blondes—Heinlein fans. (I managed to put up with it.) But the star of the evening was "the Honorable Jane." Jane is a BOAC hostess and looks just the way an airline stewardess should look—petite and pretty and shapely.

[She] was wearing an evening dress—but it was London mod. Micro skirt—and she had nice legs but nobody noticed because it was cut clear to the waistline in front. No question of a body stocking in this case. Un-possible! Nor any possibility of foam rubber. Silicone? A bare possibility, but I don't think so. Everyone got cross-eyed, including me, and Jane clearly enjoyed the sensation she was creating. (I should add that styles in Houston are much more conservative than those in New York.)

From there we went to New Orleans, with reservations at the St. Charles—and I was asked for identification as we were checking in . . . which I refused to give (this is not yet Russia) and we had our bags put back into a cab and went to the Pontchartrain where we wound up in the Mary Martin suite without being asked to produce IDs. I can see why Mary Martin stays in that suite; the Aga Khan would be quite comfortable in it. It was late, we were exhausted, so we had a bite from room service (soft shell crabs Amandine, oysters and bacon en brochette, parfait praline), bathed, and so to bed.

The next morning there was a bowl of fruit waiting for us, compliments of the manager, and enclosed with it was a little carton of personalized matches with my name spelled correctly. This was followed by a phone call from the manager asking us to have a drink with him that afternoon. (Heinlein fan? Not at all. He asked me what sort of writing I did.) The moral of this is: Don't stay in hotels that demand IDs.

I must now explain that I had avoided the Pontchartrain because Eberhard Deutsch [a New Orleans attorney] lives there and I had been trying to avoid moving into his place when I knew he was out of town. Having told his office that we would be at the St. Charles, I then had to phone again and tell them that we were at the Pontchartrain. Eberhard was returning from Europe by a plane that got in at just past noon the next day—so shortly after noon I received a call: "Young man, what are you doing downstairs? My housekeeper is expecting you."

So we moved up to the penthouse. He was not there but his housekeeper was indeed expecting us, and settled us in.

The penthouse makes the Mary Martin suite look like substandard housing—

—which I had known and which was a major reason why I was

reluctant to stay in it with the owner away. Eberhard's little cabin in the pines occupies the entire roof of the hotel; that portion which is not house proper being terraces, gardens, "landscaping," and a spectacular (pump-driven) waterfall. It is, of course, surrounded on all sides by dazzling views of the city and of the Mississippi—and best of all, it is so high up it is quiet; we could sleep.

❖ ❖ ❖

New Orleans was tiring fun and endless gourmet food . . . Bourbon Street in search of real Dixieland jazz, which we found.

ANTARCTICA

Virginia Heinlein—report 1983

This is an enormous continent, barely known, but actually inhabited by mammals and birds, on the coastline at least. There could be almost anything there and we went to learn something about it.

We were outfitted with thermal underwear to outermost layers of waterproof clothing. Recommended (by those who know) is the "layer theory" of dressing for the cold weather to be expected. And it is COLD. The worst day we encountered, including the wind chill factor, was 45 degrees *below* Fahrenheit. Otherwise, we managed to keep relatively warm.

A few words about the Zodiacs, which will often be mentioned. They are rubber boats with outboard engines, very shallow in draft, drawing only inches, made of rubber-coated fabric glued together, descendants of the life rafts of WW II. They have lightweight wooden floors; seating space for passengers was on the float tubes, which were about fourteen to sixteen inches in diameter. One held onto ropes festooned along the sides of these craft. We could be taken into beaches with no jetties, where it was possible to mingle with the local wildlife. "Wet" landings meant that we had to step into a shallow surf onto rocky beaches.

Lindblad Explorer was a small ship, built with icebreaking prow. Once we toured through an ice pack, looking at the local fauna. Groups of seals lie around on the ice, soaking up the sun or just resting; some-

View from the *Lindblad Explorer*,
the ship the Heinleins took on
their trip through Antarctica in
1983.

Heinlein on board the *Lindblad
Explorer.* The ship was very small
and all resources were limited—
and the temperature was 45
below!

times they became a bit wary at our approach and slipped into the water, but many of them just looked up and stared at us.

We embarked in *Lindblad Explorer* in Punta Arenas on the Straits of Magellan. The first warning we had was about water conservation—the showers had "minutieres" on them, to time the flow of water, and we were warned about conservation, since the ship could not make up enough fresh water from salt water to keep up the supply, if we used too much. Water in the shower would run for only about a minute, then shut off. Eventually, we both found that about two minutes in a shower would cleanse, if we did it Japanese style, soaping down first, then washing off the soap.

The ship was a bit spartan, but after a period of adaptation, satisfactory.

Lindblad Explorer carried a number of lecturers. They are specialists in various disciplines and there are daily lectures about various aspects of the things which we were about to see, or had seen. Talks on the mechanics of glaciers, about sea mammals and birds, the history of Antarctica, from the first exploration to the latest are all parts of this tour.

Getting into all those pieces of clothing in a small space was quite interesting, but we learned. The boots were the most difficult, as they had to be donned after the trousers, and the waistline bulk made it difficult to lean over to lace them up. We looked like teddy bears.

The first beach we landed on had penguins galore, of the chinstrap variety. They have one marking which gives them their name, a black strap of feathers which goes under their bills. Think of a dark sandy beach with small surf breaking on it, rocks on each side, and several harems of seals lying around, and dozens, hundreds, thousands, hundreds of thousands of penguins and you have the picture. Penguins walking into the surf, penguins returning from their fishing expeditions, walking around and paying little or no attention to us as we walked up to see the rookery. If you got down to something approaching their level (about knee height) they might just walk right up to you, inspect you, turn their backs, and walk off. One inspected us, first with one eye, then with the other, turned his (her) back, waggled its tail, and stalked off.

(I got too close to one of the seals and was chased off by the master of the harem. It must have been quite a spectacle, me flying off in those heavy boots and clothing—very slowly, as it was impossible to move very fast—chased by a seal.)

We hiked back into the rookery, through a small stream of very cold water, just barely melted, accompanied by penguins. Those poor little creatures walk about a mile to go fishing, for the purpose of feeding their young.

The penguin walk is quite clumsy, but they have another method of locomotion on snow. They flop down on their bellies and toboggan, which is relatively fast.

They sometimes cluster in groups on rocks at the water's edge, trying to decide whether to go into that water at all. When the cluster reaches a certain size, one brave individual will dive into the water, then most of the others follow. Then another group congregates, and they go through it all again. When returning, they get smashed against rocks, eventually mount them, and proceed awkwardly to their young.

Locomotion in water is by means of porpoising. Up and down, each time garnering some krill for their food, then presently they return to feed the young.

Their white fronts are often dirty with the pink color of the krill, but mostly the white is spotlessly clean. Penguin nests are built of small stones, which they shamelessly steal from each other. One experimenter put a stack of small stones painted red in one corner of a colony, and when he returned, the red stones were scattered all over

The Antarctic was heavily
populated by friendly penquins.

the colony. One mating habit is for the male to give his chosen a small stone. Another is for two birds to stretch their necks straight upward, making mating sounds.

Rookeries are quite noisy and rather dirty with guano. (And smelly, as well.) However, we found ourselves quite taken with those birds and their ways. After hatching from the egg, the baby penguin is covered with down, which it keeps for some time, shedding it in favor of the fancy dress. Some varieties leave the young with a nursemaid when they are off fishing, and you can see aggregations of those very young birds together. I watched one of the nurseries—the "nursemaid" kept after any stragglers, chivvying them back into the group, where they stayed until the parents returned.

Leopard seals eat penguins, when they catch them swimming. So one encounters orphaned baby birds. Skuas will eventually eat those. Rookeries can be vast; one we saw was estimated by experts to have about a million birds in it.

We looked on penguins as little people. They manage to endear themselves to anyone who comes into contact with them. Perhaps it is their upright posture, perhaps it is their clumsy locomotion on their feet—or possibly the "academic processions" going to and from the shore.

There were many Adelies, chinstraps, gentoos, and some of the larger species, as there were royals and the emperors, which are about four feet tall when standing upright. They look for all the world like elderly professors.

We were taken on Zodiac cruises, which didn't land at all, but simply watched for wildlife from the boats. During one such, whales appeared on the water surface. Humpback whales, weighing thirty tons, we were told. They were playing around during and after feeding. What an amount of krill such creatures must eat. (Krill are tiny shrimplike things—pale pink and almost transparent, with great black eyes. One figure I recall is that it takes thirty krill to make a gram.) Those large whales take in a great gulp of sea water, full of krill, and strain it through the baleen. Their throats pouch out with each gulp, and the water comes cascading out as they strain out the krill.

Several whales came swimming over to the boat and swam under it. We could see their flippers in the water under the boat. Then one breached and we could see its back and finally the flukes, which had barnacles on it in a pattern. Everyone was a bit scared by these demonstrations . . . with those flimsy boats being so close to those huge animals.

Most Weddell seals have scars from contact with killer whales—we saw them. Seals slide into the water without any splash, swim away with a gliding motion. In the water, they sometimes allow their curiosity to overtake them, and they stick up their heads and watch.

Cormorants (skuas) nest on sheer cliffs—there were many nests clinging to those cliffs—all of them with young cormorants watching.

There was a barbecue dinner at the Argentine station in Paradise Bay. It was about to close for the winter, when the scientists would go home. Unfortunately for us, the ship had had a batch of hand-knitted watch caps for sale, each of us had one. Knitted into them was the motto "Falklands War, 1982." We had forgotten about that, and went in with those caps on our heads. I told Robert about it, and he turned his backwards, but hairpins anchored mine in place. I felt apologetic toward our hosts.

Leaving, our boat driver was a fanatic whale chaser, and we spent an hour and a half chasing some fin whales which we never got close to.

The ship stopped at Paulet Island in the Weddell Sea, Deception Island, which is supposed to have the only Antarctic swimming pool—water in that area is warm enough for people to swim in, because of some underground heating (thermal activity). Antarctica has some working volcanoes, such as Mount Erebus, which is where there was a fatal New Zealand airline crash several years ago. Mount Erebus normally has a plume of smoke coming out of it.

Summers, the U.S. has about 1,200 people down in Antarctica, most of them at McMurdo Sound, our chief base there. But we also have Palmer Station, which we visited, Siple Base, and bases at the South Pole.

Probably the visit to McMurdo was the coldest day we encountered—going ashore in the Zodiac, our cheeks almost froze. We struggled up the hill to the base, finding it necessary to sit down for a rest several times. Then I finally commandeered a bus to take us to headquarters.

Robert found many fans among the people in Antarctica. At Palmer Station, one man was sleeping at the time of the ship's visit. When he heard that Robert had been among the tourists, he phoned the ship, and they talked.

Heinlein met a fan of his at Palmer Station, a U.S. base in Antartica.

On one Zodiac cruise, there were sea lions which played games with our boat. Their heads would come up above water and they would watch us, but when we steered toward them they would go under and pop up in a different place. Sea lions differ from seals in their gait, being able to walk in a fashion with their hindquarters.

One cruise was among icebergs, to see the sculpturing done by the winds, freezing and thawing and melting. Some of the bergs might be as much as a hundred years old, they told us. Bergs come in various shapes—tabular (squared off—just calved from the Ross Ice Shelf), which, after some melting, became castles, medieval monsters and all sorts of imaginative shapes. One evening, while we were at dinner, the captain spotted two huge bergs, and toured the ship all around them. At one point, it was estimated that we were in a field which contained sixty of the monster bergs.

A champagne party was held on a glacier. Ice is a marvelous substance, ice sculpture beautiful, but it's difficult to describe.

There were albatrosses of various sorts, including the wandering albatross—probably the largest bird known. We also saw petrels, and could go up to the nests and look at the young.

On approach and departure, there is a sea area called the Antarctic

Convergence, where the water is quite rough. Many of the passengers had to use seasickness remedies, but at most times during these passages, lifelines were rigged permanently around the ship.

EDITOR'S NOTE: Robert and I took one further trip in the Lindblad Explorer *through the Northwest Passage to the Orient. Although thirty-three other ships had managed to reach the Bering Strait, this was the first ship to go all the way to Japan, having navigated the Northwest Passage.*

CHAPTER XIII

❖

POTPOURRI

❖

March 30, 1956: Robert A. Heinlein to Lurton Blassingame

I am acquiring sunburn and backaches putting in a completely new and very complicated irrigation system. When I get that and some [Colorado Springs] house repairs completed I'll tackle a new story. My intention is to try to turn out some short stories this summer and not start another novel until about Labor Day.

April 14, 1956: Robert A. Heinlein to Lurton Blassingame

We are still gardening like mad and I ache in every bone from days and days of pick, shovel, and wheelbarrow work. I've just finished an enormous irrigation project. Well, it felt enormous to me, but it does not look like much now that the pipes are covered up. Today we have rain, snow, sleet, hail, and gropple, and I am catching up on paperwork. I expect to resume writing two weeks from Monday and plan to turn out several shorts and short-shorts before tackling another novel.

July 25, 1956: Robert A. Heinlein to Lurton Blassingame

Ginny has worked out a shenanigan with [a friend] to let you shoot on a resident permit if I don't get one . . . Ginny put in for a license, too—if you shoot on her license all that will be necessary is for you to convince the warden that you are female and redheaded.

Lurton Blassingame, Heinlein's agent, was an expert hunter.

P.S. I did my first pistol shooting (aside from one tomcat) in twenty-two years last Saturday. Three 10's and two 9's for a 48 on my first group. I should have stopped there, for I dropped as low as 42 for 5 shots later—averaging around 45.

August 20, 1956: Robert A. Heinlein to Lurton Blassingame

Take it easy on the stone masonry; it can make you old before your time. But I enjoy it more than any other form of mechanics, except that it half kills me.

October 3, 1958: Robert A. Heinlein to Lurton Blassingame

Thanks for the pic of Socrates, the super-giraffe. He is not here yet: he is still in quarantine in Hoboken and in the meantime they are trying to plan a route to Colorado Springs which will not involve bridges or tunnels too low for him—if it were up to me, I'd shoot him full of barbiturate, stretch him out flat, and fly him here in a Flying Boxcar. They'll kill him getting him here—if not from bridges, then from pneumonia. In the meantime, two widowed lady giraffes are awaiting him here; their deceased husband managed to hang himself—quite a trick for a giraffe. [This is in response to Lurton Blassingame's sending a picture of the giraffe that was to come to the zoo at Colorado Springs.]

July 14, 1961: Robert A. Heinlein to Lurton Blassingame

I'm in good health but Ginny is not. We've been having atrocious weather, which led to a set of cracked ribs for her. Like this—I've been building an irrigation dam for her garden and designed it to be a large ornamental pool as well as useful. We had been pointing towards a big fourth of July party and, since I had installed an electric pump for irrigation, I also rigged it to operate as a recirculating fountain—a jet thirty feet in the air with spotlights on the jet and floodlights on the sea green pool—very pretty and just right for a garden dinner party.

The rains came.

Golly, how the rains came! And on 2 July the pond silted up with brown slime. Ginny helped me clean it out—and slipped in the slime and fell against a boulder and cracked her ribs. Now she is strapped like a mummy and won't hold still and isn't getting well and everything hurts her—and I am finding out how really useful a wife is when she is well.

(But the party came off prettily anyway. We served sixty-four people—we now have enough picnic tables for a beer garden—Ginny had sewn about a hundred yards of bunting, I made an easel for a full-sized replica of the Declaration of Independence, we had martial and patriotic music over the outdoor sound system, and I set up a bar that could serve anything from a mint julep or a Sazerac cocktail to a Singapore sling. Fine time!—and Ginny ignored her wounds until the next day.

Shamrock is going to have kittens again.

PATRICK HENRY AD

EDITOR'S NOTE: *One morning in early April, I fetched the newspaper down to read along with breakfast, in my usual fashion. Robert was still sleeping, and there were standing orders never to disturb him until he woke up. But this day was different.*

There was a full page ad by the SANE people, signed by a number of local people we knew . . . I flew in the face of the standing orders, and woke Robert up. "What are we going to do about this?" I asked.

I fixed him breakfast and he read the ad while he ate.

There was no discussion about what we would do. Robert sat down at his typewriter and wrote an answer. When he was finished, I read the full-page answer and suggested that he rewrite it, using the same ideas he had used, but not mentioning the opposition. He did that, and the ad is re-printed in Expanded Universe.

Colorado Springs had two daily papers, one morning and one afternoon. We took the ad to the latter, paid for a full-page ad, and later went to the other and also took another full-page for our ad.

These ads caused a sensation. The telephone kept ringing, the mail was filled with a few pledges, and one or two contained checks to help the cause. We ordered extra copies of the page and sent them out to our mailing list, which was not very large at that time.

With the assistance of a wet paper copier, I made copies and sent the originals in to the President, registered, return receipt requested. I strung up a drying line in the kitchen and suspended the copies to dry. For weeks the kitchen was difficult to get around in.

Some people took an ad in the San Francisco Chronicle and sent us a copy. A few more pledges came in.

I sat down and did some figuring. Not counting the time we both put into the project, it cost us $5 each to send those pledges to the President. Our backfire had failed, and we never heard a word from President Eisenhower.

The President then signed an executive order suspending all testing without requiring mutual inspection.

Robert had been working on The Man from Mars *[Stranger in a Strange Land]. He set that aside and started a new book—*Starship Troopers. *Both books were directly affected by this try at political action—*Starship Troopers *most directly, and* The Man from Mars *somewhat less directly. The two were written in succession; they are quite different stories from what Robert might have written otherwise.*

(Robert's version of this can be found on pages 386 to 396 of Expanded Universe.*)*

April 26, 1958: Robert A. Heinlein to Lurton Blassingame

I don't know when I'll get any more fiction written—maybe never. This effort is taking up all of our time. On the other hand, we are spending money on it even faster than we spend money in traveling, so I may be flat broke soon and forced to go back to cash work.

But I refuse to worry about personal aspects of the future. I am convinced in my own mind that the United States is washed up and we will cease to exist inside of five to fifteen years—unless we quickly and drastically pull up our socks, both at home and in foreign policy. This opinion has been growing in my mind for years: I was simply triggered into doing something about it by this pacifist-internationalist-cum-clandestine Communist drive to have us treat atomics and disarmament in exactly the fashion the Kremlin has tried to get us to do for the past twelve years.

I wish some of those starry-eyed internationalists would go take a look at the illiterate, unwashed uncivilized billions whose noses they want to count in a "world state"! And also explain to me how you get a world state of "peace with justice" while dictators, both Red and garden variety, control the "votes" of a billion and a half out of two and a half. Somebody ought to tell them that "politics is the art of the practical." Me, maybe.

❖ ❖ ❖

Enough, too much—but it is much on my mind. The Patrick Henry League has been getting more response than I expected, much less than is enough to be effective. But we shall persevere.

MISCELLANEOUS

May 15, 1963: Robert A. Heinlein to Lurton Blassingame

Thanks for that full house of checks. Ginny took 'em all. You will be pleased to hear that I bought her another emerald ring, a quite expensive one, which will insure that I go back to work again before too long.

❖ ❖ ❖

Ginny is about the same and is so beat down from hand-watering her [Colorado Springs house] garden that she doesn't really know whether she is sick or exhausted. After every bath the bucket brigade starts,

Ginny bailing, me toting. I have placed four barrels around the garden and there every bit of wash water goes—hands, baths, dishes—and from these she waters with an old-fashioned watering can. In the meantime, I am digging a drainage ditch all around the house to carry all rainwater (if it ever rains!) from the driveway and the roof to my reservoir pond. I am lining it with concrete tile to keep silt out, so that it will not clog my pump. After that I am going to work out a (very expensive!) underground tank and immersion pump deal to use septic tank water for irrigation. This is no temporary emergency here; this county has doubled in population in ten years—and the area is semi-arid. (Remember that range on which you hunted antelope.) Things will get worse, not better, and I intend to make us as nearly independent of the water company as possible. No other news. We don't do a damn thing but haul water.

July 5, 1963: Robert A. Heinlein to Lurton Blassingame

. . . and it has slowed up my letter writing; I owe letters to everybody and am just barely managing to answer urgent business mail and send off checks for bills. Yesterday I celebrated the Fourth of July by bringing Ginny home from the hospital. Nothing to do with the mysterious ailment which has plagued her for so very long (which is as bad or worse than ever); this was an operation on her right wrist, orthopedic surgery to correct damage she did to it by endless toting of a heavy watering can when she was trying to save her garden. Yes, she saved the garden and, sure, I have now built a water works which makes us independent of the water company and permits her to water with a pump and a hose—but the damage was done during the month when every drop of water was applied by hand. It got so bad that she could not even sign her name with that hand, so they opened up her wrist and corrected it.

Since she is right-handed to the point that she can hardly hold a fork with her left hand, since her right hand is useless until it heals, and since I am a slow and inefficient housewife, not too much is getting done around here that does not simply have to be done at once—especially as I continue to try to get in as many hours of mechanical work as possible. The Heinlein Water Works is finished to the point where it operates, but I still have endless masonry and carpentry jobs to do before it will be utterly safe from flash floods and landscaped so that it does not look like an abandoned slum-clearance project.

September 3, 1963: Robert A. Heinlein to Peggy Blassingame

I won't send him [Lurton] flowers; his doctor has almost certainly forbidden roughage. I would like to mail him a blonde, but there
is some silly regulation about livestock. I suppose the best thing for
him to do is to get out of that ulcer-making business. (I would go crazy
in it.) But when Count does retire, I, and almost certainly a lot of others,
will perforce retire, too.

It might do him some good to come out here and fish for a month—
there aren't enough fish in Colorado streams to bother anybody.

In the meantime, he should avoid newspapers, authors, publishers,
and editors.

August 23, 1964: Robert A. Heinlein to Lurton Blassingame

[Concerning the arrival of a letter addressed to "Robert A. Heinlein, United States of America."]

The empty envelope herein is for your amusement . . . It was delivered with no delay at all, being postmarked the 9th and reaching me
on the 11th, via surface mail. It need not be returned.

POLITICS

June 15, 1964: Robert A. Heinlein to Lurton Blassingame

I am still getting no professional writing done and our household continues to be stirred up night and day by politics. I had intended to take no real part in this campaign other than donation of
money, while Ginny devoted practically full time to it. But I find myself
in the situation of the old retired fire horse downgraded to pulling a
milk wagon—a school bell rings . . . and milk gets scattered all over
the street! Last week I found myself, for the first time in a quarter of a
century, presiding at a political rally—co-opted without warning at the
last minute. I must admit that I rather enjoyed it. And I find myself
pulled in on many other political chores and devoting perhaps half as
much time to it as Ginny does.

EDITOR'S NOTE: *The preceding fall I had become much taken with politics—
a group of us had started a "Gold for Goldwater" campaign. We set up a*

Colorado Springs headquarters in a donated storefront, and gathered to-gether campaign literature, buttons, and all the trappings.

Six of us agreed to take one day a week at the headquarters, and there were all sorts of meetings and speeches to be given. Robert gave his blessing to my endeavors and I was allowed to spend as much money as I thought we could afford.

He accompanied me to political dinner parties and other doings, and presently he could no longer stand the political inactivity, so he joined me. His activities were a revelation to me. Instead of simply charging the price for a book, he set up a goldfish bowl, and asked for contributions, getting more out of each customer. He set up a dinner party, at $50 a head, and sold it out. Some bought tickets, and returned those to him to sell again, and he sold them, sometimes two or three times each, garnering a lot of "Gold" for the campaign.

The telephone rang constantly, and he could get no copy written. We were fully involved in an already lost campaign. Eventually we recognized that, and made plans to leave for South America after voting on Election Day.

October 2, 1964: Robert A. Heinlein to Lurton Blassingame

We still miss Shamrock but her little golden tomkitten is healthy and full of beans. Now I must run, get dressed, and rush to still another political dinner.

STUFFED OWL

April 15, 1967: Robert A. Heinlein to Lurton Blassingame

Ginny fetched home a stuffed owl and gave it to me. She was almost hysterical from self-panicking, laughing harder than I have seen her laugh since the time in Oct '65 when we were blockaded on a 70 mph freeway in Utah by 5,000 milling sheep. For some years I have used a family cliché concerning useless gifts: "Just what I've always needed—a stuffed owl." So she gave me one. The cliché dates back to my childhood. Do you remember Hairbreadth Harry, the Beauteous Belinda, and Rudolph Rassendyl the Villyun? Well, one Christmas about forty years ago Belinda gave Harry a smoking jacket that fitted him like socks on a rooster, and he gave her a stuffed owl—to which she said glumly: "Just what I've always needed."

So now I have just what I've always needed, and the stuffed owl (now named "Pallas Athena") is perched facing me just beyond my type-writer.

READER

December 10, 1968: Lurton Blassingame to Robert A. Heinlein

. . . However, not all people love you. I had a call this morning from a frantic mother in Minnesota whose fourteen-year-old son had run away from home for the third time. On his desk she had found your name, care of me. He has read all your books and she thinks he may be out to find you. Before taking off he had gone through his mother's purse and his father's store, so he has about $2,000 on him.

EDITOR'S NOTE We never saw the boy.

VIP

March 20, 1969: Robert A. Heinlein to Lurton Blassingame

This almost fractured me. Our tickets arrived marked "VIP." No fooling. I thought "VIP" was just an idiom—but swelp me, our tickets are so marked. I laughed until I was hoarse.

EDITOR'S NOTE In early 1969, an invitation came from the Brazilian government to attend a film festival to be held in Rio de Janeiro. All expenses would be paid by that government—we would be guests. The only payment would be that Robert give a talk.

Robert wrote this as a P.S. to Lurton in a business letter. His talk was given at the theater at the French Embassy.

As I recall, this was the only free trip Robert ever accepted; it even
included courtesy of the port—no customs or immigration needed. The re-
turn to New York was another matter!

APPRAISAL

November 21, 1968: Robert A. Heinlein to Lurton Blassingame

Did I tell you about the appraisal on my donation of mss., et
al. to the U of Calif[ornia]? If not, I must—for I am astounded. The
appraisal was made by Robert Metzdorf of New York and Connecticut,
and the IRS has been fidgeting about the long delay in getting an appraisal. But the university librarian wanted this appraiser and no one
else, because of his high prestige and his past successes in making his
appraisals stand up in court. So at last Metzdorf had a couple of other
jobs out this way and did my small job while he was here.

What he appraised was just the fraction of the total gift which is now
actually in the university's library, to wit, about two-thirds of my mss.
plus a couple of boxes of foreign editions and some [paperbacks] in
English. The valuation he placed on this fraction was $30,230.00—

—and I was flabbergasted.

Sure, Ginny had placed a guesstimate of $25,000-plus on the whole
gift—but that was for all mss., plus our entire library, plus several valuable paintings, plus several other things. Since the IRS permits deduc-
tions for gifts of chattels only after the physical property is delivered, I
had been fretted that the valuation on what I had been able to deliver
(some mss. plus a few not-very-valuable books) might be less than the
cost of appraisal—i.e., leave me with a net loss in cash and much loss
of professional time spent in cataloging and preparing the stuff for the
library. I never thought of my old mss. and notes as being worth much—
hell, to me they were simply papers that cluttered up my files but which
I did not dare throw away for business reasons. As for the foreign
editions and paperbacks, for years I have been giving them away to
anyone who would take them.

I still expect the IRS to scream about the appraisal. I'm very glad—
now—that we got the number one appraiser. If the IRS won't accept it,
I now feel safe in taking it to Tax Court.

EDITOR'S NOTE: The IRS did not object to the valuation placed on these papers.

CATS

January 12, 1957: Robert A. Heinlein to Lurton Blassingame

Pixie is dying . . . uremia, too far gone to hope for remission; the vet sent him home to die several days ago. He is not now in pain and still purrs, but he is very weak and becoming more emaciated every day—it's like having a little yellow ghost in the house. When it reaches the stage of pain, I shall have to help him past it and hope that he will at last find the door into summer he has looked for. We are pretty broken up about it . . . we have become excessively attached to this little cat. Of course, we knew it had to be when we first got him and I would much rather outlive a pet than have the pet outlive us—we're better equipped to stand it. Nevertheless, it does not make it any easier . . .

March 23, 1959: Robert A. Heinlein to Lurton Blassingame

Polka Dot had her kittens on St. Patrick's Day—like this: Ginny and I had been standing almost heel and toe watches as Pokie has not been at all well during this. About one o'clock in the morning I was up, Ginny had just gone to bed. Pokie comes dragging herself into my study, all cramped up in labor. So I held her paw for about an hour, whereupon she had one tortoiseshell female—Bridey Murphy. For the next three hours she has lots of trouble, so we get her vet out of bed and he comes over. He gave her a shot of pituitary extract; shortly she starts to deliver another one—a black and white male (Blarney Stone); poor little Blarney didn't make it . . . hung up in delivery, dead by the time we could get him out, although as lively as could be as he came part way out. And Ginny got her hand terribly bitten (Ginny screamed but didn't let go . . . and the cat didn't let go either). About dawn the three of us and Pokie went to the hospital and she had a Caesarean section for the third and last (Shamrock O'Toole, another tri-colored female, a close twin of Bridey). About 8 A.M. we fetched mother and daughters home, Ginny having had only a nap and myself no sleep at all. All three are doing fine now and the kits have doubled in size or more in six days. The thing that impressed me the most about the whole deal was the surgery—aseptic procedure as perfect as that used on humans, utterly different from animal surgery of only twenty years ago.

April 10, 1961: Robert A. Heinlein to Lurton Blassingame

Things have been confused and this is late. First we had kittens. Then Shamrock turned out to be the kind of mother who holes up in a tavern while her brats slowly freeze in the car, i.e., she takes vacations from the kittens without warning, as long as twenty-four hours, which finds us, Ginny especially, down on our knees feeding formula to kittens with a doll bottle that holds just an ounce. Then some Icelanders came to town, guests of the State Department, and I, as a member of

The Heinleins had many cats over the years; this one is Taffrail Lord Plushbottom, in the early 1980s.

the Air Power Council, was drafted to entertain them. Whereupon Ginny decided to give a dinner party for all of them, a dinner of some twenty people, at the drop of a hat. Fine time, but it killed three days, what with preparations, cleaning up, and recovering. Then the superintendent of the Naval Academy, a classmate of mine, came to town and we did it all over again—and had a blizzard. During which the wings of Ginny's new greenhouse came down under the snow load. Not much dollar damage and no plants lost, but Ginny was sad and it was quite a nuisance. I had been dubious about the design when I saw it first and had ordered modifications to beef it up, but the mechanics had not done it as yet.

Then the galley proofs on *Stranger in a Strange Land* arrived and that killed three days of the time of each of us; it's a long book. Ginny has just taken them to the post office and I am now writing to you a letter that should have gone days ago.

May 20, 1962: Robert A. Heinlein to Lurton Blassingame

The new kittens are two weeks old and fat and healthy. A hawk or an owl got Ginny's ducks.

April 17, 1964: Robert A. Heinlein to Lurton Blassingame

No more news here, save that Shammie, immediately following the adoption of her latest litter last Sunday, at once went out and set a new crop—so we should have more kittens ca. 17 June. A busy body, that one—thirty-one kittens so far and she has just turned five.

August 16, 1967: Robert A. Heinlein to Lurton Blassingame

Both Ginny and I are temporarily physically debilitated and emotionally depressed; we lost our little tomcat. He has been gone one week now and must be assumed to be dead. It is barely possible that he is out tomcating after some female and living on the land—but it is extremely unlikely. Two or three days, yes—a full week, no. A bobcat, a fox, a raccoon, an automobile. Sure, he was just a cat and we have lost cats many times before. But, for the time being, it hurts and keeps us from sleeping and leaves us emotionally unstable. Ginny continues to work hard, although she is not sleeping at all well—me, I'm so damned short on sleep that I can hardly type and can't concentrate.

PROBLEMS

December 18, 1950: Robert A. Heinlein to Lurton Blassingame

The novelette I planned to write as soon as the Puddin' story (enclosed) for *Senior Prom* was out of the way has been jeopardized by the headlines as it has a historical tie-in which calls for World War III holding off for a little while at least. I am shelving it and will start immediately on the next boys' novel for Scribner's and I'll write it so that the above point is not material! I will complete it as rapidly as possible because of those same headlines. A purely personal and selfish note in the present turmoil is that I need, somehow, to complete this [Colorado Springs] house as rapidly as possible so that I will be ready for whatever comes. Mrs. Heinlein may be called up at any time; she has already received correspondence about it—and one married female reservist here in town has already been called up ahead of her husband, so that we know the threat is real. I myself must have a minor operation before I can possibly pass the physical examination, but I hope to be able to get around to that before very long. Two of my brothers are now in uniform and the third is likely to be called up soon—and I might as well get ready for anything. In the meantime, I intend to turn out copy and lots of it as long as possible.

April 7, 1951: Robert A. Heinlein to Lurton Blassingame

Just at present any proposed work brings a feeble response. I am in a very rundown condition and have been and may still be on the ragged edge of nervous breakdown. I had purposed spending a couple of months or a bit more supervising the completion of my house, doing some of the work myself as a therapeutic measure, then when finished, taking a look at the war news and making up my mind as to whether I was morally obligated to go at once back into laboratory work rather than continue with writing. Ginny is in reserve; if and when she gets called up, I don't want to be tangled in contracts I can't shuck off—I want to be in research that will help to win the war as quickly as possible and thereby bring her home again. (I myself cannot possibly pass the physical exam; laboratory work is all I'm good for.)

March 1, 1953: Robert A. Heinlein to Lurton Blassingame

. . . We are all well again—even the cat, as I finally got the big black tomcat that had been beating him up. Ginny woke me one morning and said that the black tom was out front. I hurried into robe and slippers, loaded my Remington .380 pistol, and went out. Got him with the first shot, fortunately, as he was moving and I wouldn't have gotten a second. Had him buried and was back in bed in under twenty minutes. A sad task, but Pixie was so crippled up that I don't think he could have survived another beating—and I prefer my own cat to a feral one.

October 8, 1953: Robert A. Heinlein to Lurton Blassingame

I tried to keep the letter factual in tone; if undue emotion has crept into it, you may charge it off (this is private to you) to the fact, among others, that ——— without consulting us, gave us as financial references all around Colorado Springs—and that Ginny was annoyed by telephone calls demanding to know when ——— was going to settle her bills. And other matters better left unsaid.

December 11, 1964: Robert A. Heinlein to Lurton Blassingame

We have a new phone number—UNLISTED—so please write it down here and there. Ginny has wanted this for years to put a stop to fan calls at all hours. I must admit the quiet is welcome.

January 9, 1968: Robert A. Heinlein to Lurton Blassingame

I am returning Art Clarke's article as you asked in your note on the face of it. I take it that Spectorsky's [a *Playboy* editor] request was made to you this time rather than direct to me. He makes this request of me almost every month; I have long since quit answering these little notes. The first one was several years ago and concerned a short story by Fred Brown—quite a good one and I wrote a nice plug for it, which Spec published.

It was a mistake; I should have ignored it. I've been bombarded with similar requests ever since. Quite aside from the time such free work

Robert and Virginia with Arthur C. Clarke in Sri Lanka.

would require, correspondence is the bane of my existence and the major interference with my working time; I've no wish to add to it by writing letters to editors. And it is indeed "free work" that Spec wants; he is soliciting unpaid reviews from well-known writers.

But, hell, I might go along with it if that were all there is to it— *Playboy* is a number one market and it wouldn't hurt me to grease Spec a bit. But here is the trouble: I will not under any circumstances write anything unfavorable about any of my colleagues—and some of the stuff Spec asks me to comment on stinks. This one by Art Clarke is a dilly. But the last request concerned a story by ——. I'm on good terms with ——and intend to stay that way—but, had I written in as —— asked me to, the letter would have read: "Dear Spec, You should be ashamed to have printed it and —— should be ashamed of having written it."

So what should I do, Lurton? Pick out only the ones I can honestly praise and ignore the others? Or do as I have been doing and never comment on the work of my colleagues?

CHAPTER XIV

❖

STRANGER

❖

June 20, 1952: Robert A. Heinlein to Lurton Blassingame

I am writing every day but, frankly, the copy stinks. This novel may involve several rewrites, followed by a decent burial.

EDITOR'S NOTE: In early 1949, Robert was searching for a theme for the short story "Gulf," which he had promised to John Campbell. During the course of the discussions, I suggested to him that it be a story about a human being raised from infancy to maturity by a race of aliens. This notion arrested him, but he thought it an idea which required more room than a short story afforded. However, he went into his study and wrote for some hours—fourteen single-spaced pages, mostly questions to be answered. That was the beginning of Stranger in a Strange Land.

July 16, 1952: Robert A. Heinlein to Lurton Blassingame

Yes, I am still having trouble with that novel. Trouble is all that I am having—with the story itself and trouble with my surroundings. I have lost almost a month to houseguests, Arthur C. Clarke followed by the [George O.] Smiths—and now we are about to spend a week in Yellowstone and Sun Valley, leaving tomorrow. I could cancel this trip, but there are reasons why it is desirable not to cancel it. Furthermore I hope that a few days away from a constantly ringing phone will help me to straighten out this novel in my mind. (Sometimes I think that

STRANGER IN A STRANGE LAND

Stranger in a Strange Land became one of the most influential novels of our century. Heinlein began sketching out the idea for *Stranger* in 1949, but it took him until 1961 to be satisfied enough to write it.

Valentine Michael Smith is the only survivor of the first expedition to Mars. He is brought up by Martians, knowing nothing of Earth's culture, but well-educated in Martian ways by the ancient and wise race there. Now the second expedition has found him and returned him to Earth. He has never seen another man—or a woman.

He is confined to a hospital at first. But a nurse frees him and takes him to wise old Jubal Harshaw, where he quickly learns and adapts. There he demonstrates Martian powers—making things or people vanish, levitation, transmutation, etc. He makes all there his "water brothers" and teaches them to "grok." Then he sets out to bring his message to all, through what seems to be a new religion.

Some object. He is fatally shot. But he has learned on Mars to survive after his body dies, as he proves.

everyone in the country passes through Colorado Springs in the summer!) When I get back, I expect to have to go to the hospital for another operation. All in all, entirely too many days this year have been eaten by the locusts. My intentions have been good. I have not been idle—far from it! But I haven't accomplished much.

The story itself is giving me real trouble. I believe that I have dreamed up a really new S-F idea, a hard thing to do these days—but I am having trouble coping with it. The gimmick is "The Man from Mars" in a very literal sense. The first expedition to Mars never comes back. The second expedition, twenty years later, finds that all hands of the first expedition died—except one infant, born on Mars and brought up by Martians. They bring this young man back with them.

This creature is half-human, half-Martian, i.e., his heredity is human, his total environment up to the age of twenty is Martian. He is literally not human, for anthropology has made it quite clear that a man is much more the product of his culture than he is of his genes—or certainly as much. And this Joe wasn't even raised by anthropoid apes; he was raised by Martians. Among other things, he has never heard of sex, has never seen a woman—Martians don't have sex.

He has never felt full earth-normal gravity. Absolutely *everything* about Earth is strange to him—not just its geography and buildings, but its orientations, motives, pleasures, evaluations. On the other hand, he himself has received the education of a wise and subtle and very advanced—but completely nonhuman—race.

That's the kickoff. From there anything can happen. I have tried several approaches and several developments, none of which I am satisfied with. The point of view affects such a story greatly, of course—universal, first person, third person central character, third person secondary character, first person secondary character narrator—all have their advantages and all have decided drawbacks. A strongly controlling factor is the characteristics and culture of the Martian race—I started out using the Martians in *Red Planet*. I'm not sure that is best, as they tend to make the story static and philosophic. This story runs too much to philosophy at best; if I make the Martians all elder souls it is likely to lie right down and go to sleep. Affecting the story almost as much is the sort of culture Earth has developed by the time the story opens. After all that comes the matter of how to manipulate the selected elements for maximum drama. And I'm not pleased with any plotting I've done so far. I've messed up quite a lot of paper, have one long start I'll probably throw away and a stack of notes so high.

If this thing doesn't jell before long I had better abandon it, much as that goes against my personal work rules. I do have about three cops-and-robbers jobs which I can do, one a parallel-worlds yarn and the other two conventional space opera. I don't want to do them; I want to do a *big* story. But perhaps I should emulate Clarence Buddington Kelland and give the customers what they are used to and will buy, rather than try to surprise them.

July 18, 1952: Lurton Blassingame to Robert A. Heinlein

The book idea sounds tremendous, but I can well understand why you would find yourself in difficulties. Put it aside, work on something else, return, and find a new perspective.

June 10, 1953: Robert A. Heinlein to Lurton Blassingame

. . . Unfortunately, I cannot report that I have cracked the novel . . .

The novel is really giving me a lot of trouble. This is the one that I told you about long ago, I believe—a Man-from-Mars job, infant survivor of first expedition to Mars is fetched back by second expedition as a young adult, never having seen a human being in his life, most especially never having seen a woman or heard of sex. He has been raised by Martians, is educated and sophisticated by Martian standards, but is totally ignorant of Earth. What impact do Earth culture and conditions have on him? What impact does he have on Earth culture? How can all this be converted into a certain amount of cops-and-robbers and boy-meets-girl without bogging down into nothing but philosophical speculation? Contrariwise, what amount of philosophizing does it need to keep it from being a space opera with cardboard characters?

I got so bogged down on it last week that I had decided to shelve it for a year or so, when Stan Mullen [a science fiction author and personal friend] gave me a fight talk and quite a lot of help. Now I am continuing to try to sweat it through. When I get through I will either have nothing at all, or I'll have a major novel. I rather doubt that I will have a pulp serial; it doesn't seem to be that sort of a story. I will continue to sweat on it and you won't get anything else from me for quite a while.

January 13, 1955: Robert A. Heinlein to Lurton Blassingame

I am now on page 68 of the draft of *A Martian Named Smith*, which will be book length and adult—i.e., more sex and profanity than is acceptable in juveniles. I cannot now estimate date of finish-draft as there are some plot kinks I am not yet sure about.

February 23, 1955: Robert A. Heinlein to Lurton Blassingame

I am sorry to say the novel aborted last week—two months and 54,000 words of ms. wasted. Ginny says that it cannot be salvaged and I necessarily use her as a touchstone. Still worse, I suspect that she is right; I was never truly happy with it, despite a strong and novel theme. I am, of course, rather down about it, but I have started working on another one and hope to begin a draft in a day or two.

March 29, 1960: Robert A. Heinlein to Lurton Blassingame

I finished a draft a couple of days ago of the novel I have been writing and I am still groggy. It is very long (800 pages in its uncut form) and about all I can say about it now is that it is not science fiction and is nothing like anything I've turned out before. I intend to work on it all I possibly can until we leave, then have it smooth-typed while we are out of the country.

I am utterly exhausted from sixty-three days chained to this machine, twelve to fourteen hours a day. Now I must rest up in preparation for a physically arduous trip . . . while accomplishing a month of chores in two weeks, studying Russian history, politics, and geography so that I will understand some of what I see, and doing my damndest to cut about a third out of this new story. In the meantime, Shamrock O'Toole is about to have kittens any moment—the period is 60 to 65 days and today is her 62nd; she looks like a football resting on toothpicks and complains bitterly about the unfairness of it all. I'll send you a kitten by air express timed so that you can't send it back. Maybe four kittens.

October 10, 1960: Robert A. Heinlein to Lurton Blassingame

I assume that you have sent *The Man from Mars* to Putnam, since they are entitled to first look. I have on hand, should we ever need it, a clean, sharp carbon of this ms. on the same heavy white bond. I am aware of the commercial difficulties in this ms., those which you pointed out—but, if it *does* get published, it might sell lots of copies. (It certainly has no more strikes against its success than did *Ulysses*, *Lady Chatterley's Lover*, *Elmer Gantry*, or *Tropic of Cancer*—each at the time it was published.)

The Man from Mars is an attempt on my part to break loose from a straitjacket, one of my own devising. I am tired of being known as a "leading writer of children's books" and nothing else. True, those juveniles have paid well—car, house, and chattels all free and clear, much travel, money in the bank and a fairish amount in stocks, plus prospect of future royalties—I certainly shouldn't kick and I am not kicking . . . but, like the too-successful whore: "Them stairs is killing me!"

I first became aware of just how thoroughly I had boxed myself in when editors of my soi disant adult books started asking me to trim them down to suit my juvenile market. At that time I had to comply.

But now I would like to find out if I can write about adult matters *for adults*, and get such writing published.

However, I have no desire to write "mainstream" stories such as *The Catcher in the Rye, By Love Possessed, Peyton Place, The Man in the Grey Flannel Suit, Darkness at Noon,* or *On the Road.* Whether these books are good or bad, they each represent a type which has been written more than enough; there is no point in my adding more to such categories—I want to do my own stuff, my own way.

Perhaps I will flop at it. I don't know. But such success as I have had has come from being original, not from writing "safe" stuff—in pulps, in movies, in slicks, in juveniles. In pulp SF I moved at once to the top of the field by writing about sociology, sex, politics, and religion at a time (1939) when those subjects were all taboo. Later I cracked the slicks with science fiction when it was taken for granted that SF was pulp and nothing but pulp. You will recall that my first juvenile was considered an experiment by the publisher—and a rather risky one.

I have never written "what was being written"—nor do I want to do so now. Oh, I suppose that, if it became financially necessary, I could imitate my own earlier work and do it well enough to sell. But I don't want to. I hope this new and different book sells. But, whether it does or not, I want my next book to be still different—neither an imitation of *The Man from Mars*, nor a careful "mixture as before" in imitation of my juveniles and my quasi-juveniles published as soi disant adult SF books. I've got a lot of things I'd like to write about; none of them fits this pattern.

October 14, 1960: Lurton Blassingame to Robert A. Heinlein

Dear Water-Brother,

I greatly admire your courage and also your intellectual virility that enables you to open up new areas of the literary globe.

October 21, 1960: Robert A. Heinlein to Lurton Blassingame

In the first place, I think Putnam's offer is one of the most generous I have ever seen; it is all loaded in my favor. Will you please tell them so?

Cutting can always be done, even though there is always the chance of literary anemia therefrom. But the changes required are another matter—not because I don't wish to make them . . . but because I don't see *how* to make them. This story is Cabellesque satire on religion and sex, it is *not* science fiction by any stretch of the imagination. If I cut out religion and sex, I am very much afraid that I will end with a nonalcoholic martini.

I know the story is shocking—and I know of a dozen places where I could make the sex a little less overt, a bit more offstage, by changing only a few words. (Such as: "Hell, she didn't even have the homegrown fig leaf!") (Slightly less flavor, too; but if we must, we must.)

But I don't see how to take out the sex and religion. If I do, there isn't any story left.

This story is supposed to be a completely free-wheeling look at contemporary human culture from the nonhuman viewpoint of the Man from Mars (in the sense of the philosophical cliché). Under it, I take nothing for granted and am free to lambaste anything from the Girl Scouts and Mother's Apple Pie to the idea of patriotism. No sacred cows of any sort, no bows and graceful compliments to the royal box—that is the whole idea of the framework.

But, in addition to a double dozen of minor satirical slants, the two major things which I am attacking are the two biggest, fattest sacred cows of all, the two that every writer is supposed to give at least lip service to: the implicit assumptions of our Western culture concerning religion and concerning sex.

Concerning religion, our primary Western cultural assumption is the notion of a personal God. You are permitted to argue every aspect of religion but *that* one. If you do, you are a double-plus ungood crimethinker.

Concerning sex, our primary cultural assumption is that monogamy is the only acceptable pattern. A writer is permitted to write endlessly about rape, incest, adultery, and major perversion . . . provided he suggests that all of these things are always sinful or at least a social mistake—and must be paid for, either publicly or in remorse. (The thing the censors had against Lady Chatterley and her lover were not their rather tedious monosyllables, but the fact that they *liked* adultery—and got away with it—and lived happily ever after.) The whole deal is something like Communist "criticism" . . . anything and any comrade may be critized (at least theoretically) under Communism provided you do not criticize the basic Marxist assumptions.

So . . . using the freedom of the mythical man from Mars . . . I have undertaken to criticize and examine disrespectfully the two untouch-ables: monotheism and monogamy.

My book says: a personal God is unprovable, most unlikely, and *all* contemporary theology is superstitious twaddle insulting to a mature mind. But atheism and "scientific humanism" are the same sort of piffle in mirror image, and just as repugnant. Agnosticism is intellectually more acceptable but only in that it pleads ignorance, utter intellectual bankruptcy, and gives up. All the other religions, elsewhere and in the past, whether monotheistic, polytheistic, or other, are just as silly, and the very notion of "worship" is intellectually on all fours with a jungle savage's appeasing of Mumbo Jumbo. (In passing, I note that Chris-tianity is a polytheism, not a monotheism as claimed—the rabbis are right on that point—and that its most holy ceremony is ritualistic can-nibalism, right straight out of the smoky caves of our dim past. They ought to lynch me.)

But I don't offer a solution because there isn't any, not to an intel-lectually honest man. That pantheistic, mystical "Thou art God!" chorus that runs through the book is not offered as a creed but as an existen-tialist assumption of personal responsibility, devoid of all godding. It says, "Don't appeal for mercy to God the Father up in the sky, little man, because he's not at home and never was at home, and couldn't care less. What you do with yourself, whether you are happy or un-happy—live or die—is strictly your business and the universe doesn't care. In fact you may *be* the universe and the only cause of all your troubles. But, at best, the most you can hope for is comradeship with comrades no more divine (or just as divine) as you are. So quit sniv-eling and face up to it—"Thou art God!"

Concerning sex, my book says: sex is a hell of a lot of fun, not shameful in any aspect, and not a bit sacred. Monogamy is merely a social pattern useful to certain structures of society—but it is strictly a pragmatic matter, unconnected with sin . . . and a myriad other pat-terns are possible and some of them can be, under appropriate circum-stances, both more efficient and more happy-making. In fact, monogamy's sole virtue is that it provides a formula defining who has to support the offspring . . . and if another formula takes care of that practical aspect, it is seven-to-two that it will probably work better for humans, who usually are unhappy as hell if they try to practice mo-nogamy by the written rules.

The question now is not whether the ideas above are true, or just twaddle—the question is whether or not there will be any book left if I cut them out. I hardly think there will be. Not even the mild thread of action-adventure, because all of the action is instigated *by these heretical ideas*. All of it.

Mr. Cady's wish that I eliminate the first "miracle," the disappearances on pp. 123–124, causes almost as much literary difficulty. Certainly, I can rewrite that scene, exactly as he suggested . . . but where does that leave me? That scene establishes all the other miracles in the story, of which there are dozens. Now I will stipulate that "miracles" are bad copy—but if I eliminate them, I must throw away the last 700 pages of the ms.—i.e., write an entirely different story. Miracles are the "convincer" throughout. Without them the Man from Mars cannot recruit Harshaw, Ben, Patty, Dr. Nelson, not even Jill—nobody! No story.

(I thought I had picked a comparatively slide-down-easy miracle, in that I picked one which has a theoretical mathematical inherent possibility and then established its rationale later in Harshaw's study. But I'm afraid this one is like atomic power: no one but professional dreamers could believe in it until it happened. I might add that if I had trapped out that miracle with fake electronic gadgetry I could have "disappeared" an elephant without a squawk.)

All I can see to do now is to accept Mr. Cady's most gentle offer to hold off six months while we see if some other publisher will take it without changes, or with changes I think I can make.

But I shan't be surprised if nobody wants it. For the first time in my life I indulged in the luxury of writing without one eye on the taboos, the market, etc. I will be unsurprised and only moderately unhappy if it turns out that the result is unsalable.

If it can't be sold more or less as it is, then I will make a mighty effort to satisfy Mr. Cady's requirements. I don't see how, but I will certainly try. Probably I would then make a trip to New York to have one or several story conferences with him, if he will spare me the time, since he must have some idea of how he thinks this story can be salvaged—and I'm afraid that I don't.

The contract offered is gratifyingly satisfactory. But I want one change. I won't take one-half on signing, one-half on approval of ms.; they must delay the entire advance until I submit an approved manuscript. It is unfair to them to tie up $1,500 in a story which may turn out to be unpublishable. I don't care if this is the practice of the trade and that lots of authors do it; I disagree with the guild on this and think that it is a greedy habit that writers should forgo if they ever expect to be treated like business men and not children.

Please extend my warm thanks to Mr. Cady for his care and thoughtfulness. He must be a number one person—I look forward to meeting him someday.

October 31, 1960: Robert A. Heinlein to Lurton Blassingame

I have thought about your suggested changes in *The Man from Mars*. I see your point in each case and do not object to making the changes . . . but it seems to me that I should leave the present form untouched until I start to revise and cut to suit the ideas of some particular publisher. If I do it for Putnam's, then the horrendous job of meeting Mr. Cady's [*of Putnam*] requirements will automatically include all the changes you mention—in fact, most of the book will be changed beyond recognition.

But I still have a faint hope that some publisher will risk it without such drastic changes and cutting.

December 4, 1960: Robert A. Heinlein to Lurton Blassingame

Lurton, I do not think I have told you what a wonderful job I think you have done in placing this ms. I wrote the thing with my eye intentionally not on the market. For twenty years I have always had one eye on the market with the other on the copy in this mill (yes, even when I disagreed with editors or producers). But I knew that I could never get away from slick hack work, slanted at a market, unless I cut loose and ignored the market . . . and I did want to write at least one story in which I spoke freely, ignoring the length, taboos, etc.

When I finished it and reread it, I did not see how in hell you could ever sell it, and neither did Ginny. But you did. Thank you.

If this one is successful, I may try to write some more free-wheeling stories. If it flops, perhaps I will go back to doing the sort of thing I know how to tailor to the market.

January 27, 1961: Robert A. Heinlein to Lurton Blassingame

. . . I told you about a week ago that I had finished the basic cutting on *Man from Mars*. In the meantime, I have had a squad of high school girls count the manuscript, word by word, and totted up the results on an adding machine. The manuscript is now 160,083 words—and I am tempted to type those excess eighty-three words on a post-card . . .

I am a bit disappointed as my estimates as I went along had led me to believe that I would finish up at around 155,000 words and then I could even sweat off most or all of another 5,000 words and turn it over to Putnam's at 150,000, which I know would please them better. But I don't see any possibility of that now; the story is now as tight as a wedge in a green stump and, short of completely recasting it and rewriting it, I can't get it much tighter. I have rewritten and cut drastically in the middle part where Mr. Minton [at Putnam's] felt it was slow, and I have cut every word, every sentence, every paragraph which I felt could be spared in the beginning and the ending. As it is, it is cut too much in parts—the style is rather "telegraphese," somewhat jerky—and I could very handily use a couple of thousand words of "lubrication," words put back in to make the style more graceful and readable.

The truth is that it is the most complex story I have ever written, a full biography from birth to death, with the most complex plot and with the largest number of fully drawn characters. It needs to be told

Stranger in a Strange Land won the Hugo Award for Best Novel of 1962, given by the World Science Fiction Convention in Chicago.

at the length of *Anthony Adverse* (which ran 575,000 words!): I am surprised that I have managed to sweat it down to 160,000.

My typist is now completing the third quarter of the ms. She is able to work for me only evenings and weekends; if her health holds up, I expect that she will finish about 12 to 15 February. In the meantime, I will work on further cutting and revision and should be able to eliminate a few words—more than a thousand but less than five thousand. If my typist finishes on time I will expect to deliver the manuscript to you by Monday the 20th of February (I doubt if you will want to reread it, but you may want to see how I have revised the sex scene that you were bothered about). That will give Putnam's in excess of three weeks more margin on production time in order to publish on or before the Science Fiction Convention in Seattle 2–4 September 1961. Or they can, if they wish, use the three weeks to read it and bung it back to me for revision of anything they don't like—and still keep their production schedule. I can't do extensive cutting in that time but I can certainly revise a scene or two, if needed.

March 17, 1961: Robert A. Heinlein to Lurton Blassingame

I've just been talking to Mr. Cady at Putnam's. He tells me that Doubleday wants to issue my Sex and Jesus book as a SF book club choice and as an alternate for some other non-SF book club. Little as I like the Doubleday SF book club, I enthusiastically okayed this plan as it makes almost certain that Putnam's will make their nut and a bit of profit even if the trade edition doesn't do very well—which has been my principal worry. However, Mr. Cady seems to think that these book club sales will materially enhance the trade book sales—also, he seems to have great confidence in the book (more than I have)—I hope he's right.

This change in plans will result, he tells me, in the book being sold by Doubleday as their June offering, with trade book publication as soon as possible, probably early July.

The final title will be set on Monday afternoon (Cady will phone me) and, Lurton, you are invited and urged to suggest titles—direct to him is simplest. (I assume that this letter will reach you in the early Monday mail.) The titles now in the running are:
The Heretic
The Sound of His Wings (which has an SF tie-in through my "Future

History" chart without being tagged as "science fiction" in the minds of the general public. All of these titles have been picked to permit the book to be sold as a mainstream novel, "Philosophical Fantasy" or some such.)

A Sparrow Falls

Born Unto Trouble (Job 5:7)

That Forbidden Tree (Milton)

Of Good and Evil (Genesis 2:17)

EDITOR'S NOTE: *At this date, no one recalls just who came up with the* Stranger in a Strange Land *title.*

CHAPTER XV

❖

ECHOES FROM
STRANGER

❖

EDITOR'S NOTE: Putnam's sales on Stranger *were not very good during the first year after publication. It went immediately into the book club edition, a two-year contract, and there was a second two-year book club contract. In the second year following publication, it was out in a paperback edition from Avon. Sales went from humdrum to medium to spectacular. This book turned out to be a "sleeper." Only word-of-mouth advertising could have accounted for this. At this time, it has been in trade edition for many years, still selling enough copies to make it worthwhile for the publisher to keep it in print. And it still sells merrily in the paperback edition, which is now with Ace. It is currently in the sixty-fifth paperback printing. The Doubleday Science Fiction Book Club recently sent a request for another reprinting under their auspices.*

October 9, 1966: Robert A. Heinlein to Lurton Blassingame

Herewith is ——'s letter to you re dramatizing *Stranger*. I have no idea what is proper and reasonable in this matter and will continue to leave it entirely up to your judgment. But I'm beginning to think that additional rights to *Stranger*, such as stage, TV, and movies, might someday be worth something—possibly through Ned Brown, possibly through other channels. The fan mail on this book has been steadily

Cults sprang up around *Stranger in a Strange Land*, and Heinlein himself was considered to be a spiritual guru.

increasing instead of decreasing and it clearly is enjoying quite a lot of word-of-mouth advertising. I recently learned that it was considered the "New Testament"—and compulsory reading—of a far-out cult called "Kerista." (Kee-*rist*!) I don't know exactly what "Kerista" is, but its L.A. chapter offered me a $100 fee to speak. (I turned them down.) And just this past week I was amazed to discover a full-page and very laudatory review of *Stranger* in (swelp me!) a slick nudist magazine—with the review featured on the cover . . . And there is an organization in the mountain states called "Serendipity, Inc.," which has as its serious purpose the granting of scholarships—but which has taken over "water sharing" and other phrases from the book as lodge slogans, sorta. Or something. And there is this new magazine of criticism, *GROK*—I have not seen it yet but it is advertised in the *Village Voice*. And almost daily I am getting letters from people who insist on looking at me as some sort of a spiritual adviser. (I fight shy of them!) All in all, the ripples are spreading amazingly—and Cady may be right in thinking that the book could be exploited in other media. (I'll settle for cash at the bedside; I want no part of the cults.)

November 6, 1966: Robert A. Heinlein to Lurton Blassingame

I think I mentioned to you that the Esalen Institute wants me to lead a seminar late in June on "Religion in the Space Age," along with Alan Watts, the Zen Buddhist writer, and an Episcopalian priest. It takes just one weekend, and the place (Big Sur) is near here, and the fee ($500) is satisfactory. Nevertheless I probably will not accept, as I do not see how I could take part without mortally offending both the priest and the Zen Buddhist. I'll negotiate it directly by telephone to the director, as I am reluctant to state my real misgivings bluntly in a letter.

December 22, 1966: Lurton Blassingame to Virginia Heinlein

. . . and to receive the *Grok* buttons. Might be news release to give additional stimulus to book.

April 15, 1967: Robert A. Heinlein to Lurton Blassingame

More about *Stranger*—
My brother Rex queried the shopkeeper from whom he had purchased several sorts of *Stranger* buttons, was told: "There are about a dozen different suppliers." He went on to say that one of them was a girl who was working her way through college making these buttons (no doubt other sorts than *Stranger* buttons).

This afternoon (now Sunday evening) a sculptor, —— of Los Gatos, called on us—to show us a figure he had just completed in bronze of the death of the Martian named Smith. He asked permission to bring it over at once as he was taking it to his agent in San Francisco in negotiating a commission for an heroic-size crucifixion job for a church. (—— is a successful sculptor, not a starving artist.) But [he] wanted me to see it first.

A young woman who came with him asked me where I had gotten the word *grok*—no, she had not read the book, *had not been able to lay hands on a copy* [my emphasis added] . . . but that she knew what it meant as "everybody uses it now."

January 26, 1967: Lurton Blassingame to Robert A. Heinlein

Checking on *Grok* magazine.

February 28, 1967: Lurton Blassingame to Robert A. Heinlein

In the 2/19 issue of the *New York Times Book Review*, there is an article you may want to see—"Where the Action Is." It mention(s) *Stranger* and *Grok*. Reference seems responsible for stirring Hollywood interest. Another call asking if *Stranger* rights available.

March 14, 1967: Lurton Blassingame to Robert A. Heinlein

Have two issues of *Grok*.

April 28, 1968: Robert A. Heinlein to Lurton Blassingame

I enclose a clipping sent to me from Toronto—please return for my *Stranger* file. "Fair Use" of course—but that book *must* have made a wide impression if a telephone company in Canada makes this use of a neologism from it. (And when I think how Putnam continues to refuse to reissue a hardcover of it, I get so annoyed I need a Miltown. Damn it, they should at least arrange a Grosset and Dunlap reprint; I get regular inquiries about where to buy it in hardcover. He's missing a lot of library sales, too.)

May 23, 1968: Robert A. Heinlein to Lurton Blassingame

Since I sent you that Canadian telephone ad I have run into three more uses of *grok*—one in a short story in *Playboy*, simply as a part of dialog with no explanation, same for a poem, and a report of a shop in Florida: "We Grok Bookshop." Oh, well, while it doesn't pay royalties, it does interest me to see this neologism spread. But the darnedest thing so far is an announcement in the UCLA *Daily Bruin* concerning "Experimental College Classes—Spring 1968" with one course billed as "J. D. Salinger, Robt. Heinlein, Lawrence Ferlinghetti and Other Personal Gurus—"!!! And I'm such a square I don't even know who the third guru is. Nor does Ginny. However, I'm new to the guru business.

January 23, 1967: Robert A. Heinlein to Lurton Blassingame

Did I tell you that [Dr.] Jack Williamson is using *Stranger* as a study text in his class in SF at U of E. New Mexico? Quote: "I'm launching new courses in linguistics and modern grammar and another in the factual literature of science. . . . (in my SF class) and we are now reading *Stranger in a Strange Land*. I was a little afraid that some of my students might not be sufficiently sophisticated for it, but the response so far is good—some class members feel that it is more successful than Huxley's *Brave New World*, which we have just finished."

Did I mention in some other letter that Stanford now offers a course in SF? Apparently SF is beginning to be accepted as a respectable genre

of serious literature. It is a pleasant feeling—but I have to keep reminding myself that seeing my name in print is nothing; it is seeing it on a
check that counts. It is still the clown business; the object is to entertain the cash customer—I shall simply have to try harder than ever.

February 3, 1967: Robert A. Heinlein to Lurton Blassingame

Did I give you the impression that the principal interest in
Stranger was from teenagers? It may be, but I hope not and do not
think so. I might be forced to drink hemlock for "teaching that the
worse is the better part and corrupting the youth of the land." *Stranger*
is definitely an adult book, and the comments in it on both sex and
religion are such that I think it would be imprudent to attempt any sort
of publicity which attempts to tie this book with teenagers.

Lurton, I myself am not the least afraid of corrupting the teenagers
of this country; it can't be done. They are far more sophisticated, as a
group, than are their parents. They take up in junior high school smoking, drinking, fellatio, cunnilingus, and soixante-neuf, and move on to
coition, marijuana, and goof balls during senior high school, then get
the Pill and join the New Left when they enter college—*or at the very
least are exposed to these things at these ages and sometimes earlier.* Plus
LSD and other drugs if they wish. Shock them or corrupt them—
impossible! If they refrain, it is voluntary, not because they haven't been
exposed.

But their parents rarely know this—parents are always certain that it
is the wild, beat crowd on the other side of town, not *their* little dar-
lings! So, while I do not think *Stranger* can corrupt any reader, no
matter how young—on the contrary I think it is a highly moral book—
I think also that it would be impolitic to exploit it as a book for teenagers.

November 17, 1967: Robert A. Heinlein to Lurton Blassingame

I finally heard from the University of Wisconsin . . . This was
the bid I heard about through —— and concerning which I phoned
you. I am about to turn it down—regretfully, since Oshkosh is so close
by. But what they want me to do is lecture about *Stranger in a Strange
Land*. I decided years ago *never* to discuss my own works on a platform
. . . and I think the pragmatic reasons behind this decision apply especially strongly to *Stranger*. A writer looks pretty durn silly "explain-

ing" his stories. He said what he had to say in the ms.—or should have. *Stranger* is a fairy tale; if it amuses the reader, he has received what he paid for. If he gets something more out of it, that's a free bonus. But I'm durned if I'll "explain" it.

(I wonder if John Barth ever "explains" *Giles Goat Boy*? If he does, I'll bet he has his forked tongue in both cheeks and intentionally leaves the listener more bemused than ever. I was much impressed and enormously amused by *Giles*, and now I want to obtain and read and keep all his other fictional works—now that I can afford things other than building materials. On the other hand, Barth's fiction is not for Ginny; she lives life in simple declarative sentences with no veiled allusions, and she wants her fiction the same way.)

I am turning down the bid from Cornell; I turned down one yesterday from U of California; and I am turning down as they come in numerous lesser bids mostly from high schools here and there. Quite aside from the nuisance of speaking in public, this is not a year when I want to cope extemporaneously with the questions period which usually follows a platform talk—undeclared wars, race riots, the drop-out generation, etc., are all matters I prefer not to deal with orally and in public; I find these matters extremely complex and am not sure of the wisdom of my opinions.

But I did find it expedient to accept an invitation for March 30 for the Monterey Bay Area Libraries Book Festival; librarians are a special category. I feel that I have to do it once, for the local libraries—then next time I can point out that I already have, and sorry, but this year I'm tied up. I waived their fee, however, as I prefer doing it free to accepting a small fee ($50)—so that I can continue to tell others that sure, I speak in public—but I'm a pro and my fees are horrendously high.

MANSON CASE

January 7, 1970: Virginia Heinlein to Lurton Blassingame

Some weeks ago, a fan letter came in from the jail in Independence, California. In a burst of generosity, Robert tried to do something about this girl who'd written him. It turned out that she was one of the Manson family. So if we're knifed in our beds like Sharon Tate, it's because of three letters from members of the family. Just tell the police. I'm leaving these notices everywhere I can, in hopes of preventing anything from happening.

PLAYBOY INTERVIEW

January 16, 1970: Virginia Heinlein and Robert A. Heinlein to Lurton Blassingame

Will you also please tell Mr. [Hugh] Hefner that the *only* reason Robert agreed to be interviewed was *not publicity* for himself, but the offer of a forum to boost the space program. Publication of this interview in an early issue might have helped. As it is, the space program is in ruins, and Hefner is attempting to make something of what might have been by the use of *Stranger* and the Manson case. We will not go along with this. He has not bought himself a tame rabbit by that contribution to the Ed White Memorial Fund. He can take his [magazine] and stuff it, having first folded it until it is all corners. Under no condition will we make any public statement about the Manson case and *Stranger*. We consider Mr. Hefner's suggestion very much out of line and an invasion of our privacy. It is not a matter of *reluctance* to discuss Robert's work, but a downright refusal to do so, which has been a policy of his for a very long time.

November 10, 1970: Virginia Heinlein to Lurton Blassingame

Believe this if you can—*Stranger* is on the Women's Lib reading list!

May 4, 1971: Lurton Blassingame to Virginia Heinlein

Doesn't think anything can be done about the Valentine Smith company. Wishes they would put their letterhead and all press releases that they're using name "from the character created by Robert A. Heinlein in *Stranger in a Strange Land*."

EDITOR'S NOTE: In 1971, a fan group that based many of its philosophies on Stranger in a Strange Land *wrote to Heinlein asking permission to use material from the book. Permission was not granted. Later, a member of that group wrote to Heinlein asking why he was unsympathetic to its aims. Here is his reply.*

January 20, 1972: Robert A. Heinlein to a Reader

Facts:

1. The last time I was present at any organized SF fandom meeting was at Seattle in 1961 plus a very brief appearance at Chicago in 1962 to accept the Hugo for *Stranger*—brief because I showed up at the last minute, having been busy at NASA Houston on some writing for the Gemini program. *Stranger* was published in 1961. If there were any "nests" or such by Labor Day 1962, I was unaware of them. My contact with organized fandom since that day has been zero.

2. Before 1962 my contact with organized fandom was slight. I went several times to meetings of the LASFS [Los Angeles Science Fiction Society] in 1939–40 and went to the convention in 1940 or '41. Check: 1941, at Denver, as I recall now that I was in the east at that time in 1940. After 1940 the next contact that I recall was (I believe) in 1958— a meeting in Newark—then again at Chicago in 1960, to receive a Hugo. I think that sums up the total of my contacts with organized fandom, although I may have forgotten some casual appearance, as the period spans thirty-three years and I kept no records on it. But I am *certain* that my last appearance at a meeting was ten years ago.

3. Contacts with individuals, fans of SF who may or may not have been part of organized fandom: There have been many of these, by letter, in my home, in other people's homes, or elsewhere. There have been more fan contacts in the past than in recent years, because of pressure of work and loss of time caused by illness. In many cases I do not know whether a stranger I have met (in person or by letter) is or is not a member of organized fandom. In some cases I've learned it later (too late!) through learning that a private letter of mine has been published in one of those fan magazines, or have found that casual, social remarks have been treated, without my consent or review, as an "interview" and published in a garbled form. . . .

4. As a result of the above we have become somewhat more cautious

in recent years in our social contacts and in the letters we write, especially as the pressure from strangers has become much greater. I have to live behind a locked gate and with an unlisted phone to get any work done at all—and this is a hell of a note as my wife and I are by nature quite gregarious and social. Mrs. Heinlein usually answers and signs all of the mail, which tends to discourage the incipient "pen pals" who would, if allowed, take up all my time and leave none for writing. A rare exception, such as your letter, I answer myself. We necessarily find our social life among people who don't read science fiction.

5. All of the above adds up to this: There are very, very few people in organized fandom who know anything at all about me in the sense of knowing me personally or in being privy to my private opinions, tastes, or habits. My published works are widespread and anyone can read them. The public facts about my life are in several reference books in most public libraries. But a member of science fiction fandom is most unlikely to know any more about me than you do, and if he claims otherwise, he is almost certainly talking through his hat.

6. But I am repeatedly amazed at the number of people who claim to be "experts" on me. (One of them even wrote an entire book about me. I have never met him in my life.)

7. I have never expressed "antagonism" or hostility to "nests" or "water-brotherhoods." This is sheer fabrication. I would like to throw such a lie into the teeth of anyone saying so, if I knew who he was.

8. On the contrary, a number of "nests" have indeed gotten into contact with me. I have treated them with politeness. I have standing invitations to visit them. I think I am on good terms with every such organization which has taken the trouble to get into touch with me. If you have any specific data to the contrary, I would like to hear it, in detail. (But I have no way to deal with malicious allegations from faceless, nameless strangers.)

Stranger: It is a work of fiction in parable form. It is not a "put-on" unless you choose to classify *every* work of fiction as such. Who are these persons who allege this? I would like an opportunity to face up to one or more of them . . . as this allegation has come back to me often enough to cause me to think that someone has been spreading it systematically and possibly with malice. But the allegation always reaches me at least secondhand and never with the name of the person. Will you tell me where *you* got this allegation? I would like to track down this "Scarlet Pimpernel" and get him to hold still long enough to ask him what he is up to and why.

Now, for some background on *Stranger* and my stories in general: I write for the following reasons—

1. To support myself and my family;
2. To entertain my readers;
3. And, if possible, to cause my readers to *think*.

The first two of these reasons are indispensable, and constitute, together, a commonplace market transaction. I have always had to work for a living, for myself and now for my dependents, and I come from a poor, country family—root, hog, or die. I have worked at many things, but I discovered, somewhat by accident, that I could produce a salable commodity—entertainment in the form of fiction. I don't know why I have this talent; no other member of my family or relatives seems to have it. But I got into it for a reason that many writers have—it was what I could do at the time, i.e., I have been ill for long periods throughout my life, and writing is something a person can do when he is not physically able to take a 9-to-5 job. (Someday I would like to find time to do an essay on this. The cases range from blind Homer to consumptive R. L. Stevenson and are *much* more numerous than English professors seem to be aware of.)

But if a writer does not entertain his readers, all he is producing is paper dirty on one side. I must always bear in mind that my prospective reader could spend his recreation money on beer rather than on my stories; I have to be aware every minute that I am competing for beer money—and that the customer does not have to buy. If I produced, let us say, potatoes or beef, I could be sure that my product had some value in the market. But a story that the customers do not enjoy reading is worth *nothing*.

So, when anyone asks me why I write, if it is a quick answer, standing up, I simply say, "For money." Any other short answer is dishonest—and any writer who forgets that his prime purpose is to wangle, say 95 cents out of a customer who *need not buy at all* simply does not get published. He is not a writer; he just thinks he is.

(Oh, surely, one hears a lot of crap about "art" and "self-expression," and "duty to mankind"—but when it comes down to the crunch, there your book is, on the newsstands, along with hundreds of others with just as pretty covers—and the customer does not have to buy. If a writer fails to entertain, he fails to put food on the table—and there is no unemployment insurance for free-lance writers.)

(Even a wealthy writer has this necessity to be entertaining. Oh, he could indulge in vanity publication at his own expense—but who reads a vanity publication? One's mother, maybe.)

That covers the first two reasons: I write for money because I have a household to support and in order to earn that money I must entertain the reader.

The third reason is more complex. A writer can afford to indulge in it *only* if he clears the first two hurdles. I have written almost every sort of thing—filler paragraphs, motion picture and TV scripts, poetry, technical reports, popular journalistic nonfiction, detective stories, love stories, adventure stories, etc.—and I have been paid for 99% of what I have written.

But most of the categories above bored me. I had enough skill to make them pay but I really did not enjoy the work. I found that what I did enjoy and did best was speculative fiction. I do not think that this is just a happy coincidence; I suspect that, with most people, the work they do best is the work they enjoy.

By the time I wrote *Stranger* I had enough skill in how to entertain a reader and a solid enough commercial market to risk taking a flyer, a fantasy speculation a bit farther out than I had usually done in the past. My agent was not sure of it, neither was my wife, nor my publisher, but I felt sure that I would sell at least well enough that the publisher would not lose money on it—would "make his nut."

I was right; it did catch hold. Its entertainment values were sufficient to carry the parable, even if it was read strictly for entertainment.

But I thought that the parables in it would take hold, too, at least for some readers. They did. Some readers (many, I would say) have told me that they have read this fantasy three, four, five or more times—in which case, it can't be the story line; there is no element of surprise left in the story line in a work of fiction read over and over again; it has to be something more.

Well, what was I trying to *say* in it?

I was asking questions.

I was *not* giving answers. I was trying to shake the reader loose from some preconceptions and induce him to think for himself, along new and fresh lines. In consequence, each reader gets something different out of that book *because he himself supplies the answers.*

If I managed to shake him loose from some prejudice, preconception, or unexamined assumption, that was all I intended to do. A rational human being does not need answers, spoon-fed to him on "faith"; he needs questions to worry over—serious ones. The quality of the answers then depends on *him* . . . and he may revise those answers several times in the course of a long life, (hopefully) getting a little closer to the truth each time. But I would never undertake to be a "Prophet," handing out neatly packaged answers to lazy minds.

(For some of the more important unanswered questions in *Stranger* see chapter 33, especially page 344 of the hardcover, the paragraph starting: "All names belong in the hat, Ben.")

Starship Troopers is loaded with unanswered questions, too. Many people rejected that book with a cliché—"fascist," or "militaristic." They can't read or won't read; it is neither. It is a dead serious (but incomplete) inquiry into *why* men fight. Since men *do* fight, it is a question well worth asking.

My latest book, *I Will Fear No Evil*, is even more loaded with serious, unanswered questions—perhaps too laden; the story line sags a little. But the questions are dead serious—because, if they remain unanswered, we wind up dead. It does not affect me personally too much, at least not in this life, as I will probably be dead before the present trends converge in major catastrophe. Nevertheless, I worry about them. I think we are in a real bind . . . and that the answers are not to be found in simplistic "nature communes," nor in "Zero Population Growth," which does not embrace the entire globe. There may be *no* answers fully satisfactory . . . and even incomplete answers will be very difficult.

I find that I have written an essay to myself rather than a letter. Forgive me—perhaps I have reached the age at which one maunders. But I hope I have convinced you that *Stranger* is dead serious . . . as *questions*. Serious, nontrivial questions, on which a man might spend a lifetime. (And I almost have.)

But anyone who takes that book as *answers* is cheating himself. It is an invitation to think—not to believe. Anyone who takes it as a license to screw as he pleases is taking a risk; Mrs. Grundy is not dead. Or any other sharp affront to the contemporary culture done publicly—there are stern warnings in it about the dangers involved. Certainly "Do as

thou wilt is the whole of the Law" is correct when looked at properly—
in fact, it is a law of nature, not an injunction, nor a permission. But it
is necessary to remember that it applies to everyone—including lynch
mobs. The Universe is what it is, and it never forgives mistakes—not
even ignorant ones . . .

❖

AFTERWORD

❖

Before the cut version of *I Will Fear No Evil* was ready for publication, Robert was taken ill. For two years he was laid up with various illnesses and operations. At last, in 1972, he was well enough and very eager to begin writing again.

His next book was *Time Enough for Love*.

In addition to changes in the times and customs, Robert now had a reputation that allowed him to do such books as he preferred to do. It is possible that, at least in part, *Stranger* had had some effects upon the sexual revolution of the sixties and seventies. It was in tune with the moods of the times. So his publishers did not object to the length of *Time Enough for Love*, and one thing I found curious—there was no objection at all to the incest scenes. Not even reviewers mentioned it.

The following two years were mostly taken up with study of advances in physical and biological sciences. How could one write science fiction without keeping up with what was being discovered in those fields? These studies were undertaken for two articles for the *Britannica Compton Yearbook:* "Dirac, Antimatter and You," and "Are you a 'Rare Blood.' "

Another serious illness occurred in 1978. Following his recuperation from that, Robert went to his computer and wrote *The Number of the Beast*. Aside from a very few flags on the copy-edited manuscript, he was asked to cut by 2,000 words (!) out of an estimated 200,000 words. That was, of course, an easy task.

Expanded Universe followed, at the behest of James Baen. To our surprise, this book generated far more mail than any other book Robert

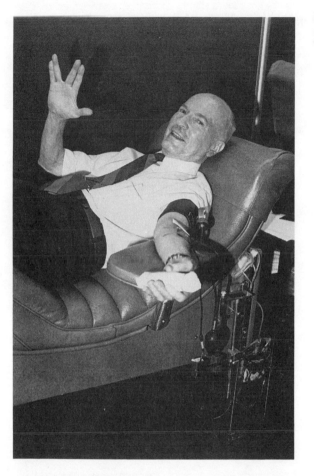

In 1977, Heinlein organized a major blood drive among science fiction fans.

had ever written. For two years, I was tied to the computer answering the fan mail which resulted from its publication.

In 1981, at seventy-four years of age, Robert decided that he would no longer do any of the special little tasks which being a well-known writer entails: no more speeches (even to librarians), no more appearances at conventions—his health would not permit the pressure. He would simply write the books he wanted to write.

So he wrote *Friday*, then *Job*, *The Cat Who Walks through Walls*, and his final book, *To Sail Beyond the Sunset*. Each of these books differed from anything he had previously done, and some displayed new techniques he had been inventing.

To Sail was published on Robert's 80th birthday in 1987, by special arrangement with his publisher. The only further item Robert wrote was the foreword for Ted Sturgeon's novel *Godbody*. While contract negotiations for *To Sail* were still going on, Robert came down with what was to be his final illness. For almost two years, he hovered between illness and frail health, but finally succumbed on May 8, 1988.

APPENDICES

APPENDIX A

❖

CUTS IN
Red Planet

❖

[Alice Dalgliesh, the editor at Scribner's, objected to anything that might be construed as having some sexual connotations and also to the use of guns by youngsters, as well as other matters. As a result, Heinlein was forced to make a number of cuts in his original manuscript. Some of these are shown here. Chapter and paragraph numbers refer to *Red Planet* as originally published.]

Between Chapter II, paragraph 13 and Chapter II, middle of paragraph 23:

The second generation trooped out. Phyllis said, "Take the charges out of your gun, Jimmy, and let me practice with it."

"You're too young for a gun."

"Pooh! I can outshoot you." This was very nearly true and not to be borne; Phyllis was two years younger than Jim and female besides.

"Girls are just target shooters. If you saw a water-seeker, you'd scream."

"I would, huh? We'll go hunting together and I'll bet you two credits that I score first."

"You haven't got two credits."

"I have, too."

"Then how was it you couldn't lend me a half credit yesterday?"

252

Phyllis changed the subject. Jim hung up his weapon in his cupboard and locked it. Presently they were back in the living room, to find that their father was home and dinner ready.

Phyllis waited for a lull in grown-up talk to say, "Daddy?"

"Yes, Puddin'? What is it?"

"Isn't it about time I had a pistol of my own?"

"Eh? Plenty of time for that later. You keep up your target practice."

"But, look, Daddy—Jim's going away and that means that Ollie can't ever go outside unless you or mother have time to take him. If I had a gun, I could help out."

Mr. Marlowe wrinkled his brow. "You've got a point. You've passed all your tests, haven't you?"

"You know I have!"

"What do you think, my dear? Shall we take Phyllis down to city hall and see if they will license her?"

Before Mrs. Marlowe could answer Doctor MacRae muttered something into his plate. The remark was forceful and probably not polite.

"Eh? What did you say, Doctor?"

"I said," answered MacRae, "that I was going to move to another planet. At least that's what I meant."

"Why? What's wrong with this one? In another twenty years we'll have it fixed up good as new. You'll be able to walk outside without a mask."

"Sir, it is not the natural limitations of this globe that I object to; it is the pantywaist nincompoops who rule it— These ridiculous regulations offend me. That a free citizen should have to go before a committee, hat in hand, and pray for permission to bear arms—fantastic! Arm your daughter, sir, and pay no attention to petty bureaucrats."

Jim's father stirred his coffee. "I'm tempted to. I really don't know why the Company set up such rules in the first place."

"Pure copy-cattism. The swarming beehives back on Earth have similar childish rules; the fat clerks that decide these things cannot imagine any other conditions. This is a frontier community; it should be free of such."

"Mmmm . . . probably you're right, Doctor. Can't say that I disagree with you, but I'm so busy trying to get on with my job that I really don't have time to worry about politics. It's easier to comply than to fight a test case." Jim's father turned to his wife. "If it's all right with you, my dear, could you find time to arrange for a license for Phyllis?"

"Why, yes," she answered doubtfully, "if you really think she's old enough." The doctor muttered something that combined "Danegeld" and the "Boston Tea Party" in the same breath. Phyllis answered:

"Sure, I'm old enough, Mother. I'm a better shot than Jimmy."

Jim said, "You're crazy as a spin bug!"

"Mind your manners, Jim," his father cautioned. "We don't speak that way to ladies."

"Was she talking like a lady? I ask you, Dad."

"You are bound to assume that she is one. Drop the matter. What were you saying, Doctor?"

"Eh? Nothing that I should have been saying, I'm sure."

Between Chapter VIII, paragraph 29 and Chapter VIII, paragraph 3:

"Sure." Jim got up. In so doing he woke Willis, who extended his eyes, sized up the situation, and greeted them. Jim picked him up, scratched him, and said, "What time did you come in, you tramp?" then suddenly added, "Hey!"

" 'Hey' what?" asked Frank.

"Well, would you look at *that*?" Jim pointed at the tumbled silks.

Frank got up and joined him. "Look at what? Oh—"

In the hollow in which Willis had been resting were a dozen small, white spheroids, looking like so many golf balls.

"What do you suppose they are?" asked Jim.

Frank studied them closely. "Jim," he said slowly, "I think you'll just have to face it. Willis isn't a boy; he's a she."

"Huh? Oh, no!"

"Willis good boy," Willis said defensively.

"See for yourself," Frank went on to Jim. "Those are eggs. If Willis didn't lay them, you must have."

Jim looked bewildered, then turned to Willis. "Willis, did you lay those eggs? Did you?"

"Eggs?" said Willis. "What Jim boy say?"

Jim set him down by the nest and pointed. "Did you lay those?"

Willis looked at them, then figuratively shrugged his shoulders and washed his hands of the whole matter. He waddled away. His manner seemed to say that if Jim chose to make a fuss over some eggs or whatever that just happened to show up in the bed, well, that was Jim's business; Willis would have none of it.

"You won't get anything out of him," Frank commented. "I suppose you realize this makes you a grandfather, sort of"

"Don't be funny!"

"Okay, forget the eggs. When do we eat? I'm starved."

Jim gave the eggs an accusing glance and got busy on the commissary. While they were eating Gekko came in. They exchanged grave greetings, then the Martian seemed about to settle himself for another long period of silent sociability—when he caught sight of the eggs.

Neither of the boys had ever seen a Martian hurry before, nor show any signs of excitement. Gekko let out a deep snort and left the room at once, to return promptly with as many companions as could crowd into the room. They all talked at once and paid no attention to the boys.

"What goes on here?" asked Frank, as he crowded against a wall and peered through a thicket of legs.

"Blessed if I know."

After a while they calmed down a little. One of the larger Martians gathered up the eggs with exaggerated care and clutched them to him. Another picked up Willis and they all trooped out.

Jim stood hesitantly at the door and watched them disappear.

In place of text between Chapter XIII, paragraph 6 and Chapter XIII, paragraph 17:

"Certainly, certainly," agreed MacRae, "but speaking nonprofessionally, I'd rather see the no-good so-and-so hang. Paranoia is a disorder contracted only by those of fundamentally bad character."

"Now, Doctor," protested Rawlings.

"That's my opinion," insisted MacRae, "and I've seen a lot of cases, in and out of hospitals."

Insert to Chapter XIV, paragraph 49:

"Everything about Mars is startling. Another thing: we've never been able to find anything resembling sex on this planet—various sorts of specie conjugation, yes, but no sex. It appears to me that we missed it. I think that all the nymph Martians, the bouncers, are female; all of the adults are male. They change. I use the terms for want of better ones, of course. But if my theory is . . .

After the current ending:

Jim took it well. He accepted MacRae's much expurgated explanation and nodded. "I guess if Willis has to hibernate, well, that's that.

255

When they come for him, I won't make any fuss. It was just that Howe and Beecher didn't have any *right* to take him."

"That's the slant, son. But it's right for him to go with the Martians because they know how to take care of him, when he needs it. You saw that when you were with them."

"Yes." Jim added, "Can I visit him?"

"He won't know you. He'll be asleep."

"Well—look, when he wakes up, will he know me?"

MacRae looked grave. He had asked the old one the same question. "Yes," he answered truthfully, "he'll have all his memory intact." He did not give Jim the rest of the answer—that the transition period would last more than forty Earth years.

"Well, that won't be so bad. I'm going to be awfully busy in school right now, anyhow."

"That's the spirit."

Jim looked up Frank and they went to their old room, vacant of womenfolk at the moment. Jim cradled Willis in his arms and told Frank what Doc had told him. Willis listened, but the conversation was apparently over the little Martian's depth; Willis made no comment.

Presently Willis became bored with it and started to sing. The selection was the latest Willis had heard, the tango Frank had presented to Jim: *¿Quién es la Señorita?*

When it was over Frank said, "You know, Willis sounds exactly like a girl when he sings that."

Jim chuckled. "*¿Quién es la Señorita*, Willis?"

Willis managed to look indignant. "Willis fine boy!" she insisted.

APPENDIX B

❖

Postlude to *Podkayne*
of Mars—Original Version

❖

[The editor at Putnam's was unhappy with Heinlein's original ending for *Podkayne of Mars*. Heinlein therefore made some changes to satisfy his requirements. In the published version, Podkayne survives; in Heinlein's original, she did not.]

POSTLUDE

I guess I had better finish this.

My sister got right to sleep after I rehearsed her in what we were going to do. I stretched out on the floor but didn't go right to sleep. I'm a worrier, she isn't. I reviewed my plans, trying to make them tighter. Then I slept.

I've got one of those built-in alarm clocks and I woke just when I planned to, an hour before dawn. Any later and there would be too much chance that Jojo might be loose, any earlier and there would be too much time in the dark. The Venus bush is chancy even when you can see well; I didn't want Poddy to step into something sticky, or step on something that would turn and bite her leg off. Nor me, either.

But we had to risk the bush, or stay and let old Gruesome kill us at her convenience. The first was a sporting chance; the latter was a dead certainty, even though I had a terrible time convincing Poddy that Mrs. Grew would kill us. Poddy's greatest weakness—the really soft place in her head, she's not too stupid otherwise—is her almost total inability to grasp that some people are as bad as they are. Evil. Poddy never has understood evil. Naughtiness is about as far as her imagination reaches.

But I understand evil, I can get right inside the skull of a person like Mrs. Grew and understand how she thinks.

Perhaps you infer from this that I am evil, or partly so. All right, want to make something of it? Whatever I am, I knew Mrs. Grew was evil before we ever left the Tricorn . . . when Poddy (and even Girdie!) thought the slob was just too darling for words.

I don't trust a person who laughs when there is nothing to laugh about. Or is good-natured no matter what happens. If it's that perfect, it's an act, a phony. So I watched her . . . and cheating at solitaire wasn't the only giveaway.

So between the bush and Mrs. Grew, I chose the bush, both for me and my sister.

Unless the air car was there and we could swipe it. This would be a mixed blessing, as it would mean two of them to cope with, them armed and us not. (I don't count a bomb as an arm, you can't point it at a person's head.)

Before I woke Poddy I took care of that alate pseudo-simian, that "fairy." Vicious little beast. I didn't have a gun. But I didn't really want one at that point; they understand about guns and are hard to hit, they'll dive on you at once.

Instead I had shoe trees in my spare shoes, elastic bands around my spare clothes, and more elastic bands in my pockets, and several two-centimeter steel ball bearings.

Shift two wing nuts, and the long parts of the shoe trees become a steel fork. Add elastic bands and you have a sling shot. And don't laugh at a slingshot; many a sand rat has kept himself fed with only a sling shot. They are silent and you usually get your ammo back.

I aimed almost three times as high as I would at home, to allow for the local gravity, and got it right on the sternum, knocked it off its perch—crushed the skull with my heel and gave it an extra twist for the nasty bite on Poddy's arm. The young one started to whine, so I pushed the carcass over in the corner, somewhat out of sight, and put the cub on it. It shut up. I took care of all this before I woke Poddy because I knew she had sentimental fancies about these "fairies" and I didn't want her jittering and maybe grabbing my elbow. As it was— clean and fast.

She was still snoring, so I slipped off my shoes and made a fast reconnoiter.

Not so good— Our local witch was already up and reaching for her broom; in a few minutes she would be unlocking Jojo if she hadn't already. I didn't have a chance to see if the sky car was outside; I did well not to get caught. I hurried back and woke Poddy.

"Pod!" I whispered. "You awake?"

"Yes."

"Wide awake? You've got to do your act, right now. Make it loud and make it good."

"Check."

"Help me up on the perch. Can your sore arm take it?"

She nodded, slid quickly off the bed and took position at the door, hands ready. I grabbed her hands, bounced to her shoulders, steadied, and she grabbed my calves as I let go her hands—and then I was up on the perch, over the door. I waved her on.

Poddy went running out the door, screaming, "Mrs. Grew! MRS. GREW! Help, help! My brother!" She did make it good.

And came running back in almost at once with Mrs. Grew puffing after her.

I landed on Gruesome's shoulders, knocking her to the floor and knocking her gun out of her hand. I twisted and snapped her neck before she could catch her breath.

Pod was right on the ball, I have to give her credit. She had that gun before it stopped sliding. Then she held it, looking dazed.

I took it carefully from her. "Grab your purse. We go, right now! Stick close behind me."

Jojo *was* loose, I had cut it too fine. He was in the living room, looking, I guess, to see what the noise was about. I shot him.

Then I looked for the air car while keeping the gun ready for the driver. No sign of either one—and I didn't know whether to groan or cheer. I was all keyed up to shoot him but maybe he would have shot me first. But a car would have been mighty welcome compared with heading into the bush.

I almost changed my plan at that point and maybe I should have. Kept together, I mean, and headed straight north for the ring road.

It was the gun that decided me. Poddy could protect herself with it— and I would just be darn careful what I stepped on or in. I handed it to her and told her to move slowly and carefully until there was more light—but get going!

She was wobbling the gun around. "But, Brother, I've never shot anybody!"

"Well, you can if you have to."

"I guess so."

"Nothing to it. Just point it at 'em and press the button. Better use both hands. And don't shoot unless you really need to."

"All right."

I smacked her behind. "Now get going. See you later."

And I got going. I looked behind once, but she was already vanished in the smog. I put a little distance between me and the house, just in case, then concentrated on approximating course west.

And I got lost. That's all. I needed that tracker but I had figured I could get along without it and Pod had to have it. I got hopelessly lost. There wasn't breeze enough for me to tell anything by wetting my finger and that polarized light trick for finding the Sun is harder than you would think. Hours after I should have reached the ring road I was still skirting boggy places and open water and trying to keep from being somebody's lunch.

And suddenly there was the most dazzling light possible and I went down flat and stayed there with my eyes buried in my arm and started to count.

I wasn't hurt at all. The blast wave covered me with mud and the noise was pretty rough but I was well outside the real trouble. Maybe half an hour later I was picked up by a cop car.

Certainly, I should have disarmed that bomb. I had intended to, if everything went well; it was just meant to be a "Samson in the Temple" stunt if things turned out dry. A last resort.

Maybe I should have stopped to disarm it as soon as I broke old Gruesome's neck—and maybe Jojo would have caught both of us if I had and him still with a happy-dust hangover. Anyhow I didn't and then I was very busy shooting Jojo and deciding what to do and telling Poddy how to use that gun and getting her started. I didn't think about the bomb until I was several hundred meters from the house—and I certainly didn't want to go back then, even if I could have found it again in the smog, which is doubtful.

But apparently Poddy did just that. Went back to the house, I mean. She was found later that day, about a kilometer from the house, outside the circle of total destruction—but caught by the blast.

With a live baby fairy in her arms—her body had protected it; it doesn't appear to have been hurt at all.

That's why I think she went back to the house. I don't *know* that this baby fairy is the one she called "Ariel." It might have been one that she picked up in the bush. But that doesn't seem at all likely; a wild one would have clawed her and its parents would have torn her to pieces.

I think she intended to save that baby fairy all along and decided not to mention it to me. It is just the kind of sentimental stunt that Poddy would do. She knew I was going to have to kill the adult—and she never said a word against that; Pod could always be sensible when absolutely necessary.

Then in the excitement of breaking out she forgot to grab it, just as I forgot to disarm the bomb after we no longer needed it. So she went back for it.

And lost the inertial tracker, somehow. At least it wasn't found on her or near her. Between the gun and her purse and the baby fairy and the tracker she must have dropped it in a bog. Must be, because she had plenty of time to go back and still get far away from the house. She should have been ten kilometers away by then, so she must have lost the tracker fairly soon and walked in a circle.

I told Uncle Tom all about it and was ready to tell the Corporation people, Mr. Cunha and so forth, and take my medicine. But Uncle told me to keep my mouth shut. He agreed that I had fubbed it, mighty dry indeed—but so had he—and so had everybody. He was gentle with me. I wish he had hit me.

I'm sorry about Poddy. She gave me some trouble from time to time, with her bossy ways and her illogical ideas—but just the same I'm sorry.

I wish I knew how to cry.

Her little recorder was still in her purse and part of the tape could be read. Doesn't mean much, though; she doesn't tell what she did, she was babbling, sort of:

"—very dark where I'm going. No man is an island, complete in himself. Remember that, Clarkie. Oh, I'm sorry I fubbed it but remember that; it's important. They all have to be cuddled sometimes. My shoulder— Saint Podkayne! Saint Podkayne, are you listening?" UnkaTom, Mother, Daddy—is anybody listening? Do listen, please, because this is important. I love—"

It cuts off there. So we don't know whom she loved.

Everybody maybe.

Mr. Cunha made them hold the *Tricorn* and now Uncle Tom and I are on our way again. The baby fairy is still alive and Dr. Torland says it doesn't have radiation sickness. I call it "Ariel" and I guess I'll be taking care of it a long time; they say these fairies live as long as we do. It is taking to shipboard life all right but it gets lonely and has to be held and cuddled or it cries.

APPENDIX C

❖

HEINLEIN
RETROSPECTIVE
OCTOBER 6, 1988

❖

Trip report—October 30, 1988

On the evening of October 6, 1988, I received on Robert's behalf, the NASA Distinguished Public Service Medal, following a small dinner party given that evening. There were approximately 700 people present for the ceremony, and the presentation was made by Dr. Noel Hinners, Associate Deputy Administrator (Institution) of NASA.

The Description and Criteria of NASA Honor Awards reads: "*NASA Distinguished Public Service Medal (DPSM)* is granted to any individual who is not an employee of the Federal Government or was not an employee during the period in which the service was performed. The award is granted only to individuals whose meritorious contributions produced results which measurably improved, expedited, or clarified administrative procedures, scientific progress, work methods, manufacturing techniques, personnel practices, public information service, and other efforts related to the accomplishment of the mission of NASA."

The citation itself reads:

The National Aeronautics and Space Administration
Awards to
ROBERT ANSON HEINLEIN
the
NASA
DISTINGUISHED PUBLIC SERVICE MEDAL

In recognition of his meritorious service to the Nation and mankind in advocating and promoting the exploration of space. Through dozens of superbly written novels and essays and his epoch-making movie *Destination Moon*, he helped inspire the Nation to take its first step into space and on to the moon. Even after his death, his books live on as testimony to a man of purpose and vision, a man dedicated to encouraging others to dream, explore, and achieve.
  Signed and sealed at Washington, D.C.
  this sixth day of October
  Nineteen Hundred and Eighty-Eight.
  /s/James C. Fletcher
  Administrator, NASA.

The medal itself can be described as a sunburst, with a globe in the center, on a ribbon with a wide center strip in navy blue, with two lighter blue stripes on the sides, and a golden strip in the center of the lighter blue. There are two buttonhole ornaments to be worn with civilian dress; one is a copy of the medal, the other a dark blue button, with the gold and light blue used as a sunburst on that background. (I've seen Croix de Guerre holders use those ribbon buttonhole ornaments on their lapels.)
  After thanking Dr. Hinners for the honor, I used Robert's "This I Believe" credo for my talk. I had tried to write a speech, then remembered this talk of Robert's and thought it would be appropriate for this occasion. So I sent the record to Ward Botsford in New York, and he put it onto tape for me. Transcribed, it is below. (Ward told me that it was lucky I had not tried to tape it myself, as it might have ruined the only copy in existence, I believe.)
  I told the audience how this particular piece of writing had come into being, and that it seemed to me to be appropriate to this occasion,

and I had consulted several people about my feeling, and they had said— "Go ahead. It's the perfect thing to do."

THIS I BELIEVE

I am not going to talk about religious beliefs but about matters so obvious that it has gone out of style to mention them. I believe in my neighbors. I know their faults, and I know that their virtues far outweigh their faults.

Take Father Michael down our road a piece. I'm not of his creed, but I know that goodness and charity and lovingkindness shine in his daily actions. I believe in Father Mike. If I'm in trouble, I'll go to him.

My next-door neighbor is a veterinary doctor. Doc will get out of bed after a hard day to help a stray cat. No fee—no prospect of a fee— I believe in Doc.

I believe in my townspeople. You can knock on any door in our town saying, "I'm hungry," and you will be fed. Our town is no exception. I've found the same ready charity everywhere. But for the one who says, "To heck with you—I got mine," there are a hundred, a thousand who will say, "Sure, pal, sit down."

I know that despite all warnings against hitchhikers I can step to the highway, thumb for a ride and in a few minutes a car or a truck will stop and someone will say, "Climb in Mac—how far you going?"

I believe in my fellow citizens. Our headlines are splashed with crime yet for every criminal there are 10,000 honest, decent, kindly men. If it were not so, no child would live to grow up. Business could not go on from day to day. Decency is not news. It is buried in the obituaries, but it is a force stronger than crime. I believe in the patient gallantry of nurses and the tedious sacrifices of teachers. I believe in the unseen and unending fight against desperate odds that goes on quietly in almost every home in the land.

I believe in the honest craft of workmen. Take a look around you. There never were enough bosses to check up on all that work. From Independence Hall to the Grand Coulee Dam, these things were built level and square by craftsmen who were honest in their bones.

I believe that almost all politicians are honest . . . there are hundreds of politicians, low paid or not paid at all doing their level best without thanks or glory to make our system work. If this were not true we would never have gotten past the thirteen colonies.

I believe in Rodger Young. You and I are free today because of end-less unnamed heroes from Valley Forge to the Yalu River. I believe in—I am proud to belong to—the United States. Despite shortcomings from lynchings to bad faith in high places, our nation has had the most decent and kindly internal practices and foreign policies to be found anywhere in history.

And finally, I believe in my whole race. Yellow, white, black, red, brown. In the honesty, courage, intelligence, durability, and *goodness* of the overwhelming majority of my brothers and sisters everywhere on this planet. I am proud to be a human being. I believe that we have come this far by the skin of our teeth. That we *always* make it just by the skin of our teeth, but that we will make it. Survive. Endure. I believe that this hairless embryo with the aching, oversize brain case and the opposable thumb, this animal barely up from the apes will *endure*. Will *endure* longer than his home planet—will spread out to the stars and beyond, carrying with him his honesty and his insatiable curiosity, his unlimited courage and his noble essential decency.

This I believe with all my heart.

Robert's talk got a standing ovation. I don't take credit for that; it was *his* speech, his ideas.

There were other speakers, too. Jerry Pournelle gave some reminis-cences of Robert; Catherine and L. Sprague de Camp did much the same thing. Tom Clancy told how Robert's work had taught him to write. Captain Jon McBride (an astronaut) gave credit to Robert for his early work on spaceflight; Dr. Charles Sheffield told how Robert was not an American writer, but a British one . . . and Tetsu Yano, all the way from Tokyo, talked about his work in translating Robert's work—weeping at the end for Robert's loss.

Then there was a showing of *Destination Moon*.

The entire evening (with the exception of the motion picture) was videotaped, and I am very anxious to obtain a copy. It has been said that if enough people write in to ask how to obtain tapes for their own use, they might be sold by NASA.

Among those present were Robert's oldest friend, Rear Admiral Cal Laning; Rear Admiral and Mrs. J. Galbraith; and Woodie Teague, who came all the way from Colorado Springs. I had all those over to the hotel for a drink afterwards. (And a few others, too.)

The following evening, Eleanor Wood, Jim Baen, and I went out to the Kondo's new home in Columbia, MD for a party. A very nice party, with lots of old friends there. Next day, Eleanor and I went up to NY, and I saw more old friends—took Margo Fischer to lunch on Sunday— she's now 87, I think, and each time I see her, I think to myself it might be the last time.

Spent the rest of the weekend and a couple of days of the following week up in the country with Eleanor and her kids; the fall colors were on display, and it was lovely.

Arrived home with a king-sized case of jet lag, got Pixel out of the kennel, and now we've settled down for the winter. No rain so far, but I do hope there will be!—we're on water restrictions now, and it could get a lot worse, if we don't get a lot of rain here.

BIBLIOGRAPHY
(In order of publication)

FICTION

"Life-Line," *Astounding Science Fiction*, August 1939. Reprinted in *The Man Who Sold The Moon*, Baen Books.

"Misfit," *Astounding Science Fiction*, November 1939. Reprinted in *The Past Through Tomorrow*, Ace Books.

"Requiem," *Astounding Science Fiction*, January 1940. Reprinted in *The Past Through Tomorrow*, Ace Books.

"If This Goes On—," *Astounding Science Fiction*, February, March 1940. Reprinted in *The Past Through Tomorrow*, Ace Books.

" 'Let There Be Light,' " *Super Science Stories*, May, 1940 (under pseudonym Lyle Monroe). Reprinted in *The Man Who Sold The Moon*, Baen Books.

"The Roads Must Roll," *Astounding Science Fiction*, June 1940. Reprinted in *The Man Who Sold The Moon*, Baen Books.

"Coventry," *Astounding Science Fiction*, July 1940. Reprinted in The Past Through Tomorrow, Ace Books.

"Blowups Happen," *Astounding Science Fiction*, September 1940. Reprinted in *The Man Who Sold The Moon*, Baen Books.

"The Devil Makes the Law," *Unknown*, September 1940, (under pseudonym Anson MacDonald). Reprinted as "Magic, Inc.," in *Waldo And Magic Inc.*, Del Rey Books.

"Sixth Column," *Astounding Science Fiction*, January, February, March

1941 (under pseudonym Anson MacDonald). Reprinted by Baen Books.

" '—And He Built a Crooked House—,' " *Astounding Science Fiction*, February 1941.

"Logic of Empire," *Astounding Science Fiction*, March 1941. Reprinted in *The Green Hills of Earth*, Baen Books.

"Beyond Doubt," *Astonishing Stories*, April 1941 (under pseudonym Lyle Monroe and Elma Wentz).

"They," *Unknown*, April 1941.

"Universe," *Astounding Science Fiction*, May 1941. Reprinted in *Orphans Of The Sky*, Ace Books.

"Solution Unsatisfactory," *Astounding Science Fiction*, May 1941 (under pseudonym Anson MacDonald). Reprinted in *Expanded Universe*, Ace Books.

" '—We Also Walk Dogs,' " *Astounding Science Fiction*, July 1941 (under pseudonyn Anson MacDonald). Reprinted in *The Past Through Tomorrow*, Ace Books.

Methuselah's Children, *Astounding Science Fiction*, July, August, September, 1941.

"Elsewhere" ("Elsewhen"), *Astounding Science Fiction*, September 1941 (under pseudonym Caleb Saunders). Reprinted in *Assignment In Eternity*, Baen Books.

"By His Bootstraps," *Astounding Science Fiction*, October 1941 (under pseudonym Anson MacDonald). Reprinted in *The Menace From Earth*, Baen Books.

"Commonsense," *Astounding Science Fiction*, October 1941. Reprinted in *Orphans Of The Sky*, Ace Books.

"Lost Legion" ("Lost Legacy"), *Super Science Stories*, November 1941 (under pseudonym Lyle Monroe). Reprinted in *Assignment In Eternity*, Baen Books.

" 'My Object All Sublime,' " *Future*, February 1942.

"Goldfish Bowl," *Astounding Science Fiction*, March 1942 (under pseudonym Anson MacDonald). Reprinted in *The Menace From Earth*, Baen Books.

"Pied Piper," *Astonishing Stories*, March 1942 (under pseudonym Lyle Monroe).

Beyond This Horizon, *Astounding Science Fiction*, April, May 1942 (under pseudonym Anson MacDonald). Reprinted by New American Library.

"Waldo," *Astounding Science Fiction*, August 1942 (under pseudonym

Anson MacDonald). Reprinted in *Waldo And Magic Inc.*, Del Rey Books.

"The Unpleasant Profession of Jonathan Hoag," *Unknown Worlds*, October 1942 (under pseudonym John Riverside).

"The Green Hills of Earth," *Saturday Evening Post*, February 8, 1947. Reprinted in *The Green Hills Of Earth*, Baen Books.

"Space Jockey," *Saturday Evening Post*, April 26, 1947. Reprinted in *The Past Through Tomorrow*, Ace Books.

"Columbus Was a Dope," *Startling Stories*, May 1947 (under pseudonym Lyle Monroe). Reprinted in *The Menace From Earth*, Baen Books.

"They Do It With Mirrors," *Popular Detective*, May 1947 (under pseudonym Simon York). Reprinted in *Expanded Universe*, Ace Books.

" 'It's Great To Be Back!' " *Saturday Evening Post*, July 26, 1947. Reprinted in *The Past Through Tomorrow*, Ace Books.

"Jerry Is a Man," ("Jerry Was a Man"), *Thrilling Wonder Stories*, October 1947. Reprinted in *Assignment In Eternity*, Baen Books.

"Water Is for Washing," *Argosy*, November 1947. Reprinted in *The Menace From Earth*, Baen Books.

Rocket Ship Galileo, Scribner's, 1947. Reprinted by Del Rey Books.

"The Black Pits of Luna," *Saturday Evening Post*, January 10, 1948. Reprinted in *The Green Hills Of Earth*, Baen Books.

"Gentlemen, Be Seated!" *Argosy*, May 1948. Reprinted in *The Green Hills Of Earth*, Baen Books.

"Ordeal in Space," *Town and Country*, May 1948. Reprinted in *The Green Hills of Earth*, Baen Books.

Beyond This Horizon (revised version), Fantasy Press, 1948. Reprinted by New American Library.

Space Cadet, Scribner's, 1948. Reprinted by Del Rey Books.

"Our Fair City," *Weird Tales*, January 1949.

"Nothing Ever Happens on the Moon," *Boy's Life*, April, May 1949. Reprinted in *Expanded Universe*, Ace Books.

"Poor Daddy," *Calling All Girls*, 1949.

"Gulf," *Astounding Science Fiction*, November, December 1949. Reprinted in *Assignment In Eternity*, Baen Books.

"Delilah and the Space Rigger," *Blue Book*, December 1949. Reprinted in *The Past Through Tomorrow*, Ace Books.

"The Long Watch," *American Legion Magazine*, December 1949. Reprinted in *The Green Hills Of Earth*, Baen Books.

Red Planet, Scribner's, 1949. Reprinted by Del Rey Books.

"Cliff and the Calories," *Senior Prom*, August 1950.

Farmer In The Sky, first serialized as *Satellite Scout* in *Boy's Life*, August, September, October, November 1950. Scribner's, 1950. Reprinted by Del Rey Books.

"The Man Who Sold the Moon," (not serialized), in *The Man Who Sold the Moon, Shasta*, 1950. Reprinted by Baen Books.

"Destination Moon," *Short Stories Magazine*, September 1950.

Between Planets, serialized as *Planets in Combat* in *Blue Book*, September, October 1951. Scribner's, 1951. Reprinted by Del Rey Books.

The Puppet Masters, serialized in *Galaxy Science Fiction*, September, October, November 1951. Doubleday, 1951. Reprinted by Del Rey Books.

"The Year of the Jackpot," *Galaxy Science Fiction*, March 1952. Reprinted in *The Menace From Earth*, Baen Books.

The Rolling Stones, serialized as *Tramp Space Ship* in *Boy's Life*, September, October, November, December 1952. Scribner's, 1952. Reprinted by Del Rey Books.

"Project Nightmare," *Amazing Stories*, April 1953. Reprinted in *The Menace From Earth*, Baen Books.

"Skylift," *Imagination*, November 1953. Reprinted in *The Menace From Earth*, Baen Books.

Starman Jones, Scribner's, 1953. Reprinted by Del Rey Books.

The Star Beast, serialized as *The Star Lummox* in *Magazine of Fantasy and Science Fiction*, May, June, July 1954. Scribner's, 1954. Reprinted by Del Rey Books.

Tunnel In The Sky, Scribner's, 1955. Reprinted by Del Rey Books.

Double Star, serialized in *Astounding Science Fiction*, February, March, April 1956. Doubleday, 1956. Reprinted by Del Rey Books.

Time For The Stars, Scribner's, 1956. Reprinted by Del Rey Books.

The Door Into Summer, serialized in *Magazine of Fantasy and Science Fiction*, October, November, December 1956. Doubleday, 1957. Reprinted by Del Rey Books.

"The Menace From Earth," *Magazine of Fantasy and Science Fiction*, August 1957. Reprinted in *The Menace From Earth*, Baen Books.

Citizen Of The Galaxy, serialized in *Astounding Science Fiction*, September, October, November, December 1957. Scribner's, 1957. Reprinted by Del Rey Books.

"The Elephant Circuit" ("The Man Who Traveled in Elephants"), *Saturn*, October 1957.

"Tenderfoot in Space," *Boy's Life*, May, June, July 1958.

Have Space Suit—Will Travel, serialized in *Magazine of Fantasy and Science Fiction*, August, September, October 1958. Scribner's, 1958. Reprinted by Del Rey Books.

"All You Zombies—," *Magazine of Fantasy and Science Fiction*, March 1959.

Methuselah's Children (revised version), Gnome Press, 1958. Reprinted by Baen Books.

Starship Troopers, serialized as *Starship Soldier* in *Magazine of Fantasy and Science Fiction*, October, November 1959. Putnam, 1959. Reprinted by Baen Books.

Stranger In A Strange Land, Putnam, 1961. Hardcover available, also reprint, Ace Books.

"Searchlight," *Scientific American*, August 1962; *Fortune*, September 1962. Reprinted in *The Past Through Tomorrow*, Ace Books.

Podkayne Of Mars, serialized in *Worlds of If*, November 1962, January, March 1963. Putnam, 1963.

Glory Road, serialized in *Magazine of Fantasy and Science Fiction*, July, August, September 1963. Putnam 1963. Reprinted by Ace Books.

Farnham's Freehold, serialized in *If*, July, August, October 1964. Putnam, 1964. Reprinted by Ace Books.

The Moon Is A Harsh Mistress, serialized in *If*, December 1965, January, February, March, April 1966, Putnam, 1966. Reprinted by Ace Books.

"Free Men," in *The Worlds of Robert A. Heinlein*, Ace Books, 1966. Reprinted in *Expanded Universe*, Ace Books.

I Will Fear No Evil, serialized in *Galaxy*, July, August, October, December 1970. Putnam, 1970. Reprinted by Ace Books.

Time Enough For Love, Putnam 1973. Reprinted by Ace Books.

"No Bands Playing," *Vertex: The Magazine of Science Fiction*, December 1973. Reprinted in *Expanded Universe*, Ace Books.

The Notebooks Of Lazarus Long, Putnam, 1978. (Taken from two chapters of *Time Enough For Love*).

The Number Of The Beast, Fawcett Columbine, 1980. Reprinted by Ace Books.

Expanded Universe, Ace Books, 1980. Reprinted by Ace Books.

"A Bathroom of Her Own," *Expanded Universe*, 1980. Reprinted by Ace Books.

"On the Slopes of Vesuvius," *Expanded Universe*, 1980. Reprinted by Ace Books.

Friday, Holt, Rinehart and Winston, 1982. Reprinted by Del Rey Books.

Job: A Comedy Of Justice, Del Rey Books, 1984. Reprinted by Del Rey Books.

The Cat Who Walks Through Walls, Putnam, 1985. Reprinted by Ace Books.

To Sail Beyond The Sunset, Putnam, 1987. Reprinted by Ace Books.

MISCELLANEOUS

(These two items defy classification.)

Tomorrow, The Stars, Doubleday, 1952. This is an anthology, which was put together by someone else, and Robert wrote the preface for it.

Destination Moon, Gregg Press, 1979, edited by David G. Hartwell. The title page says it is by Robert A. Heinlein, with a new introduction by David G. Hartwell. This book contains a novelette titled "Destination Moon," and an article called "Shooting *Destination Moon*," which originally appeared in *Astounding Science Fiction*, July 1950. It also contains a number of still pictures from *DM*, and photocopies of many newspaper and magazine clippings.

NONFICTION

"Discovery of the Future," Guest of Honor speech at Denver, Colorado, 1941 World Science Fiction Convention. Printed in *Vertex*, issue #1.

"Man in the Moon" ("Back of the Moon"), *Elks Magazine*, 1947.

"Flight Into the Future," *Collier's*, August 30, 1947.

"On the Writing of Science Fiction," published in *Of Worlds Beyond*, Fantasy Press, 1947.

"Baedecker of the Solar System," *The Saturday Review of Literature*, December 24, 1949. Review of Bonestell and Ley's book, *Conquest of Space*.

"Where To?" article, *Galaxy*, February 1952.

"Shooting *Destination Moon*," *Astounding Science Fiction*, July 1950.

Article about writing, *Writer's Digest*, March, 1950.

"This I Believe," radio article written for Edward R. Murrow series of the same title. [Broadcast December 1, 1952]

"Ray Guns and Rocket Ships," published by the *Bulletin of the School Library Association of California*, 1952.

"The Third Millennium Opens," *Amazing Stories*, April 1956.

"Science Fiction: Its Nature, Faults and Virtues," Advent Publishers, 1959.

"Who Are the Heirs of Patrick Henry?," published April 12, 1958, *Colorado Springs Gazette Telegraph*. Also in *Expanded Universe*.

" 'Pravda' Means 'Truth'," *American Mercury*, October 1960.

"Inside Intourist," published in *Expanded Universe*.

"Appointment in Space," *Popular Mechanics*, 1963.

"The Happy Road to Science Fiction," *McClurg's Book News*, 1964.

"Science Fiction: The World of 'What If?' ", *World Book*, 1964.

Foreword for *Beyond Jupiter*, by Chesley Bonestell and Arthur C. Clarke, Viking Press, 1972.

Forrestal Lecture, 1973, published in *Analog*, January 1974.

"A United States Citizen Thinks About Canada," *Canada and the World*, April 1975.

"Dirac, Antimatter and You," *Compton Yearbook*, 1975.

"Are You a Rare Blood?" *Compton Yearbook*, 1976.

Testimony before joint session, House Committee on Aging and House Committee on Science and Technology, August 19, 1979, published in *Expanded Universe*, 1980, as "Spinoff."

"Larger Than Life," written for MosCon I, published in *Expanded Universe*, 1980.

Preface for Ted Sturgeon novel, *Godbody*, Donald I. Fine, 1985.

INDEX

PHOTOGRAPHIC CREDITS

Photographs on pages xii (bottom), xiii (top), xiii (bottom), xiv, xvi, xviii, 27, 32 (left), 32 (right), 39, 56, 84, 85, 92, 95, 98, 107, 115, 116, 118, 122, 124, 127, 130, 132, 147, 184, 185, 190, 194 (top), 194 (bottom), 199 (top), 199 (bottom), 201, 204, 207, 217, 221, 232 are from the personal archives of Virginia Heinlein.

Del Rey would like to thank Charles N. Brown of *Locus* magazine for the photographs on pages xviii, 14, 32 (right), 38, 42, 56, 59, 64, 68, 70, 73, 77, 80, 82, 84, 158 (top), 158 (bottom), 159 (top), 159 (bottom), 162, 167, 168, 170, 172, 173, 174, 179, 223, 179, 194 (bottom), 223, 232.
Thanks also to Matthew Berger, Kenneth R. Sharp, and Alexander Klapwald for lending items from their collections.

Astounding Science Fiction covers and illustrations:
"Life-line" (page 4) copyright 1939 by Street & Smith Publications, Inc.,; "If This Goes On" (page 5), "Blowups Happen" (page 8) copyright 1940 by Street & Smith Publications, Inc.; "Methuselah's Children" (page 19), "By His Bootstraps" (pages 21 and 48) copyright 1941 by Street & Smith Publications, Inc.; "Goldfish Bowl" (page 16), "Beyond This Horizon" (page 24) copyright 1942 by Street & Smith Publications, Inc.; "Double Star" (page 169) copyright 1956 by Street & Smith Publications, Inc.; "Citizen of the Galaxy" (page 78) copyright 1957 by Street & Smith Publications, Inc. All reproduced by permission of Davis Publications, Inc.

Jackets of *Starship Troopers* (page 82), *Stranger in a Strange Land* (page 233), *I Will Fear No Evil* (page 179), *The Moon Is a Harsh Mistress* (page 173), *Podkayne of Mars* (page 87), *Glory Road* (page 170), and *Farnham's Freehold* (page 172) photographed by permission of Putnam Publishing. *The Past Through Tomorrow* (page 175) reprinted by permission of the Putnam Publishing Group from the jacket of *The Past Through Tomorrow* by Robert A. Heinlein Copyright © 1967 by G.P. Putnam's Sons. The "Future History" chart (pages 176–77), copyright The Putnam Publishing Group, reprinted by permission from the publisher.

Rocket Ship Galileo (page 42). Reprinted with permission of Charles Scribner's Sons, an imprint of Macmillan Publishing company from *Rocket Ship Galileo* by Robert A. Heinlein. Illustrations by Thomas W. Voter. Copyright 1947 by Robert A. Heinlein; copyright renewed © 1975 Robert A. Heinlein.
Space Cadet (page 45). Reprinted with permission of Charles Scribner's Sons, an imprint of Macmillan Publishing company from *Space Cadet* by Robert A. Heinlein. Illustrations by Clifford N. Geary. Copyright 1948 Robert A. Heinlein; copyright renewed © 1976 Robert A. Heinlein.
Red Planet (page 46). Reprinted with permission of Charles Schribner's Sons, an imprint of Macmillan Publishing Company from *Red Planet* by Robert A. Heinlein. Illustrations by Clifford N. Geary. Copyright 1949 Robert A. Heinlein; copyright renewed © 1977 Robert A. Heinlein.